SUBSTANTIAL
EVIDENCE

SUBSTANTIAL EVIDENCE

BILL HUBBARD

An imprint of New Horizon Press
Far Hills, New Jersey

Expanding Horizons books are published by

New Horizon Press
P.O. Box 669
Far Hills, New Jersey 07931

All Kensington Titles, Imprints, and Distributed Lines are available
at special quantity discounts for bulk purchases for sales promotions, premiums, fund-raising, and educational or institutional use.
Special book excerpts or customized printings can also be created
to fit specific needs. For details, write or phone the office of the
Kensington special sales manager: Kensington Publishing Corp.,
850 Third Avenue, New York, NY 10022, attn: Special Sales Department, Phone: 1-800-221-2647.

EXPANDING HORIZONS is a trademark of NEW HORIZON
PRESS. EXPANDING HORIZONS and the EXPANDING HORI-
ZONS logo are trademarks of NEW HORIZON PRESS and the
EXPANDING HORIZONS logo is a registered trademark.

ISBN-13: 978-1-933893-03-7
ISBN-10: 1-933893-03-6

First New Horizon Press Hardcover Printing: 1998
First Expanding Horizons Mass Market Printing: March 2007

10 9 8 7 6 5 4 3 2

Printed in the United States of America

To Debbie—I worship the water you walk on!

Author's Note

This book is based on the experiences of Bill Hubbard and reflects his perceptions of the past, present, and future. The personalities, events, actions and conversations portrayed within the story have been taken from his memory, and conversations have been reconstructed using extensive interviews, research, court documents, letters, personal papers, press accounts, and the memories of participants.

Events involving the characters happened as described; only minor details have been changed.

Contents

Acknowledgments

I am very aware that when anyone accomplishes something meaningful, it is usually not just the work of that one individual. Therefore, this book chronicles not only my story but the stories of many people whose roles were large and small, who believed in me and banded together to accomplish a common goal. I was the beneficiary of their combined efforts.

This also is the story of the faithfulness of God to those who give themselves to Him. I believe the promises of the Bible to be true, and they were fulfilled in my life during these trying times. We got the right information at the right time, and the right breaks when they were most needed. This information and these breaks were the result of the diligence of many people and they were far beyond coincidence. We were very aware of the Architect who was really running it all and so, many times, were able to hang on when there seemed little hope.

It would take another volume to thank all of those who had a part, but some deserve special mention.

To my parents, Jim and Lorraine Hubbard, I owe my thanks for a terrific childhood in an environment that lived out their teachings. I saw firsthand what integrity was and that doing the right thing often has a price tag attached. When it came to my turn, doing the right thing and being willing to pay the price was the most natural thing in the world to do.

To my wife, Debbie, you own my life! When I have no strength of my own, I can always depend on yours. Your unconditional love and unwavering belief in my character and integrity make me try harder each day to be the man you already believe I am.

To Denette Vaughn, my Lubbock, Texas, attorney, I owe so much. Her career has never been about money.

It is about people and causes. More than a first-rate attorney, she is a true friend, plus a source of strength and encouragement. Her advice—both legal and personal—has never led me astray.

To Bill Kerns, of the *Avalanche-Journal* in Lubbock, Texas, and friend extraordinaire, who lived this episode in my life beside me hour by hour—thanks. In the early stages of writing this book, your insight and criticism were always helpful and on target.

To attorneys J. Mark Lane of New York, Millard Farmer of Atlanta, Jed Stone of Chicago, Dan Hurley of Lubbock, Steve Losch now of Houston, Cynthia Orr, and Gerald Goldstein of San Antonio, your selfless and tireless efforts in taking on my fight were the most remarkable I have ever witnessed. I owe all of you not only my career, but also my thanks for broadening me as a person and expanding my horizons. I am a different person because I encountered you.

Probably most important for the purpose of this book, I owe a debt of gratitude to my manuscript consultant, editor, and agent, Wanda Evans of Lubbock, Texas. Your enthusiasm in taking on this project and in taking what I thought was a finished manuscript and making it into a book is acknowledged with my humble appreciation. Your creative insights and sharp pencil truly breathed life into the pages.

Finally, to my brothers and sisters in law enforcement and especially to those of the Lubbock Police Department: thanks for the wonderful years I spent in your ranks and for the strength and encouragement you gave me as this ordeal ran its course. May this story encourage you always to do the right thing even in the face of seemingly insurmountable odds. Integrity is everything and you will persevere.

Bill Hubbard
August 1997

1

A Bad Spell

West Texas is said to have four seasons, but seasons unlike most parts of the country. It seems like winter lasts six months and summer lasts six months, while spring and fall last about a day each. It was October 21, 1992. The nights had been cool enough that the lawns had stopped growing and turned brown, but the first freeze had not yet come, so leaves still clung to the trees. Looking out the window, I realized that it must be the one day of autumn for that year.

It was 7:00 A.M. After a power breakfast of black coffee, I shaved and showered and headed for the office, where the detectives were making their first stop at the coffeepot and dropping into each other's offices to discuss the upcoming day. It was a typical morning. If there was no news on outstanding cases, the conversation would inevitably turn to department gossip or the latest police humor.

Today the coffee conversation was of a serious nature. One of our own, a Lubbock police officer, was the subject of a case being presented to a grand jury. The case had been kept quiet by the investigators working on it, but it had been entered into the police department computer system a day or two before, so by now most of the second floor—home of the detective division—had read about it.

Now each officer was giving his evaluation of the case, what he felt the chances were that the grand jury would indict, and what he felt had really happened. It was not a pretty case. An off-duty patrol officer had admitted to having sex with a woman who worked at the apartment complex where he had a second job providing security. That was the fact. The speculative aspects were what the actual relationship was between the man and the woman, if the woman was a willing participant in the act, and what force or threats the officer might have used. The still-predominant white male Texas attitude of the department was evident in the oft-repeated comment in the next twenty minutes: "He'll skate on it because he's a minority."

With the speculation out of the way and the last of the coffee, officers dispersed. It was time to get to work. Three days a week, one of my officers would come in early and go to the jail to collect the mug shots and fingerprint cards of suspects recently booked. I had the tedious chore of meticulously analyzing the fingerprint cards, classifying them by the Henry classification system, and filing them in a manual card file. Not exciting, but necessary.

Scanning them quickly but intently, I found an error on one of the cards. The jail deputy who had taken the suspect's prints had inadvertently printed the left index finger twice and had neglected to print the left middle finger. I knew it was a simple matter of inattention or distraction. I made a photocopy of the card and told the others that I would have a laugh with that deputy the next time I went over to the jail.

This Wednesday seemed to be starting off as the classic "typical day in the life of a police officer." Nothing special was going on, no high profile cases and no looming disasters. As a supervisor, I had learned to appreciate a normal day on the occasions when one occurred. Days such as these gave investigators an opportunity to catch up and note progress on cases already assigned, reflect on old, unsolved cases for anything overlooked, and make plans and policies for the future.

After finishing the fingerprint analyses, I moved on to other routine chores and was not upset at all when I was interrupted by a phone call.

"Hi, it's me," said a voice. "Me" was Denette Vaughn, not only my friend but also my attorney. I had met Denette briefly several years before when she first came to work for the city as a prosecutor in municipal court. From there she had gone to the district attorney's office as a prosecutor, and eventually had been in charge of the prosecution of all drug cases generated by the Lubbock Police Department. During that time, I had been the sergeant in charge of the undercover Street Crimes Unit. Denette and I got along well. We would bark at each other and fight over the merits of various cases, but when the fight was over, it was over. There were no grudges, just a lot of work. I could argue with her and not have to pay for it six months later by her nitpicking my cases. In that respect, she was unique in my experience with prosecutors.

On this October morning, however, there was not that much pressing to talk about. We just chatted. Denette was a widow in her early thirties, a single parent of a twelve-year-old son, an instructor in mass communication at Wayland Baptist University, and now an attorney with her own private practice. I had barely replaced the receiver after saying good-bye to her when the phone rang again.

"Hi, Bill. This is Joe." I recognized the voice of Joe Gulick, a reporter for the *Avalanche-Journal.*

"Hey, Joe," I said. "What's up?"

"Have you heard the results of today's grand jury?" he asked.

Thoughts of the police officer we had been discussing earlier that morning flashed through my mind. I thought Joe was looking for a quotable reaction from me or some direction for a story he was doing on it.

"No, Joe. I haven't heard anything."

"You don't know, do you?" he asked.

"Know what?" I asked, puzzled by the sound of urgency in his voice.

"Bill, I really hate to be the one to break this to you, but you've been indicted on felony charges."

An awkward silence followed.

Stunned, I finally blathered, "I have to go," and slammed down the phone. My mind was racing. Indicted? Why? What for? What had I done that a grand jury would consider a felony? Or, for that matter, what had I done that anyone could consider even a misdemeanor? I didn't have a clue.

Dazed, I stepped from my office into the common area of the homicide section. Captain Wiley, my department chief, was passing by. I shook my head in disbelief. "I've just been indicted by a grand jury."

The look on his face told me immediately that he also knew nothing about it. I saw Detective Doug Davenport, one of the investigators, and walked over to him.

"Have you testified before a grand jury today?" I asked Doug.

"No. Why?" he replied.

"I've been indicted." The words sounded foreign coming from my lips. "Bill Hubbard" and "indicted" simply did not go together in the same sentence. I had been a cop long enough to know that the first order of business for someone charged with a crime was to get a lawyer. I had just talked to Denette, but I had to reach her again and fast. A sheriff's deputy with an arrest warrant is usually on his way as soon as a grand jury acts. I strongly suspected that he would be the very next person in my office and would be accompanied by an army of television cameras and reporters—whoever was behind this had most probably activated the press to get a full measure of publicity.

It is impossible to adequately describe my feelings. Through all the years I had sought persons who had outstanding arrest warrants, I had never known how it felt to actually be that wanted person. It is unnerving to say the least.

I got back to my office phone and called the number where Denette had just been. She is famous for being in a place one minute and gone the next. "Please still be there! Please!" I murmured. Much to my relief she answered the phone.

"Denette, I've been indicted."

"What!"

"Joe Gulick just called and said today's grand jury has indicted me on two felonies."

She didn't flinch as I had. That's what I liked about Denette—her calmness when it was needed. "Can you get out of there and over here right away?" she asked. "Meanwhile I'll find out what this crap is all about."

"Yeah, I can leave. I've got my beeper if they need me."

"Then do it and come to my house. Then stay put until I can get downtown and figure out what's going on here."

With that, I hung up the phone, approached the status board in front of the secretary's desk, moved my magnetic dot to the out column, and strode out the door. As I drove my unmarked city detective car across town, I still could not think what I possibly could have been indicted on. I did know, though, that whatever it was, it was a lie and I was going to set the record straight—and fast. I also knew I had to call my wife and tell her before someone else did. I picked up my cell phone and dialed. Unfortunately, the line was busy. I drummed my fingers on the dashboard anxiously, waiting a few minutes before placing the call again.

My wife Debbie was working as the marketing director on a promotional project for Lubbock's South Plains Mall, one of the largest malls in Texas. At that moment, Debbie was taking the phone call of Bill Kerns, who was not only a good friend, but was also the entertainment editor at the *Avalanche-Journal.*

"Debbie, have you heard from Bill?" Kerns asked.

"No. Why?" she said, suddenly wary.

"The scuttlebutt here is that a grand jury indicted him this morning."

"Indicted?" Debbie's mind went blank for a moment. "How could they indict him? What for? What were the charges?"

"I don't know, but that's what Gulick said. If I—"

"Debbie, Bill is on the phone." Debbie's assistant stood in the doorway.

"I've got to go. Bill is on the other line," Debbie told Kerns.

Bill's voice was agitated as he told Debbie, "All I know is I've been indicted. Can you meet me at Denette's house right away?"

"I'll be right there." Debbie replaced the receiver, grabbed her purse, and ran for the office of her boss, Vic Hines. Hurriedly, she told Vic she had to leave and why.

"Let me know if there is anything I can do to help," he told her. She nodded, already halfway through the door.

On the drive from the mall to Denette Vaughn's home,

Debbie thought of all the situations for which, as a police officer's wife, she had mentally and emotionally prepared herself, such as Bill's getting hurt—or worse. Never in a million years would she have expected criminal charges to be filed against her husband. Some said his strident manner and rigid moral and professional code made him difficult to get along with. But he was the most honest, dedicated cop anyone could ask for. She racked her brain for a reason that could account for this disaster, and could think of nothing.

Meanwhile I was more than halfway to Denette's. By the time I got there Denette had her "lawyer clothes" on and was ready to go out and do battle for me.

"Put your car in the garage," she ordered. "If they come looking for you at least your car won't be in front of my house. They can't come inside without probable cause and a warrant, so don't answer the door for anybody. If I need to talk to you, I'll either call on the private line or on your pager."

Somehow, I felt better now that Denette was in charge. I had an immense amount of respect for her abilities, but I also felt like what I was—a fugitive.

Denette left quickly. I put the car away and then was left alone in her house. I knew Debbie was on the way there but I was also aware of being alone—very alone. Only the barking of the dog in the backyard once in a while broke the silence. Then it got quiet. While "afraid" was not the emotion I was feeling, I was quite insecure.

It seemed like forever, but it was only a few minutes before I heard a car in the driveway and looked out. Debbie's familiar gold Cougar had just stopped, and she was getting out.

Suddenly it was guilt I was feeling, and a lump rose in my throat. It seemed that all of the crises we had faced as a couple were because of me: the fear of some of my dangerous life-and-death assignments, the twenty-four-hour duty at times, and a recent internal investigation by the department in which I was cleared. As always, Debbie was with me through all of it.

Just seeing her get out of the car made me feel better. Willowy, compassionate, giving, nearly perfect in every sense, she had immediately dropped what she was doing and hurried to be with me in order to show her support. It was amazing that she never resented the demands made upon her as the wife of a police officer.

We had been introduced by mutual friends on a blind date in 1979. Convinced that marriage and police work do not mix, I had kept our relationship in a dating mode for more than five years until I finally got brave enough to ask her to marry me. Now, seven years and some changes later, this was one terrific marriage. No one was more amazed than I was.

I knew two things for sure as she walked to the front door: how much I loved her and how glad I was she was there.

"What's going on, Hon?" she asked.

"I wish I knew," I replied. "Denette has gone down to the courthouse to see if she can find out what it's all about."

"What about the P.D.?"

"Well, the few people I spoke to before I left today claimed to know nothing. Wiley looked like I'd hit him with a brick when I asked him about it, so I am pretty sure that whatever it is didn't come through the P.D. The way that place leaks, if it had started in the building, I'd have heard something before it all hit the fan."

We moved on into the living room and Debbie sat down on the sofa. She tried to initiate a conversation a couple of times, but my answers were curt. I wanted her to be there but I just did not feel like talking.

The next couple of hours were the longest of my life. At least Debbie was able to sit still. Not me. I paced. And paced. And paced.

There was a lot of time to think, but not much to think about since I had no information. All I could do was walk and wonder and pray. There wasn't any holy praying going on here, either. These were real down-to-earth prayers, from deep inside of me.

Lord, help me. HELP me. I'm so uncertain and confused. Help Denette to find what's going on and give us the strength to deal with it.

The deafening silence was broken by the barking of Denette's dog. Then Debbie spoke. "I've been thinking. Do you think this could be . . . ?"

"I don't *know!*" I said shortly. I was immediately ashamed of my curtness, but I was not in any kind of mood to talk about it, and playing a guessing game as to what this could all be about seemed fruitless to me until Denette called from downtown and we knew for sure.

More silence. More pacing.

Denette had driven directly to the courthouse and marched into the third floor office of the district attorney. "I'm representing Bill Hubbard," she said, "and I would like to know what's going on."

At the D.A.'s office she was given copies of the indictments, and she flipped through them. "This is just a rehash of last year's internal investigation at the police department," she said. "Bill was cleared. What is going on?"

No one could answer her questions, so she decided to pay Police Chief Don Bridgers a visit. First, though, she needed to call Bill and let him know the little she had found out.

* * *

I'd decided not to answer Denette's phone if it rang (which it didn't) just in case the news hounds figured out where I was and wanted to catch me at my worst. After an hour and a half my pager went off. I went to the phone and called the number in the pager window.

Denette answered with the familiar, "Hi. It's me."

"What's going on?"

"Relax," she reassured me. "This is just a rehash of the internal stuff that we saw a few months ago and you were cleared of any wrongdoing. What I'm not sure of at this point is why anyone would bring all that junk up again to torment you. I have to find out who's behind it and exactly how it happened. Everybody's being real secretive over here, so all I can guess is that someone appears to have a vendetta against you. But what makes me mad is that this was kept so quiet and nobody let us know that this was coming down."

"Okay. So what do we do?"

"Well, I don't know anything definite as yet. I still have to get my hands on some of the paperwork, and then I intend to see Chief Bridgers. I don't think warrants have been issued for your arrest yet, but we'll beat them to that. I'll arrange for your bond and we'll turn you in at the jail. Just hang tight until I get some more work done."

"Okay," I said, feeling deflated.

Denette must have heard the worry in my voice because she ended with, "It'll be okay, Bill. You'll be fine."

"I know, but . . ."

"Gotta go. But," she added as an afterthought, "go home and put on your best suit. Let Debbie stay at my place in case I have to call."

Oh swell, I thought, the Internal Affairs investigation again. In my mind I rehashed the nine weeks that began in early May of 1991. It began with the written complaint of disgruntled members of the Street Crimes Unit. The complaint basically detailed a personality conflict and problems with my uncompromising management style. The commanding officer had determined that, since the complaint had originated within the police department, it would be handled by my chain of command rather than by Internal Affairs.

Unfortunately for me, my division commander and I had, in the past, vehemently disagreed on the way police inquiries were to be conducted. He'd not only had me investigated, but drastically broadened the scope of the investigation. It escalated from a personality squabble between me and some of my men to include complaints by other officers. Some of these officers took issue with my strident methods, while others I had called on the carpet. There were also some who disagreed with the uncompromising and sometimes, I had to admit, obsessive way I battled to get criminals off the streets and to right the wrongs victims suffered.

During those nine weeks, my supervisors conducted interviews and allowed those wanting to do so to make statements against me. The possible punishment I faced ranged from a reprimand to a suspension, to a demotion, to being terminated from the department. After I responded to all the garbage that was thrown at me, the department rendered its verdict. I got a reprimand for the original personality clash and for "being inconsiderate to a subordinate." Other than that I was cleared—no suspension, no loss of pay or seniority, and no reduction of rank. Nothing.

Now, apparently someone had resurrected some of the complaints I had already answered in order to torture me anew.

As I hung up the phone and turned back toward the living room where Debbie was anxiously waiting, I could see that she had a very good idea of what was going on, having listened to my end of the conversation with Denette.

"It's back," I said. "The internal investigation that never goes away. How many times do I have to answer and be punished for stuff I didn't do? This is nuts."

Debbie sat very still, looking stunned. "It will be all right, Bill. You're honest and honorable. That's what will come out once again."

But the seemingly unending wait continued as I paced. And paced.

Okay, I mumbled to myself. *Same old stuff. No problem. Tell my side of it, get it all straight once again.* Not easy to go through. Tough, in fact.

However, in my favor, a West Texas storm was brewing in the form of Hurricane Denette Vaughn.

To say that Denette Vaughn is short is an understatement. Denette is very small. She is also very pretty, quick-witted and usually conveys good-natured friendliness in kind of a Brett Butler way. But it is a big mistake to cross this woman. She does her best work when she is angry. She uses the term "mad" to define her attitude. Cross her, cross someone she cares about or commit an act of injustice toward a client and be prepared to pay the price. And today Denette Vaughn was mad—*really* mad.

The secretary in Chief Don Bridgers's outer office stared in stunned silence as Denette Vaughn stormed in. Eyes set straight ahead, through clenched teeth she hissed, "Where's Don?" Without breaking stride to wait for an answer she sailed past the shocked secretary and strode down the hall to Bridgers's office, went in, and none too gently closed the door.

Denette Vaughn, petite, feisty and breathing fire, confronted Don Bridgers, tall, reserved and caught off guard. It looked something like a Chihuahua treeing a Great Dane.

Waving the indictment papers in front of the chief of police, Denette was at her best. In tone and volume she was direct and lionlike. "Just what the hell is all of this about?"

The mild-mannered chief immediately braced himself. "Denette, we had no idea over here that this was happening," he assured her.

"You mean to tell me that somebody can just come in here and help themselves to information kept in internal files and go running off to have a grand jury indict one of your best officers, and *you have no idea what's going on?*" Denette raged.

"Believe me, Denette," Bridgers said, "whatever and however the police administration—"

"So," she interrupted, "what you are saying is that this information, that is supposedly stored under lock and key here in this office, is somehow taken out, given to whomever, a grand jury indicts my client and you have *no idea it's going on?* What are you doing here anyway? Are you running this place or is it running you?"

"Well—"

"Well," Denette's one-woman riot continued, her words steel-edged, "if that's truly the case—that you had nothing to do with all of this—I'll tell you a couple of things. First of all, you had better get out from behind that desk and get out there in your police department and find out what's going on. And secondly, you can be sure that when I find out how this happened and who all's responsible, there's going to be hell to pay. I don't care if it's you, or your administration, or some of your officers, or the D.A.'s office, or whoever—I'm going to find out who they are and they're going to answer for this."

When Denette had made her point, she jerked the office door open. Then she got a bit of a surprise. While she had been in with the chief, members of the local media had gathered in the lobby of the chief's office, looking for some follow-up on this unfolding story. Evidently, Ms. Vaughn had broken the sound barrier between them in expressing to Chief Bridgers how she felt about all of this, because the news teams were just sitting there, saying absolutely nothing, but smiling broadly.

I was back at her house. On Denette's orders I had rushed home, put on my best suit, and rushed back. Soon her new, white Grand Am pulled into the driveway. At this point I had more control over my emotions, although the scope of the situation had not completely sunk in. In my naivete, I still thought that when "whoever" realized what a horrible mistake this was, the horror would go away. That shows just how little I knew about the criminal justice system after working in it for so many years.

"Bill," Denette said carefully when she came inside and brought us up to date, "you don't think this has anything to do with your investigation of those suspicious autopsies of Doctor Erdmann, do you? Your testimony against Erdmann did cast some doubt on the actions of the district attorney."

I looked at her to say no and stopped. "You think that might be behind all this?"

"Don't you?"

"God, I don't know." My voice was anguished. "Maybe. But I had to do it. It's not only my job, but I believe it's my responsibility to do what's right for the public and myself." I wondered if Denette was right.

"I know."

We used Denette's car to drive downtown so I could surrender myself. On the way, she turned into my public relations coach. "You look great," she said. "Keep your head up. Look confident. *You have done nothing wrong here, so look like it.* Try to look relaxed."

"Yes, ma'am," I said obediently. During the coming days, with Debbie running my personal life for me and Denette ramrodding the legal end of things, "Yes, ma'am" would be my theme song.

On my arrival at the county jail, three television crews and a reporter from the *Avalanche-Journal* followed us all the way in, asking questions with every step. After all, this was *news*—a cop going to jail!

I found myself standing at the booking desk where I had brought so many criminals so many times before. But now I was on the other side of the table. I was face to face with the deputy who had made the error on the fingerprint card I had classified just that morning. Through my emotional haze, I watched to make sure he took *my* fingerprints correctly.

Although there was a palpable tension in the booking area, it was unusually quiet. Captain David Gutierrez, the chief of the Lubbock County Jail, had cleared out all nonessential personnel and was watching me be booked. I tried to joke with the jail staff members who were still present, but could not help the bitterness in my voice. "I want you all to know that I'm not angry with any of you, and when I own this county, you can still have your jobs."

After the booking, I signed papers that would secure my release on bond. Even though I had lived in this community for more than thirteen years, owned a home in the city and was married to a woman who was gainfully employed in Lubbock, Judge Blair Cherry, in whose court my case had landed, and who worked for Travis Ware in the D.A.'s office before becoming a judge, would not allow me to be released on my personal recognizance. Whoever had set me up had obviously done a good job of poisoning the waters.

Denette had put up her own security to make my

bond. She teased that she had never put up her own property to secure a client's release before, so I had better not jump bail! I assured her that I had every intention of sticking around. With the bond officially posted and all of the booking complete, I walked outside. A battery of reporters had assembled in front of the jail. I kept my statement to a minimum. Denette wanted to do my talking for me. But I could not help saying, "I find this all to be really incredible. In my law enforcement career, I've made some hard choices. Going into law enforcement at all, you make some sacrifices. I never dreamed that working so hard for justice would have a price tag attached to it."

I also made it plain that I believed these were bogus charges and promised the reporters, "I'll be back soon wearing a badge."

Denette met the charges head-on. "It's too coincidental not to be related to the Erdmann thing," she told them. "The time and the way it happened are highly suspicious. I'll know more when I know who is involved."

At the mention of Dr. Ralph Erdmann, the reporters scurried off. The person they wanted to talk to was District Attorney Travis Ware, who pointedly denied that he was retaliating against me for exposing his role in the pathology scandal. He said emphatically that officers from my own department had "come forward" to his first assistant, Rebecca Atchley, with the allegations. According to Ware's statement that day, Atchley then brought the information to him and he referred it to the attorney general's office. Ware told the reporters he had been complaining about me to the police department "since 1987."

As the day ended, what had started as a beautiful, typical October day had turned into a nightmare. I was still reeling and unable to fully grasp what was happening to me. *I'm a cop. Cops put people in jail. They don't go to jail.* I repeated this reassurance to myself as a sort of mantra.

How does one go from Officer of the Year and nominee for Texas Peace Officer of the Year to indicted felon? Had I abused my authority and used excessive force? Helped myself to drug money? Planted dope on someone in order to make a case? No. I had done my job, followed orders, and told the truth. But, in doing so, I had angered some very powerful and vindictive people. I went home that night fully believing that a knife had been put in my back, but not fully understanding how corroded it was or how deeply it had penetrated.

I hated the labels that had been attached to me that day. Felon. Criminal behavior. Indicted. Booked to jail. Posted bond.

Me! Bill Hubbard. Christian. Good guy. Former ministerial student. Husband. Friend. It just didn't stack up.

Ironically, the officer whose case was originally taken before the grand jury for a sexual offense was no-billed. He went back to work. I had gone to jail.

My only crime, as far as I could tell, was that I had conducted a long, arduous investigation and eventually uncovered criminal activities within the criminal justice system. The problem was that two prominent and powerful men in that system, Dr. Ralph Erdmann and District Attorney Travis Ware, might just be the perpetrators. It was becoming obvious that blowing the whistle on powerful people who commit unethical and/or illegal acts could get a person, even a police officer, into a pile a trouble. When I had first started the investigation more than a year earlier, and followed the grisly trail left by Dr. Erdmann, I would never have believed it would lead me to my own indictment on felony charges. I thought back to the day it all began, August 26, 1991. . . .

2

Past Pain

Ahh, Lubbock. It's a town of just under 200,000, and the word is that you either love it or you hate it. There are reasons for doing either, or both. Most people think the weather is great—even when it reaches 100 degrees in the summertime, it usually cools off at night. Winters generally are mild, although occasionally we experience a severe one with snow and ice and below zero temperatures. February is typically the worst winter month.

I wish it could be October all year. With balmy days and cool nights, it is the harvest time for the cotton farmers, who produce a significant amount of the nation's cotton. Consequently, gin smoke and the smell of burning cotton burrs hang heavily on the small, outlying towns.

Lubbock is a young town in more ways than one. It is less than 100 years old, and the pioneer spirit of independence and fortitude still prevails to a great degree. So does the patriarchal mind-set. It is staunchly conservative.

Most say that business—private and government—is conducted by the good old boy network, which operates at almost every level. The county government and the judicial environment are more subject to this cronyism than the city government.

Lubbock has much going for it, though. Designated as Hub City, Lubbock is the core of wholesale and retail trade for the region. A first-class airport and excellent highways connect Lubbock with surrounding counties which depend on the city as a regional distribution and warehousing center.

Lubbock has one of the state's lowest unemployment rates, due in part to its top billing as the largest health care provider from the Dallas/Fort Worth Metroplex to Phoenix to the west and Denver to the northwest.

The town also provides numerous educational opportunities. It is the home of Texas Tech University, with 24,000 students, including both a law school and a medical school, Lubbock Christian University and Wayland Baptist University, both private universities, and South Plains College, a two-year community college. Texas Tech has a strong record as one of the top law schools in the state.

The population is almost one-third Hispanic, with a large black community. However, neighborhood integration is rare. Because of the universities, there are also sizeable settlings of Middle Easterners, Vietnamese, Turkish, and other nationalities. Many feel it is a great place to live. In the heart of the Bible Belt, it advertises clean, wholesome living, good schools, good medical services, and many, many churches.

Its detractors point out that there is little to do, and everything that is offered has a cost. There are no facilities for contemporary concerts, and no money to pay the prices hot performers command. City ordinance prohibits the sale of liquor, wine or beer, except by the drink in clubs and restaurants. So you can't go to your

corner convenience store and buy a six-pack to enjoy
while you watch the Cowboys play on TV.

Although there is a fairly healthy cultural climate, fea-
turing ballet, the symphony, Broadway touring shows,
and performances by an excellent drama and music department at Texas Tech, these appeal only to a small
percentage of the population. Country western and classic rock are the prevailing musical preferences.

As for the press, at most newspapers the daily controversy is over whether a sports story rates a banner on the
front page. Although the *Avalanche-Journal* has first rate
editorials and reporters, there is no question. When
there is a sports story, it gets a banner. Lubbock resi-
dents are great sports enthusiasts, to say the least.

The perfect end-of-summer morning accounted for only
a portion of my excitement as I drove to work. I was eagerly
anticipating my first day as sergeant assigned to the identification section of the Lubbock, Texas, police department. And I was relieved that my wife, Debbie, and I had
just survived one of the toughest periods in our lives.

In mid-May we had lost Debbie's oldest brother to brain
cancer. My mother had been hospitalized with heart problems and within hours of my arrival at her bedside in Albuquerque, New Mexico, she had undergone bypass
surgery. Two weeks after that I returned to Albuquerque
to be with my dad when he had cancer surgery. Mom was
not even able to be at the hospital with Dad. The morning
after Dad's surgery, my beloved grandmother, Nannie,
who was ninety-nine years old and lived with Mom and Dad,
died in her sleep. The day Dad was released from the hospital, I conducted a grave side service for my own grandmother. It was more difficult than anything I had ever
done during those years when I had been in the ministry
prior to entering law enforcement.

During this time, I had been subjected to an intensive nine-week internal investigation concerning my supervision of the Street Crimes Unit before being cleared. Then after a difficult competitive examination I had been named to this new position in homicide.

We weren't sorry that the summer was drawing to a close. However, we really felt that we had put our trust in the Lord and He had seen us through a very difficult time. Debbie and I had joked, "If we make it through this, we can make it through anything."

On this glorious August 26th morning, no one could have convinced us that looming over the horizon were events that would make the past few months pale by comparison.

It was only 6:45 A.M. I didn't see anyone as I carried my box of office supplies and personal decorations to my new second-floor office and began unpacking. Wherever I officed, I surrounded myself with some favorite memorabilia and my Texas Rangers collection. One of the few good things I could say about the past several months was, "Well, at least it is baseball season!" Like the other citizens in Lubbock, I was an ardent fan. Along with my Rangers photos and Nolan Ryan regalia were the plaque I had received as 1985 Police Officer of the Year, and the certificate of recognition from the State Senate for the same honor.

First things first, however. A favorite slogan of police officers is, "To protect and serve . . . after coffee." Standing at the coin-operated machine, I filled my brand-new mug that bore a bold inscription: "To err is human; to forgive is against departmental policy."

Frank Wiley, my new captain, came up as I turned from the coffee machine.

"Got a minute?" he asked. Wiley, a thirty-year veteran of the Lubbock Police Department, was tanned, although not as fit looking as one would expect from such

an avid golfer. Perhaps because he also was an avid cop.
He reminded me a little of my grandfather, had my
grandfather been prone to wear pointed toe western
boots.

"Sure." Who is going to tell his captain he doesn't
have a minute? I followed him into his office, which was
strategically located by the coffee machine. He closed
the door, always a bad sign. He sat down behind his
desk. I remained standing.

He wasted no time. "I know since you were nominated
as officer of the year and survived an investigation and
now been promoted, you think you wear a Teflon overcoat, but I want you to know your Teflon days have
ended today. You have to prove yourself all over again
here." I couldn't believe it! Evidently all Wiley knew
about the summer's investigation was what he had heard
via the grapevine.

"Captain," I said, "I have never felt I was Teflon-coated
but I know I can be steel-edged. I've just tried to be the
very best police officer I could."

Wiley wasn't fazed. He began questioning me about
particulars of the internal investigation. I had already answered them fully and completely to the authorities, so
I wanted to tell him that all this stuff was history, but I
didn't think that was a good idea. I went over it again
with him and reminded him of the result.

Finally, he said, "Well, welcome, but remember what I
said about proving yourself here. It's good advice."

With that, Wiley dismissed me. Back in my office, I
met my new crew: a corporal and two officers. Corporal
Jimmie Riemer, stocky, his dark hair touched with gray,
had joined the Lubbock Police Department in 1959 and
had been in the identification section since 1964. Detective Gaylon Lewis, or "Buffalo" as he was known because
of his size, had joined L.P.D. about a year before I did.
We were about the same age (mid-thirties) and he had

been in I.D. for several years. Detective Wesley Shields was younger than I and had been a dispatcher when I joined the force.

They were all standoffish but polite. I knew that the only way to get along with these men was to get to know them, treat them fairly, and put in a lot of hard work at their sides.

The next order of business was a meeting with my predecessor, Lieutenant Thomas Esparza. He was about my age with quick dark eyes that missed nothing and which frequently glinted with humor. Esparza had been my classmate at the Lubbock Police Academy. As a sergeant he had been assigned to I.D. for a little over a year before he succeeded on the promotional exam and was moved up to lieutenant. My situation was complicated even more, because the men in I.D. had liked working for Thomas, who was a really good guy.

Esparza spent a lot of time helping me get oriented and showing me the ropes. He gave me the vacation book and explained to me the various operating policies for the unit. We also discussed at length each of the three officers assigned to the unit—their personality traits, their individual skills, strengths and weaknesses. I knew I had a challenge ahead of me, since two of these men I outranked were senior to me in time on the force. The third tended to follow the lead of the other two. This was a close-knit unit because they had particular skills that no one else in the department possessed. If, for example, you wanted a fingerprint analysis and comparison, you had to come to them. Consequently, an often heard complaint about I.D. was that they were primadonnas.

As our meeting drew to a close, Esparza reached into the file drawer of what was now my desk, and took out a manilla folder that had the word ERDMANN handwritten in red on the tab. Lubbock County had no coroner or medical examiner, so Dr. Ralph Erdmann had been hired as a forensic pathologist for the county.

"This file was started because of complaints about Doctor Erdmann," Esparza told me. "Most of the problems are in regard to his forgetfulness or incomplete autopsies. For example, we've had some detectives complain that Erdmann didn't open the head of a victim when they thought he should have, and that in certain instances he whisks over procedures that some detectives thought he should have performed more thoroughly," Esparza continued. "As a result of these complaints, I decided to start this file. You can do with it whatever you like, but my suggestion is that you keep an eye on him."

Thomas opened the file and showed me the contents. It was a single sheet of paper in the form of a memo dated May 15, 1991, and was from Detective Shields. Shields wrote that Dr. Erdmann had contacted him and requested assistance. It seems that Erdmann had "lost" his notes from a particular homicide autopsy and needed them to complete the autopsy report. Erdmann had asked Shields to bring the police photos that had been taken during the autopsy, along with the police reports, and meet with him so that Erdmann could go over it all and be able to complete his report.

Shields had made an appointment with the doctor, but the doctor had not shown up for the meeting. Erdmann then called Shields that afternoon and said he would meet with Shields later in the week. When the memo was written about this incident, eight days had passed and Erdmann had not made additional contact. Shields did not know how, or if, Erdmann had completed his autopsy report nor, if he had, what it said.

After I finished reading the memo, Esparza went on to tell me that he and the other homicide sergeant, Randy McGuire, had gone to see one of the justices of the peace, Jim Hansen, just after Hansen had taken office in

January of that year, and talked to him about Erdmann. In Lubbock County, it is the justice of the peace who orders autopsies and receives the autopsy results from the pathologist so he can rule on the death.

I told Esparza I would keep my eyes open.

"Good luck," he said, offering his hand.

As I went about my duties after my meeting with Esparza, I could not get Erdmann, who had a reputation as a strange duck, off my mind. It seemed ludicrous that something as important as the autopsy of a homicide victim could apparently be treated so lightly by Dr. Erdmann, especially since that autopsy could be a huge factor in determining whether or not someone was guilty or innocent of a crime. A botched autopsy could send a killer on his way or convict an innocent person. On top of that, with my tail feathers still smoldering from the events of last summer, I was determined that if Dr. Erdmann's problems began to reflect on the identification section of the police department, I would document events to the point that the blame would be put where it belonged—on the doctor, not on us.

3

Learning The Ropes

The early days of my new assignment had been some of the best I ever had as a police officer. Although I was a sergeant and technically in charge, the truth of the matter was that every officer under my supervision had much more knowledge about the various aspects of major crime scene investigation than I. And these officers were very good at what they did.

One of them was Jimmie Riemer. The amazing thing about Jimmie was that he was not a dinosaur. Though he had been in the unit forever, he still kept current on the latest advances in police science and was able to speak knowledgeably about all of it. Fortunately for me, he and the others were very patient in breaking me in and in showing me how to do the many different tasks.

Under the watchful eyes of the other unit members, I began to learn about two of the most important jobs we performed—photography and fingerprints. Each person arrested by the Lubbock Police Department had his or her prints taken at the Lubbock County Jail, and one set of them came to my office. There the prints were classified according to the Henry classification system and filed in a manual card file. Learning the Henry system and being able to classify cards is a very tedious but necessary first step in becoming an expert at comparing and matching prints. So, early on, I learned to define the print types, classify a ten-print card, and file those cards. I also learned to take the fingerprints of arrestees and suspects, which looks a lot easier to do than it is!

I had never operated a single lens reflex camera prior to this new assignment. The others in the outfit were all in agreement that the best way to learn was by taking pictures. For days, I was the terror of the police department, always popping up with camera in hand. I kept a running log of my camera settings, sent the film to be developed, and then met with the other members of the unit who compared the pictures with the log and gave me lessons on how to improve.

Slowly, things began to settle down. I was no expert, but I was no longer the obtuse freshman sergeant who didn't know his way around. I realized though, I still needed experience in my new position.

I took a couple of days off, and Debbie and I went to visit our ailing family. While we were away, the first homicide occurred since I became head of the identification unit. The other officers worked the scene as they always had, and things probably would not have been any different if I had been there. I was still learning, but when I got back a day later and found out about the murder, I really wished I had been there.

The case, which is still open and so must be reported rather cautiously, concerned a woman who had returned home somewhat late one evening and was attacked in her living room. She fought her assailant to a front bedroom where she was choked down onto a bed and killed. The woman's husband and son were spending the night trying out a motor home the husband wanted to purchase, so the murdered woman was not discovered until the husband returned home the next morning.

As soon as the murder was reported, the detectives scoured the area and conducted intensive interviews. They knew that the chances of solving the case would diminish greatly after the first forty-eight hours. In conducting the interviews, the detectives developed a likely suspect, who had offered what they believed to be a weak alibi that involved what the suspect said he and the victim had eaten prior to her return home.

Suddenly, the contents of the victim's stomach emerged as being of major importance. As in most of our cases, Dr. Erdmann performed the ordered autopsy within hours after the discovery of the crime scene. The detectives rushed to him for help when they heard the suspect's alibi. Unfortunately, in doing the autopsy, Erdmann had not bothered to look at the contents of the stomach, let alone make an inventory or save them.

Because of this, our chances of nailing the suspect came to a screeching halt. "Angry" does not begin to express the rage I observed in some of our top investigators, when their case broke down because of Erdmann's failure to provide the key evidence they needed. To this day, the prime suspect walks free, with police unable to piece together enough evidence to file charges.

Erdmann. There was that name again.

In light of the slim file on him that Thomas Esparza had given me, I decided that a second page should be added, based on the shortcomings of this latest homicide autopsy. Since I was new to the identification unit and was only beginning to get a handle on my job, I had much inexperience and many unanswered questions concerning autopsies. I had never even attended one, so I had no idea what was supposed to take place! But the question which now resounded in my mind seemed simple: Would a standard homicide autopsy performed by someone other than Dr. Erdmann require an inventory of the stomach contents? Unfortunately, I just didn't know.

During the next ten days I talked at length with the men in my unit, as well as my lieutenant and captain, trying to figure out an answer to this question. Every break I got, I read forensic pathology textbooks and had more discussions. I concluded that the stomach contents question probably would have been addressed by other pathologists.

Captain Wiley had backed off considerably after the "Teflon overcoat" welcome he had given me to the division. He had gotten to know me better, and recognized that despite my admitted single-mindedness on getting criminals off the street, I was a hard worker who was trying to get the job done right. And, during the middle part of October, our common goal was to get at the real truth about our autopsies. Though the official file was only a few scant pages, we both had bad gut feelings about the pathologist's activities and skills.

"However," Wiley told me, "if we go to Erdmann and try to straighten him out, he'll just go to Travis Ware." Criminal District Attorney Travis Ware was a staunch defender of Erdmann. And it was rumored that, whatever Ware wanted from Erdmann, Ware got. The district attorney's prosecutors provided the findings, testimony and expert opinions for the cases, while Erdmann's autopsy reports and testimony made the pieces of the case fit perfectly. Maybe a little too perfectly, some thought.

Wiley was convinced that if we were to effect a change in Erdmann's methods, we would need to accumulate sufficient evidence to convince Ware there was a problem, and then enlist Ware as an ally for a change. If we went to Erdmann, Erdmann would go to Ware, Ware would side with Erdmann, and we would end up right where we had started. Except that we would then also have made Ware angry because we were picking on his friend Dr. Erdmann.

Much speculation was made as to what the Erdmann-Ware connection really was. Was it merely that of pathologist/prosecutor? Or was it friendship or a financial connection, or something more sinister? No one seemed able to answer these questions with any certainty, but the speculation grew.

As a result of discussion among the supervisors in the homicide section, Wiley gave me the task of researching autopsy standards by contacting medical examiners around the state of Texas and trying to answer the question, "What are the standard procedures in a homicide autopsy?" If we could find that there were standards in forensic pathology and that Dr. Erdmann did not adhere to them, then we could present sufficient information to Ware to convince him that there was a serious problem. So here I was, a rookie sergeant in the division who had never yet attended an autopsy, calling all over the state after having read as much as I could in the available textbooks, trying to determine exactly what should occur in a homicide autopsy! I had quite a job before me, but was resolved to get it done before we had yet another murder case go unsolved.

At Captain Wiley's suggestion, I decided to contact some of the larger medical examiners' offices, because they had been in operation a long time and presumably had established longstanding procedures. My initial queries were directed at Tarrant County (Fort Worth), Dallas County, Bexar County (San Antonio), and Harris County where Houston is located. I found representatives from these offices to be cordial, concerned and helpful. The talks I had with the people from Tarrant and Bexar counties were especially candid and enlightening.

I spent quite a while on the phone with Assistant Chief Investigator Darrell Thompson of the Tarrant County

M.E.'s office. Thompson told me that actual M.E.'s offices were governed mostly by Chapter 49 of the Texas Code of Criminal Procedure. Since Lubbock was not under the M.E. system, the standards of the C.C.P., though desirable, were not always attainable.

In a county such as Lubbock, the justices of the peace are the officials who have the responsibility for conducting inquests into deaths, ordering autopsies, and making the rulings in those deaths. For counties with a medical examiner, the J.P.'s are relieved of the responsibility for making death rulings. It becomes the responsibility of the doctors in the M.E.'s office, with their greater medical expertise, to make the rulings. In Lubbock, the J.P.'s are often at the mercy of whatever information has been provided to them by whatever pathologist is on contract with the county to do their autopsies.

Investigator Thompson also provided me with some of the standards used by their office. I learned that the law allows two types of autopsies: "full" autopsies and "cause-of-death" autopsies. The cause-of-death autopsy is normally done in home deaths of the elderly, industrial accidents, suicides, and the like. It is mainly done to establish that foul play was not involved in the death. The pathologist assures himself of the cause of death and rules out the possibility of homicide. In homicides, however, full autopsies are always done, and in all full autopsies the procedure followed is always the same.

The full autopsy always involves a complete external exam and documentation of wounds, marks, tattoos, etc. The chest cavity is then opened for a thorough internal examination, and an external and internal examination is made of the head. Weights, tissue samples, and blood screens are all part of the standard of the Tarrant County office for the full autopsy, Thompson informed me.

Although at this time I had never been to an Erdmann autopsy, one of the frequent comments I was hearing

from the L.P.D. detectives was that no two Erdmann autopsies were ever the same. Procedures that were standard in two or three consecutive autopsies were ignored
in the next. I got the impression that many of Lubbock's
homicides were getting only a cause-of-death autopsy
when a full autopsy was warranted. As I understood
things from my interviews thus far, in a homicide the
pathologist must not only establish what caused the
death, but also what did not cause the death. In a courtroom, that pathologist must be prepared to answer whatever questions or hypotheses are raised by either the
prosecution or defense. In the case of capital murder,
which is punishable by death in Texas, someone's life
may very well ride on what the pathologist does or does
not do.

I felt I was making real progress and gathering information that would be helpful to us. But everything I had
learned so far was just a grain compared to what I
learned in my communications with the Bexar County
Medical Examiner's Office in San Antonio. I found that
the Chief Medical Examiner there was a man named Dr.
Vincent DiMaio. Dr. DiMaio was already familiar to me,
in that he and his father literally wrote the book on
forensic pathology. The senior DiMaio, Dominick, for
years had been the Chief Medical Examiner in New York
City. It had been their book that I had obtained soon
after taking my new assignment in homicide in order to
better understand what Dr. Erdmann was and was not
doing.

I spoke at length by telephone to an assistant M.E. in
DiMaio's office, Dr. Suzanna Dana. She confirmed many
of the things that I had already learned from others.
After talking to all these experts, I had to conclude that
in homicides in other counties, a full autopsy was always
done, and those full autopsies always entailed the same
procedures.

Dr. Dana volunteered Dr. DiMaio's assistance even though he was out of town at that time. She said Dr. DiMaio was concerned with substandard work in his profession and was always ready to critique the reports of other pathologists and give his findings in writing. I also found that news about the reputation of our Dr. Erdmann had already traveled as far as San Antonio. And it wasn't good. It was even suggested that the Lubbock Police Department immediately start sending our homicide victims to another county such as Bexar so that reliable findings could be obtained and standards could be established.

On October 22nd I put the findings of my research into a memo for Captain Wiley and presented it to him. In working with Wiley, I had already learned that submitting the results of one completed task often led to two or three new assignments. This time my new task was twofold. First, I was to construct a sample protocol of what a homicide autopsy should entail. Second, I was to contact law enforcement personnel in jurisdictions where Dr. Erdmann had once practiced but no longer did, and find out why his services had been discontinued.

This was ironic. I, a guy who had studied seven years for the ministry and who was now a cop and had never even attended an autopsy, was assigned to write a protocol that would set forth the standards for a doctor to follow in performing a full autopsy! As I got started, I felt like a person writing a driver's manual who had never seen a car. On the plus side, I had at my disposal all kinds of written material, and on call were experts in the field who were willing to help me with my monumental task. The first thing I received was a long fax from Dr. DiMaio's secretary. The document, written by Dr. DiMaio, addressed the very subject at hand. Then I plunged into reading, researching and writing.

After I completed each draft, I ran it by my officers

(who had all been to many autopsies) as well as Lieutenant Summerlin and Captain Wiley. I spent about two weeks writing while keeping up with my daily responsibilities. Each time major revisions were needed, the previous draft hit the trash can. By the third draft I felt I was beginning to get somewhere. I decided to give the sample protocol the real acid test, so I faxed it off to Dr. DiMaio. He wrote all over it and zapped it back to me. By mid-November I had what looked like a viable autopsy protocol to submit.

In the meantime, I contacted officers of the Potter County and Amarillo Police Departments to find out why Dr. Erdmann's services had been discontinued, and why he no longer worked in the northern part of the Texas panhandle. What I learned and passed on to my supervisors came as no surprise. Again and again I heard that there were three main problems with Dr. Erdmann: He was not accessible, he was not timely in turning in his autopsy reports, and his autopsies were inconsistent, since Erdmann did not always perform the same procedures in each autopsy, particularly in doing internal head examinations.

At the time, Dr. Erdmann was doing autopsies for more than forty counties in the Texas panhandle. He was under contract with Lubbock County for a base salary of $140,000, and he was paid by other counties on a per-autopsy basis. Erdmann's fee normally was in the $750 range for each autopsy, with additional charges for copies of autopsy photos and certified copies of the autopsy report. It seemed extremely logical to me that because of his widespread practice he was always late, was cutting corners and was anxious to end one autopsy in order to get to the next. It also didn't take much of a mathematician to see that this was a real money-making operation for Dr. Ralph Erdmann.

4

The Erdmann File

By the middle of November word of the Erdmann investigation had traveled throughout not only the detective division, but the entire police department. Officers who had knowledge of errors, oversights or worse by Dr. Erdmann began bringing them to me. No matter how old the incident was, we included it in the file. Virtually everyone who had ever had dealings with Erdmann was convinced that we had to have a more reliable pathologist. The question presently at hand was whether Erdmann could change to meet the need, or if bringing in a new forensic pathologist should be considered. The problem was complicated by the fact that Erdmann was employed not by the L.P.D. but by Lubbock County. And District Attorney Travis Ware was widely rumored to be Erdmann's number one fan.

We at the police department had also been led to believe by Ware and other officials that finding any pathologist willing to practice in West Texas was a very difficult chore. It was Ware who had recruited Erdmann, and it was Ware's signature, along with that of the county judge, that was on Erdmann's $140,000-a-year contract. However, in doing my research, I found out from the Amarillo Police Department that their replacement for Dr. Erdmann had been recruited from the New Mexico Medical Examiner's Office for a salary of $89,000, and they were happy with him.

On November 13, 1991, L.P.D. Officer Pat Kelly came to my office. I had known Pat since my first day at the police academy in 1979. We had been classmates, two of the eleven cadets who were sworn in that day. However, to say that we were not close while in the academy would be an understatement. Although we both were committed to police work, we really did not like each other. We came from completely different backgrounds, with completely different friends and likes and dislikes.

Nevertheless, although his methods and mine were different, after graduating from the academy Pat established himself as a good cop and a hard worker, despite what many saw as an abrasive personality. While I was head of the Street Crimes Unit after I made sergeant, Pat was one of the officers who worked for me for a time.

The Street Crimes Unit had been created because the town of Lubbock had developed a serious house-burglary problem. Several factors contributed. The prisons were full, and parole was easy to get after only a small fraction of a sentence had been served. And drug abuse among the criminal element was on the rampage. This meant that drug-addicted crooks were committing property crimes in order to sell the goods and support their habits. One of the crimes of choice was the daytime house burglary. This normally occurred between 8:00 A.M. and 5:00 P.M. Monday through Friday, when the fewest number of people were home in the residential neighborhoods. Since most people were at work, few witnesses were around. If the burglars could find homes with poor security—and that was easy—their chances of finding easily fenced goods and getting away undetected were strongly in their favor.

Worried about this problem, the police department applied to the State of Texas for a grant to fund a program and special position to try to get the burglaries under control. The funding was made available. The police department took applications from throughout the various divisions to fill this new position. At first it was called the Selective Law Enforcement Unit, and later it became the Street Crimes Unit. It was a division of one officer, and I was tapped for the job.

In the unit, I worked in uniform from a marked police car and was given a desk with a phone. My only directive was, "Go catch burglars." I decided that though that directive, given the conditions, was hard to carry out, it would be the key to any success I might have. If I went out by myself in a marked car trying to catch burglars, I would get only limited results. However, if I used my position to disseminate information and thereby alert all the officers on the force, there was the potential for great success.

I installed a bulletin board in the patrol briefing room. On it I listed the particulars about every daytime house burglary that occurred, including the address, time of occurrence, type of entry, type of goods taken, and any suspect information or description. From the start certain trends were apparent. Officers on the beat were able to see the trends where they patrolled every day, and they started to address the problem. They knew what was going on, at what time, and what to look for. Burglars are creatures of habit, so they generally did their work from the same vehicles, in the same neighborhood, in the same manner, at the same time of day.

Though mine was a crude effort at crime analysis, it created the potential where an officer could be waiting for a burglar when he appeared. The burglary problem in Lubbock was rampant, but in every possible instance I was there. Since I had the luxury of not having to respond to radio calls, I was able to arm myself with the information I had generated and take to the streets. The early days of the program were punctuated by some impressive arrests.

Another tactic we used was to conduct surveillance on known drug hangouts, since we knew a large percentage of the addicts were burgling to support their habits. Sure enough, cars that had been listed as suspect vehicles in burglary reports began to show up at these places, and an investigative stop as the addicts were leaving gave me an opportunity to identify who was using which vehicle. Often, after identifying the occupants of the car, when I submitted their names on a fingerprint comparison request to the guys in the identification section, they would match prints lifted at the burglary site to the people who occupied the car I had stopped earlier.

Once a week I compiled everything I had learned from reading reports, from surveillance and from investigative stops. I published the information in an intelligence report that was distributed throughout the department. I wanted to arm every officer with information that would help him do his job better.

The brass of the department were very complimentary on the success that was achieved in the early days. They were able to see a decline in the number of burglary occurrences, as well as a rise in the number of cases we were able to solve by arrest. I was convinced that by adding a few men to my unit and by switching us to street clothes and unmarked cars, we could really make a dent in the burglary problem.

Shortly after the first of the year of 1986, my wish was granted. The unit now became three strong, and the uniforms and marked cars were left behind for good. I considered the unit to be more covert than undercover. We continued to assimilate and distribute a huge amount of intelligence information, but since we were now able to move about on the streets without being recognized as police, we began to make some big arrests.

At the slightest observation of a burglary or any other crime being committed by a career criminal, we did not hesitate to move in, identify ourselves as police, and make the arrest.

We broadened our horizons, too. By profiling known active criminals, we got to know their homes, their cars, their associates, their hangouts, and their criminal files. If Joe Crook was known to have so much as a traffic warrant out on him and if we saw him, he went to jail. Many times, a simple stop and arrest yielded either a car full of stolen goods from a crime that had just been committed but not yet reported, or the arrestee had dope on him. What started as a simple misdemeanor arrest more often than not turned into a solid felony charge.

Occasionally, one addict-crook's name would appear over and over as a suspect on burglary reports, but even with our best efforts we could not catch him. In those instances, we worked to find out where the person was staying. Early in the morning, we would set surveillance on that place and, when the suspect came out, we would follow. The reasoning was we knew that the suspect was a known drug taker and had to go out and commit a crime to support his habit. He would either shoplift, commit a burglary or go buy dope. We would follow, observe, and arrest.

This method also had the secondary benefit that it played on the paranoia of an addict. From our informants, we learned that most addicts thought they were being followed. As a result, some criminals actually stopped their unlawful activity and sought help in detoxification centers. I transported and assisted several of these individuals to find help.

Not only had my efforts in combating burglary been rewarded by the Downtown Optimist Club, when I received their Police Officer of the Year Award for 1985, the police chief of that time, Tom Nichols, had nominated me for the Texas Peace Officer of the Year Award given by the attorney general's office. I was one of sixteen nominees statewide. Even though I was the nominee, I was very aware that the work of my fellow officers contributed largely to the award. Their hard work had made the unit succeed.

As the burglary work continued to progress and then stabilized, I became eligible for promotion to sergeant, and I decided to go for it. By January of 1987 I had a new gold sergeant's badge, number 13, a number that would have great significance in my life. The promotion had a downside, however, in the form of a new assignment. At that time the police department had a policy of assigning all new sergeants to the front desk for a period. I thrived on street police work, so putting me at the front desk to handle an endless line of dissatisfied citizens and ringing phones was not unlike taking an eagle who has spent his life free and locking him in a cage.

After thirteen months, two weeks and four days on the desk, relief came. While I was assigned to the desk, Sergeant Pat Nesbitt took over the unit I had founded. The success was so great that the brass decided to combine a less effective plainclothes squad with the highly effective burglary unit. When Nesbitt was promoted to lieutenant, he told the bosses that Bill Hubbard was the sergeant to fill his vacancy. I was sprung from my cage and put back on the work I loved so much. We combined the Selective Law Enforcement Unit with the Tactical Unit and adopted the new name of Street Crimes

Unit. By now the unit had grown in size to seven officers, including Pat Kelly and me.

Though some considered his methods somewhat unconventional, Pat had been extremely successful at fighting crime and getting crooks off the street. Unconventional or not, Kelly regularly worked twelve to fourteen hours a day, got the job done, had an impressive network of informants, and did his job within the law and within the guidelines of the unit.

When, despite this, local media became critical of an intensive investigation he spearheaded, Pat was incensed by the press batterings. Nothing illegal or in violation of department policy had occurred, but it had not turned out the way originally intended. Pat got tired of the criticism, and, when a position in accident investigation opened up, he took it, relieved to leave the headlines behind. My advice at the time had been for him to hang in there and let the storm pass, but he opted for the transfer anyhow.

Pat Kelly and I had another thing in common besides having been classmates at the academy. We both were intensely disliked by Travis Ware, and the dislike stemmed from our work on the Street Crimes Unit. If I felt my case or the case of one of my men had merit, I was quick to spring to its defense in the office of any prosecutor in the Criminal District Attorney's office. I was not intimidated by the fact that they were lawyers and I was, as they said, just a cop. I did my homework, studied case law and recent court rulings, and governed the unit's activities and reports accordingly. I had no patience with a prosecutor who was not up on the latest rulings, who put down and demeaned police officers, or who did not seem to be doing his job to the fullest so that a criminal could get a full measure of the law. I feel to this day that I owed this to my fellow officers and to the victims of the crimes. On more than one occasion, my conversation with the prosecutor degenerated to a shouting match in the hallway of the D.A.'s office. Criminal District Attorney Travis Ware eventually came to view me as a royal pain in the rear.

In fact, I had supported Ware both verbally and financially in his initial bid to become D.A. With the passage of time, however, I recognized that he was a nonflexible individual who had to have things his way or not at all. He didn't like it when a two-bit police sergeant stood up to him or one of his staff. However, I believed in our task to stop criminals from victimizing the public and felt it was a righteous cause, and we worked hard to accomplish it.

Pat Kelly, like me, would argue the merits of his cases with prosecutors. The lawyers in Ware's office did not like being challenged by him, either.

After Pat transferred to accident investigation, he again distinguished himself as a tireless worker. Any time of the day, any day of the week, Pat was ready to respond to the gruesome automobile crashes where sometimes a life had been lost. He also did detailed follow-ups on hit-and-run accidents, so most of his work actually was detective work, but in crimes where vehicles were involved.

In November, Pat came to my office to retrieve from our files some photographs that he had taken at an Erdmann autopsy of a 1991 traffic accident victim. Apparently, a lawsuit had arisen over the accident and Dr. Erdmann had been tabbed to testify. Erdmann had contacted Kelly because he could not remember if he took photos during the autopsy. Erdmann told Kelly that if he had, he could not find them now.

This was another disturbing example of Erdmann's not following an established procedure. Wondering whether he had taken photos in any autopsy was a disgrace because that was something very fundamental that needed to be done in all cases. On top of that, if he had an organized filing system, the whereabouts of any photos should not ever be an issue.

My unit—the I.D. unit—was the custodian of all photos taken at crime scenes, accidents, autopsies, and follow-up investigations. If there was a photograph, we had it. Pat gave me the case number in question, and I located the envelope containing the pictures Pat had taken at the autopsy. What we saw in the photos absolutely blew us away. The edge of several of Pat's photos showed Dr. Erdmann with his camera taking pictures!

We now knew for a fact that Erdmann had taken photos at that autopsy and must have lost them. This discovery was disturbing and indicated to us that Erdmann could also be mislabeling, losing or misplacing other autopsy items such as tissue samples, blood for toxicology, notes and diagrams. Considering the large number of autopsies the doctor was performing, the veracity of any autopsy he performed could be in jeopardy if his files were disorganized. This new revelation, combined with all the other information which I had been accumulating since coming to the unit three months earlier, increased my doubts about Erdmann's practices and procedures.

After Kelly and I finished studying his photos, we discussed Erdmann. Pat told of a case which occurred many months earlier, where a prosecutor in the district attorney's office who had been drinking and driving had hit and killed a pedestrian, Darlene Hall. It had been a strange case from the start, because Ware and several of his associates had either witnessed the accident, or come upon the scene immediately afterward.

The involvement of Ware and members of his office at the scene gave rise to many questions at the police department as to whether the investigation had in some way been misdirected or hampered. Unfortunately, few of our questions could be answered since the evidence showed the assistant prosecutor was legally intoxicated.

Pat Kelly had attended the autopsy of Darlene Hall performed by Dr. Erdmann. Kelly said that Erdmann had commented during the procedure that there was no strong odor of alcohol coming from the body, adding that an odor was usually present if someone was drunk.

The body had been so badly damaged on impact that finding uncontaminated blood in the chest cavity for toxicology purposes would have been a difficult task. However, if blood was in fact taken, Kelly did not witness it. But Erdmann must have kept some for use in a blood alcohol test. Days later, when Kelly got the results of the test, he was stunned to learn that Dr. Erdmann now contended that the victim had not only shown alcohol in the blood, but a very high alcohol concentration—if a reeling, drunken pedestrian is hit and killed by a mildly intoxicated driver, that driver is usually in a less precarious position both criminally and civilly.

Kelly told me he had approached his lieutenant about this matter, and told the lieutenant he wanted to send a letter to Travis Ware drawing attention to his knowledge of this apparent Erdmann indiscretion. Kelly said the lieutenant told him to stay out of it and leave the matter to Ware and Erdmann. Kelly strongly suspected that Ware, or someone in his office, had given some kind of direction to Erdmann as to what Mrs. Hall's desired intoxication level should be.

The Erdmann file in my desk drawer was growing larger and larger, and my knowledge of the doctor broadened on a daily basis. I also had growing doubts about the nature of the relationship between Erdmann and Travis Ware, although at the time I had nothing solid upon which to base my suspicion. I did know, however, that officers with more exposure to the Erdmann/Ware connection were concerned that without an avalanche of information about the pathologist's inefficiency, Ware would stay firmly entrenched in the doctor's corner.

I knew when I was promoted to the detective division that I would have to be present at an autopsy in the not-too-distant future. Only a few days later my knowledge not only of autopsies, but of Dr. Erdmann, became firsthand.

Ten minutes before midnight on Saturday, November 16th, the phone call came. Cops hate late-night phone calls. I knew who would be on the other end before I even said "Hello."

"Sergeant Hubbard, this is Amy at the communications center. There's been a shooting at 2915 Colgate, and the officers are calling for detectives."

"Okay," I said. "Call Detective Shields and get him started over there. I'll be en route."

I turned to Debbie. "I'm going to work. It's late now, so don't wait up." I went to get dressed. Another Saturday night cut short, but Debbie always understood that this is my life. I dressed in jeans and a shirt, and put my badge on my belt, along with my Glock 9mm pistol. A light jacket over that, and I was out the door.

The time it would take to get from my house to the crime scene was less than ten minutes. As I drove, I tried to get an idea of the neighborhood in my mind. I had spent many hours in that area, especially during my stint in Street Crimes. The predominantly Hispanic neighborhood seemed to have an overabundance of drug dealers, gangs, junkies, and thieves. Sprinkled in among that were really good folks who had owned their homes for years and could not afford to move out when the less-desirables moved in to take over. Those good folks often ended up being the real victims by being captives in their own homes, and when they did get out, their homes were robbed. It was a neighborhood in transition.

I drove east on Colgate from the nearest main street and looked ahead the three blocks to where my crime scene was supposed to be. As I drew closer, I could see the yellow crime scene tape, cop cars, and cops. I parked at the closest intersection and got out of my car. Lt. Ricky Cross, a classmate of mine from my academy days and the ranking patrol officer on the scene, was in the intersection.

"What do we have here, Ricky?" I asked.

"Not much is here that I can tell," he answered. "The people here aren't being real helpful. They always want to take care of it themselves. Anyhow, the house is up there on the right, second from the corner. Some kind of a party was going on there when some rival gang members drove up in a white Camaro. Two guys got out of it, went up to the group outside, produced a gun and started shooting. Two were hit, and the guys in the Camaro split. The partyers loaded the two wounded in a red pickup and drove them to the hospital."

"How are they doing?"

"One of them's in pretty bad shape, from what I've been told, but the other is expected to be okay."

"And the guys in the white Camaro?"

"We've got them," Cross said. "Savell and some others found it moving just a little way from here. We've got four in custody and we have the gun."

This was looking promising. Great work by Patrol Division always makes a detective's life easier. Wesley Shields drove up as Cross finished briefing me.

"Hey, Wes. I hope you weren't doing anything important."

"You know me Sarge, I live to come to work on Saturday night." His sarcasm was not lost on me. "What have we got?"

As Shields loaded his 35mm camera, I relayed to him what I had learned from Cross. "I'll get a wrecker on the way for the Camaro, and we'll lock it up at the police garage so we can deal with it later," I said. "Savell has the gun, and the Suits are headed to the P.D. to deal with the ones in custody."

With suspects in custody, witnesses, glass from the scene, glass from the Camaro, the bullet and the gun that fired it, this case already was beginning to look ready for a courtroom. There was still a lot of work to be done, but, even at this early stage, it appeared to be a prosecutable case. However, the stakes quickly increased when one of the victims died at the hospital.

The autopsy of this victim would be vital to the case. Not only would the track of the bullet need to be traced in order to determine an exact cause of death, but when the bullet was recovered from the body, it could be matched by an expert to the gun that fired it. The next day Shields and I went to the morgue at University Medical Center where the autopsy was to be performed.

I approached this with some measure of fear and trepidation. There are several of these morbid occasions that come along during a police career that you really don't know how you will handle until you are faced with them. One is your first arrest. Another is your first homicide call. Still another is your first body that has been dead for a while before it was discovered. I was at the brink of another of those morbid rites of passage—my first autopsy. Would I handle it okay? Would I get sick? If I did anything but handle it well, you could bet it would be all over the police department by the next day.

When Shields and I got to the morgue that day, Dr. Erdmann was already there, scalpel in hand, about to start. I reminded him curtly that police identification officers had to be present in a homicide autopsy. "You do understand that, don't you?" I said.

He answered, "I do."

Though I had seen the man on the television news, this was our first face-to-face meeting. He was smaller than I expected, having a somewhat military appearance with neatly

arranged attire and a short, flattop haircut. He spoke with
a thick German accent. I had been told by Detective
Shields that Dr. Erdmann was a big fan of the University
of Texas, and I had observed the university's burnt orange
decal and the "Hook 'Em Horns" insignia on the doctor's
Cadillac parked outside the hospital.

"Have X-rays been taken?" Shields asked as Dr. Erdmann prepared to cut. All of my research indicated that
X-rays are standard procedure, and here Erdmann was
set to get started without seeing to what I felt was a basic
matter.

Shields reminded Dr. Erdmann that the body had the
entrance wound of a bullet in the chest but no exit wound,
which indicated that the bullet was still in the body. Especially in a case like this, X-rays are of the utmost importance
in order to know where exactly in the body the bullet is located so it can be recovered. Since we had the gun we believed fired the bullet, the bullet's recovery without further
damage to it was imperative.

Putting aside his scalpel, Dr. Erdmann went to the
phone and ordered the portable X-ray unit sent to the
morgue. Once the X-rays were taken and read, Erdmann
again took out his scalpel and was ready to proceed. Only
after Shields took out his photography equipment and
began shooting pictures did Dr. Erdmann get his own
camera out and take some reference shots of his own.

"What is your theory about what happened here?" Dr.
Erdmann asked. I had been warned that this was a tactic
he used. It was said that in order to stay in good with law
enforcement and those who paid his salary, the doctor
would usually ask the police what their theory was in the
homicide. And in most, if not all, of those cases, his autopsy would prove the theory. Just like that. Short and
sweet. Cut and dried.

I wasn't about to be a party to such a practice. Politely,
I said, "Dr. Erdmann, you're the pathologist. You tell *us*

what happened to the body. Then we'll determine if the autopsy results are consistent with what we saw at the crime scene." When I told Dr. Erdmann this, I could see that he was not pleased. However, he remained businesslike and proceeded with the autopsy.

Dr. Erdmann did not have an assistant, but did the autopsy all himself. Common sense would indicate that handling something as large, heavy and bulky as a limp human body is more than one person can handle. Erdmann remarked how expensive it was to keep help on a per-autopsy basis. I then found that attendance at a Ralph Erdmann autopsy was often a hands-on experience for police officers. As Dr. Erdmann prepared to retrieve the bullet which had entered the front of the chest, pierced the heart, and lodged between two ribs in the back, I found myself wearing surgical gloves and helping with the bullet removal. I was quite sure that Shields was getting a real charge out of this. His new sergeant was not only attending his first autopsy, but getting the full treatment as well.

As he called out instructions, I helped Dr. Erdmann roll the body onto one side. While I reached into the open chest cavity and put my gloved finger into the bullet track toward the back, Dr. Erdmann felt the place where I was pushing. He made a small incision at that point, and the bullet came out into his hand. Shields documented the procedure with photographs.

With the bullet recovered and the cause of death ascertained, I could see by his expression and body language that Dr. Erdmann was about through. I had not seen him perform other procedures that I knew from my research were standard in a homicide autopsy, such as the removal, dissection and weighing of major organs. In fact, there was no scale in the autopsy room. I knew that every autopsy report I had ever seen had listed the weights in grams of each of the major organs. If his final report contained organ weights, they would only be guesses. I had seen absolutely no lower tract or stomach exam. No eye or eye fluid recovery had been done.

Finally, Dr. Erdmann had not so much as made a cursory external examination of the victim's head, no less done an internal exam. As he was putting his instruments away, I asked him about it. "In a situation like this, the head is not normally opened," Dr. Erdmann snapped.

From my interviews and reading I knew that in a homicide autopsy just the opposite was true, and I told him so.

"Do you want the head opened?" Erdmann demanded irritably.

"You are the forensic pathologist, and if the head should be opened, you should do so."

"Where did you get your expertise?" Erdmann asked.

"I have no expertise. I know only what I have read."

"And what is that?"

I mentioned the DiMaio book. Erdmann then began interpreting the Code of Criminal Procedure for me, saying that the autopsy only had to proceed to the point where the doctor could determine the cause of death.

"In a homicide there is much more to consider than just how the person died," I reminded him. "The pathologist must do a full autopsy in order to be ready to answer any and all questions that may be raised by either the prosecution or the defense."

Then I changed my approach. "If this case were being handled by any medical examiner's office around the state, would they open the head?" I asked.

He said he did not know.

"I do know," I fired back. "It seems to me that without a thorough examination of the head, the defense could claim that the victim had earlier received a head injury that had made him combative and that the suspect shot him in self-defense," I said defiantly. As the autopsy stood at this point, Dr. Erdmann could not successfully answer such questions and thereby defeat a defense theory. I did know from Erdmann's furious expression that he did not like having a first-time visitor to the morgue telling him how to do his job. He grew quite angry and summoned the morgue manager to assist him in preparing to do the cranial examination. By this time I think Detective Shields had moved off to the side for fear that objects might start flying across the room.

At that moment the morgue manager, Woodson Rowan, came in and diverted Erdmann's attention from me. They prepared to do the cranial. Due to the tension and the fact that another witness was now present, I felt it best if Shields and I left and let Dr. Erdmann finish up. I could check with Rowan or the funeral home later to ascertain if a thorough cranial had been done. We left, and I later verified that the procedure had been completed.

I knew I had angered Dr. Erdmann and fully expected some backlash, especially if Erdmann took the matter to Travis Ware. So the next day, I wrote a three-page memo to Lieutenant Summerlin and Captain Wiley detailing the events at the morgue. In the memo I commented that Dr. Erdmann either did not know or did not care what the standards of his own profession were.

The expected backlash did not happen right away. With my first two drafts of the protocol in hand, together with the input of Dr. DiMaio of Bexar County, I was able to complete a third draft by the third week of November. I sent it with a cover memo up my chain of command.

The protocol spelled out the steps to be followed by the investigative agency as well as the pathologist performing the autopsy. I purposely kept it generic so that no names or personalities would enter in. And, so that both the police and pathologist would have a complete picture of what was going on, the protocol began with

the officers' on-scene investigation and continued
through every step of the full autopsy procedure. It left
no doubt that in a homicide a full autopsy would be required. I wondered but did not ask why a protocol had
not been drafted in the five years Erdmann had been
doing autopsies so haphazardly.

I decided not to complain. I was relieved that the project was completed and was out of my hands. It would be
up to my superiors if something was to come of it. After
I handed it in, I went back to my main tasks of getting
my job done, being trained and gaining expertise in my
new field. But I still kept track of Erdmann, adding new
elements and reports to his file.

The early winter was a busy time for the homicide
unit. No sooner had we begun to make headway on cases
we were working than we were slapped with another
case. On the last Sunday of November, Buffalo Lewis
and I worked an East Lubbock stabbing death of a
woman whose live-in boyfriend was the immediate suspect. As we processed the scene for physical evidence
and did the photography, Detective George White conducted interviews and did the leg work that would eventually lead to the boyfriend's arrest.

The next morning Lewis and White made plans to
attend the autopsy by Dr. Erdmann. White was still red
hot about the October autopsy where Erdmann had
failed to check the victim's stomach contents and brought
the case to a screeching halt. He was not about to let this
one be messed up, so he attended the autopsy himself.

When they returned, I called Buffalo into my office to
interview him about the procedures Erdmann had done
so I could take notes and put them in my file. When
Buffalo told me it was a typical Erdmann autopsy, I was
not encouraged. Apparently, my exchange with the
doctor the week before had no effect on him. Buffalo
told me that, basically, Erdmann had done a cause-of-

death autopsy and not a full autopsy. Again, no organs were removed, examined and weighed. And once again, Dr. Erdmann had not done a cranial exam until Detective White strongly insisted on it. White believed there was a possibility the victim had been hit in the head before receiving the fatal stab wounds. The Erdmann file grew.

The following Thursday I was looking forward to my first Thanksgiving Day off in six years, but it wasn't to be. Just before sunup, the telephone on my nightstand rang. I responded with Detective Shields to the scene of a beating in northern Lubbock near the airport. A night of drinking and arguing had set brother against brother armed with knives and baseball bats. Our suspect had fled, and the victim was barely alive in the hospital with massive head wounds. He was being connected to a respirator. It appeared to be only a matter of time before the case was raised from aggravated assault to murder. Shields notified Dr. Erdmann that the victim was in bad shape and that when he was finally disconnected from the respirator, we would need to be present for the autopsy.

The weekend came and went. On Monday, Shields contacted Dr. Erdmann's office only to find that the victim had been taken off life support on Saturday. Dr. Erdmann had gone ahead and performed the autopsy without anyone present. We were stunned, because we at least thought Dr. Erdmann was clear on the need for identification officers to be present for the procedure, especially in homicide cases. That had been the one thing we thought we had gotten across to him. Apparently we had not. As poor as Dr. Erdmann's procedures and documentation had been to this point, I could only imagine what he would do (or not do) if witnesses were not even there.

Dr. Erdmann then apologized to Detective Shields

and claimed he did not understand that we wanted to be present for all homicide autopsies.

"We are still new at this and still learning," he said. When Shields asked him for a copy of the autopsy report, Dr. Erdmann told him that the request would have to be a formal request on a department letterhead.

I did not like the smell of the case. With Dr. Erdmann not having the police present at the autopsy and then being cagey about providing a routine copy of a report, I got the feeling that he was getting suspicious that something bad was brewing. I wondered if because his last two homicide autopsies had been actively challenged in-progress by detectives present, he had solved that little problem by not notifying those detectives that he was going to do a homicide autopsy. Going to my bosses, I urged them, "Please move the protocol ahead before the situation with Dr. Erdmann explodes and causes us serious problems."

By the second week of December, the actions of our pathologist progressed from giving me cause for concern to scaring the living daylights out of me. Detective Lewis and I worked a double murder where one victim was known to have AIDS and the other was believed to be HIV positive. It was a bizarre and gruesome scene, and we were extremely careful in conducting our investigation and gathering evidence, much of which was blood evidence. Dr. Erdmann notified us when and where the autopsies were to take place, and that he would do them both on the same evening.

When Buffalo and I got to the University Medical Center morgue, Dr. Erdmann was attired as he always was for an autopsy in plastic apron and gloves. He was ready to proceed. On the wall in the morgue and also in the outer office were guidelines for a "high risk" autopsy, which included victims even remotely believed to be HIV positive. The belief was that it was better to be safe than to risk environmental contamination or infection of those present. Looking around, I concluded that Dr. Erdmann had not taken one of the specified precautions that were posted on the wall fewer than six feet from him!

I asked him about this, and he told me not to worry. "The HIV virus cannot live for more than about ten minutes after a body dies, and these bodies have been in refrigeration most of the day." Thoughts of infections that occurred after mere blood transfusions flashed through my mind, and this unsubstantiated revelation did not sway me from my resolve not to assist him this time, but to keep my distance. I would get in there only when necessary for photographic documentation.

Without further ado, Dr. Erdmann began the autopsy, cutting four pairs of surgical gloves off his hands as he went. Once, a back-splash of fluid got him right in the face and he dove to the sink to wash it off.

Since both of the victims had apparently died of massive head wounds, Dr. Erdmann had no choice this time but to do cranial examinations. However, as we watched in shocked silence, in blatant violation of the posted procedure, he approached the task with power instruments. His first cut sent visible bloodlets flying fifteen feet to either side of the autopsy table. I wondered what kinds of unseen bloodlets could now be airborne, so I motioned to Buffalo and we got out of there until things could calm down. I was both sick and disgusted. And I had to admit that Dr. Erdmann had found an effective way to keep the police away from his autopsies!

Within a few days of Christmas, Dr. Erdmann called me at my office saying that he had been chastised by the hospital management for leaving the morgue messy after his last autopsies. He asked for a letter from me to defend him. He got a letter from me, all right, but I am sure my angry words about his inadequacies were not at all what he expected.

At about this time, Lieutenant Summerlin and Captain Wiley were finally able to get the protocol I had drafted looked at by the district attorney. I never was able to learn the particulars of the meeting, but I was advised of the outcome. Captain Wiley reported back to me that Travis Ware had recommended that his staff write a protocol, and that the police department go ahead and complete their protocol. At some later date we would meet to formally mesh and adopt the resulting plan.

The agreement to have two protocols to "mesh" into one was just another example of the lengths the police department was willing to go to appease Travis Ware, hoping to get something done about Ralph Erdmann. If we had to let Ware run the show and make it all look like something he thought of and orchestrated, we would have to accept that. What we needed was a new set of regulations for conducting homicide autopsies properly, not an ego struggle over whose idea it was or who could get the credit or blame.

Captain Wiley directed me to telephone Travis Ware. The conversation was cordial and businesslike. I agreed to add even more details to the protocol I had written, so that it would cover the whole sequence of events and "who was to do what and when" from the time the police first discovered a homicide through the autopsy.

Within days I had added twenty paragraphs to the paper I had authored and retitled it, "Homicide Protocol." I then sent my proposal to Ware's staff. Apparently, Ware was to do the "meshing" himself, because the protocol the D.A.'s staff was to write never did make it to the police department, until we met some seven weeks later to formally adopt it. That meeting would turn out to be quite a memorable event.

5

"Have I Told You. . . ?"

Detective George White had pretty well had his fill of
Ralph Erdmann. White's problems with the pathologist
dated back much further than just the recent stomach
contents case and the case where White had insisted Erdmann do a complete cranial examination.

One day, White stopped by while Detective Doug
Sutton was in my office sharing "Erdmannisms" of his
own. The case White wanted to talk about dated back to
November of 1990. White had been so concerned about
it at the time that he had made extensive notes in his
police computer file. He had now printed those notes
and gave them to me for inclusion in the rapidly growing file on Erdmann. This expansive collection made my
office the place detectives would come day after day with
cups of coffee in hand to offer, "Have I told you the one
that Dr. Erdmann . . . ?"

According to White's notes, a death which appeared
to be a suicide had been ordered for autopsy by Justice
of the Peace L.J. Blalack. This was standard procedure.

However, about three weeks later when the judge received Erdmann's autopsy report, it listed the cause of death as asphyxiation caused by a plastic bag covering the head. Blalack called Detective White to let him know that Dr. Erdmann's report was not consistent with the police report. White did some checking and could find nothing even remotely to do with a plastic bag in regard to the death.

White then contacted Erdmann and got a vague explanation that "someone" had told the doctor about the involvement of a plastic bag. Backtracking, White contacted every person who had been involved with the case who had also communicated with Dr. Erdmann. He could find no one who made any mention at all concerning a plastic bag. Detectives Lewis and Riemer had both been present at the autopsy and had explained the circumstances surrounding the death to Dr. Erdmann before he started. No mention of a plastic bag was made in the conversation.

White set up a meeting to be held in Judge Blalack's office to get the problem cleared up. Erdmann, Lewis, Riemer, White and Blalack were to attend. Dr. Erdmann did not show up. The meeting concluded with Judge Blalack saying that he would have Dr. Erdmann remove the incorrect pages from his autopsy report and replace them with correct information. Blalack told the officers that Erdmann had done this sort of thing in the past, and he had used the same procedure to get Erdmann to correct the problem.

Reading White's notes, I was stunned. I wondered how a problem of this magnitude which had been exposed to a county official as far back as 1990—apparently not a first occurrence, either—had not been thoroughly investigated. And I wanted to know why Erdmann was still doing Lubbock's autopsies more than a year later! No wonder White was so upset over the two recent homicide autopsies. So far as he was concerned, it was just a lot more of the same old incompetence. And to this day no one knows how or why Erdmann came up with the theory about the bag.

"Shoot, I can top that," Sutton said. He told of investigating a home death where he had been contacted by the victim's family who believed foul play was involved. Initially, it looked to police like a drug overdose. When Sutton asked the victim's mother why she felt it was foul play, she said that Erdmann, with family permission, had released autopsy information to the victim's psychiatrist, and the psychiatrist had found indicators in the autopsy report that possibly could lead to a conclusion of homicide. Hearing this, the mother called Dr. Erdmann directly, and the pathologist told her he had not conferred with anyone concerning this autopsy. The victim's mother then became concerned that Dr. Erdmann might have confused information from another autopsy with that of her daughter. She asked Sutton to check into it.

Erdmann told Sutton that the case appeared to be a simple drug overdose. Erdmann did not recall conferring with the psychiatrist about it. He then launched into his familiar explanation of why such a mistake might have occurred. He was extremely overworked, he said, and he had gotten far behind in his paperwork.

Wanting to know more, the detective telephoned the psychiatrist, who said that Dr. Erdmann had told him of bruises about the victim's neck that might lead one to suspect strangulation. In the police world, there is quite a distance between a drug overdose, which could be either an accident or a suicide, and strangulation, which would mean that it was a homicide and a killer was running around loose.

The psychiatrist told Sutton he had talked to Dr. Erdmann and felt the man definitely was referring to the right person, because Erdmann spoke of physical characteristics that matched the psychiatrist's knowledge of his patient. The psychiatrist also complained that Dr. Erdmann had questioned him as to whether the patient was known to be a lesbian. The psychiatrist told Sutton, "I believe I told Dr. Erdmann that this questioning was completely out of line, since it had nothing to do with establishing the cause of death and whether or not the physical evidence indicated homicide, accident, or suicide."

Within a few days of talking to Sutton, another crisis of a different sort, also revolving around Dr. Erdmann, occurred. I was notified by the chemists at the Lubbock state police laboratory that blood Dr. Erdmann was drawing at autopsies for testing and toxicology purposes was being submitted to them in tubes that contained no preservatives. By the time the blood got to the lab to do the necessary analyses, it was often putrefied or had deteriorated in such a way that the results were compromised. Concern was also expressed that the same problem might be occurring in the blood testing Erdmann was doing himself or submitting to other labs. To prevent this happening again, we went to the local health department and obtained the kind of tubes the chemists told us should be used. From then on we took these empty tubes to autopsies and made sure that the blood samples went into them.

It almost got to the point that I wondered why we didn't go and do the autopsy ourselves and leave Erdmann completely out of it! The extreme measures we had to use to ensure accurate autopsies and complete results were getting ridiculous.

The subject of blood samples and testing opened up a new avenue of investigation into Erdmann's incompetence. By February of 1992, the beating death Detective Shields and I had worked the previous Thanksgiving had returned to the foreground. State police chemists examining the suspected death weapon contacted us for control samples of blood from both the victim and the suspect, so they could tell whose blood was on the items we had submitted for testing. Shields contacted Erdmann to ask for a sample of the victim's blood to take to the lab. Dr. Erdmann said he did not know the whereabouts of the blood at that time, but he would check and call us back. Several days passed and the doctor did not call back, even though two additional messages were left with his secretary.

Shields had been trying for more than two weeks to get this blood sample from Erdmann when he brought the situation to my attention. I called Erdmann and requested the blood. Dr. Erdmann told me he had given the blood to the officers who had attended the autopsy and they had probably already submitted it to the police laboratory. I reminded the doctor that this was the case from Thanksgiving where we had made several contacts with him and his office requesting to be notified when the autopsy would be. He had done the procedure on his own, without notifying us, though.

At that point, he changed his story and said he must have sent it to the "toxicology laboratory," but would not specify which toxicology laboratory. He said he would find out the name and call me back.

By the third of February we had not heard anything more from the pathologist; so I notified the chief investigator at the D.A.'s office of the situation to see if they could get Erdmann on the stick. Within hours another investigator called me back, saying he had talked to Erdmann, who told him that the blood in question had been "sent to an independent toxicology laboratory and that all of the blood had been used up."

I did not have the means to prove it, but his story did not seem likely. This threw yet another stumbling block in the way of prosecuting yet another murder case. "I am becoming really weary of Ralph Erdmann's detrimental effect on so many of our major cases," I said, as I made my position absolutely clear to those in authority over me at the police department.

At about the same time—late January—Erdmann found himself in a predicament a little farther north, in Canyon, Texas. He had been subpoenaed to testify in a capital murder case and things were not going too well for the doctor.

According to articles in the *Lubbock Avalanche-Journal,* defense attorneys for Johnny Lee Rey, a capital murder defendant, sought to disqualify Dr. Erdmann as an expert witness. The defense made a motion in 251st District Court asking the judge to allow admission of evidence about the reputation, truthfulness, or untruthfulness of Dr. Erdmann. The lead defense counsel, C.R. Daffern, wished to question Erdmann under oath to find out if Erdmann had ever falsified any autopsy reports. If Erdmann replied no, Daffern sought to pursue with additional questioning.

Erdmann spent nearly an hour on the witness stand. What really astounded courtroom observers was that Erdmann could not answer specific questions concerning when he graduated from college, what year he went into the armed forces, and when he was licensed to practice medicine in the United States. Regardless of these shortcomings, the judge ruled that Erdmann could serve as an expert witness.

Despite this startling decision, I still had hopes that some light would appear at the end of our Erdmann tunnel. The staff of Travis Ware's office had completed work on their suggested homicide protocol and Ware had contacted the police department to set the meeting to "mesh" the two protocols, even though the one written by the D.A.'s staff had never been revealed to us.

On February 5, 1992, at 10:00 A.M., the whole chain of command of my unit went to the D.A.'s office to meet with Ware and his staff. With me were Colonel Ewing, Captain Wiley and Lieutenant Summerlin. With Ware were two of his investigators, Tom Loper and Dewayne Haney. These two investigators were the ones tabbed to come to crime scenes for videotaping and they had done the bulk of the work on the D.A.'s protocol.

At the meeting, copies of the D.A.'s protocol were distributed. Ewing, Wiley, Summerlin and I looked them over during the half hour Ware kept us waiting. The D.A.'s protocol consisted of four pages dated January 30, 1992. The first page was a cover memo from Haney and Loper while the last page was marked "special notes." That left two pages of any substance at all and those pages were titled, "Autopsy Protocol." The problem was that the two pages concerned only when the investigators from the Criminal District Attorney's office would or would not attend an autopsy. That was it. Not one word was included as to what the procedure should be during an autopsy. The title "Autopsy Protocol" was misleading to say the least. However, this four-page document had been validated by a one-inch tall signature at the end: Travis S. Ware.

I felt their protocol was extremely weak. In addition, it contained a lot of outs for the D.A.'s investigators. It held such stipulations as, "Under no circumstances will the C.D.A. investigator touch the deceased victim's body or any item containing or having a residue of blood or body fluids," and "C.D.A. investigator is not to take custody of any evidence at the autopsy." This protocol indicated that all the dirty work would be left to the police department. However, I knew it would be just fine with my men if the C.D.A. investigator simply shot his video and left.

I really did not see anything to "mesh" between the two documents. The one done by the D.A.'s staff was so thin that it certainly did not conflict with the lengthy, detailed document that the police department had constructed and forwarded to them.

Finally, we were ushered into Ware's office. As always, the district attorney projected the image of a male model. Tall, good looking and lean, he wore his expensive suit, power tie and Rolex watch well. His heavily starched white shirt sparkled against his perennial tan.

Officers from the police department who visited Ware's office had come to expect being subjected to a monologue. Ware loved to lecture cops and he always did it from a mind-set of superiority. Today was no exception.

For fifteen minutes Ware went on and on extolling the virtues of Dr. Erdmann, telling us how the pathologist had pulled Lubbock County out of a hole because he took the job when no one else seemed interested in it. We heard over and over about how hardworking Erdmann was and how he was "one hell of a witness who has gotten us some great convictions."

With what I had already seen and heard, I had no doubt that this was indeed the case. Dr. Erdmann was putty in a prosecutor's hands, and was so eager to please that he could tailor-make an autopsy and testify just about any way the prosecution desired. Finally, when the lecture was over, I said, "Look, we are tired of Erdmann's constantly asking the police at the autopsy what we want. He is the pathologist and should know what needs to be done and that it should be done the same way in all homicide cases."

Ware ignored me. I mentioned that Erdmann's autopsy reports often were not timely and that I believed that in situations such as the listing of organ weights Dr. Erdmann was simply guessing. I had never seen him remove one single organ and place it on a scale, even though every one of his reports listed the weights of the organs in grams. "I believe that if he is not doing a procedure as simple as that and his report says that he is, there is a high likelihood that he is not doing other things but is reporting as if he had."

Ware interrupted. "If a guy died of a gunshot wound to the head, it shouldn't matter what his liver weighed."

"That is not the point," I insisted. "The point is that he is reporting as fact a procedure he has not done."

"I have checked around and it is standard among forensic pathologists to estimate organ weights," Ware said. "Almost no one actually puts them on a scale."

Ware wouldn't name his source of information, and that fact would come back to haunt him a year later in the presence of a federal judge. Nevertheless, Ware assured us he would "straighten Erdmann out." I remembered Captain Wiley's advice and was glad I'd followed it. Going to Ware with sufficient hard data seemed to be the correct route. If we had gone to Erdmann and he in turn had gotten Ware to side with him, we would be out in the cold.

Still, I felt a concern that I couldn't stifle. "I am worried that Dr. Erdmann will not comply with the step-by-step autopsy protocol that we are adopting," I said.

"He'll either comply or I'll fucking fire his ass," Ware said.

As the meeting drew to a close, Ware observed, "It is not the practice of my office to air internal matters outside." He mentioned the newspaper article from a couple of days earlier that had told of Dr. Erdmann's troubles on the witness stand in Canyon and urged us to keep all of this quiet. "If we don't, the defense attorneys will have a field day," he said.

I sensed then that truth and doing the right thing were not nearly as important as avoiding anything that might reflect poorly on him or his office. As our delegation from the police department walked the two blocks back to the police station, I mused out loud, "Ware must believe defense attorneys can't read, because even if we do keep the matter quiet, it has already been exposed in

the newspaper. It's interesting that Ware has the audac-
ity to believe that he can dictate to us what we should or
should not keep quiet. His name certainly is not on my
paycheck."

An investigator at Ware's office told me later that on
the afternoon after our meeting, Ware called Dr. Erdmann in for a closed door session that lasted at least two
hours. The morgue manager said that later that same
day Dr. Erdmann was running around holding the protocol Ware apparently had given him, and the pathologist was not the least bit happy about it.

Unfortunately, I speculated, it was probably too little
too late. Too many instances of Erdmann foul-ups had
already occurred over too long a period of time. Too
many cases had his signature on them. The damage
could not be controlled at this late date by simply insti-
tuting a specific protocol and insisting that he adhere to
it, even if he would. . . .

And he wouldn't. Within three days of the meeting
in Ware's office, I attended another autopsy. Dr. Erdmann acted as if no protocol had ever been instituted.
He used the same few procedures he customarily performed in the same old way. No removal and examination of organs, no weighing of organs. No difference at
all, and no comment on what had happened just three
days earlier. I made no confrontation at this point,
opting instead not to say anything directly to Erdmann
about it, and see if Ware would make good his promise
to "straighten Erdmann out."

Meanwhile, as I waited, other important issues and
cases were about to be put on my schedule. They too
were related to Erdmann. I will always be amazed at the
sources of information that certain news people have.
Sometimes they know things even before the people
who are directly involved. On those occasions they get to
spring the surprise, then sit back and record the reac-

tion. Such was the case in mid-February when I received a telephone call from a local television reporter who told me I was about to receive a subpoena to testify in a capital murder case in Canyon. He even gave me the date of my scheduled court appearance: April 2, 1992.

I knew very little of the case except that six young men had been accused in the beating death of Raymond Merriman, Sr., an elderly Randall County man, during the course of committing a burglary at his home. Dr. Erdmann had done the autopsy. One of the six had already been tried, convicted and sentenced to death. Erdmann had testified in the case back in January. The hearing at which I was to appear was a pretrial hearing requested by the defense in order to argue for an exhumation of the victim, Mr. Merriman, so that a second autopsy could be done. It was the contention of the defense that the victim had not died as a result of the injury inflicted by the suspects, and they believed that a second autopsy could prove their point.

As soon as I got off the phone with the newsman, I strode through the halls of the detective division looking for any of my bosses. It was a couple of minutes after 5:00 P.M. so things were rather quiet. However, I found Colonel Ewing and Chief Don Bridgers, who had succeeded Nichols, visiting in Bridgers's office with the door open. After making sure I was not interrupting anything, I told them what I had just learned. "I have no idea how anyone as far north as Randall County could have any clue about what I know about Erdmann."

Bridgers and Ewing immediately began discussing what officers could and could not testify to so far as autopsies are concerned.

"You can say what you saw only if you are specifically asked," Bridgers pointed out. "You aren't a pathologist so you have no ability to evaluate what was or was not done."

I did not agree with the chief but I did not challenge him. I could read, and I knew from my reading that what Dr. Erdmann was doing at our autopsies was not correct procedure.

What I did voice was another worry. "I have a grave concern in particular regarding something Erdmann does regularly. In every instance where Erdmann has done a cranial exam in my presence, he has placed the brain in a container of preservative, and I believe that in each of those instances he has sent an empty-headed body off to the funeral home to be buried. Once I asked Erdmann about it, and he said matter-of-factly, 'The medical school gets the brains.'"

That had occurred so early in my tenure in homicide that I was not aware that permission for keeping organs was given only on a case by case basis. At this point, I wondered just how many brainless bodies Erdmann had sent on to be buried by unsuspecting families?

Uneasily, I waited to be served. Sometime later, the subpoena I had been told was coming arrived. It demanded my appearance on April 2nd. It also ordered me to bring with me any or all notes, written complaints, files and records pertaining to Dr. Ralph Erdmann. Even if the defense in this case had been tipped in some roundabout way that I was keeping an Erdmann file, I was sure they had no idea what a jackpot they were about to hit. Another uneasy wait began.

In the meantime, our department's business went on as usual. Unfortunately, this meant more Erdmann headaches. We were back to problems concerning the whereabouts of blood samples. Two cases were involved, both of which occurred around the previous Christmas. Not surprisingly, one of them was the case Detective Sutton had told me about, where Erdmann had communicated erroneous information to the victim's psychiatrist.

Toxicology results in this suspected overdose case had

never come back. The victim had died on December 23rd. Here it was February 17th, and we still had no idea what the toxicology screen was. In effect, the whole case was still up in the air. Captain Wiley instructed me to meet Dr. Erdmann at his office, obtain another sample of the victim's blood, and deliver it to the local state police laboratory.

I contacted the doctor by phone to set up a suitable time to meet him. Erdmann informed me that in this case, as well as another case he did about the same time, he had no toxicology results because the laboratory in California where he had sent the blood had lost both samples. Erdmann asked that when I came to receive some of the blood he had retained in the first case, if I would also receive a sample from the second case and deliver it to the police lab. I told him I would.

Before my meeting with Erdmann, I went to the police computer, and obtained and read the reports from the second case. I learned that one of my own men, Jimmie Riemer, had attended that autopsy, received the vial of blood at the time, and delivered it to the police lab on the very day of the autopsy! I had caught Dr. Erdmann in a second lie.

I did not tell Dr. Erdmann that there already was a toxicology report in the second case. I simply went to meet him as arranged and listened to him rant and rave about the California laboratory that had lost the blood he had sent them. When he let up for a moment, I told Erdmann, "I want the name and address of this lab so I can write and lodge a formal complaint because their ineptitude is harming our cases." As I expected, Erdmann became quite angry and could not seem to remember the name of the lab or locate the address.

Mumbling, he checked his log for the two cases in question and located the correspondingly numbered vials of blood he kept in a bucket in the refrigerator in his office.

For almost eight weeks both of those vials had been in the same refrigerator where he kept his lunch. Neither vial had any preservative in it. I followed the doctor to the morgue where he obtained, to my discomfort, a previously used and rinsed syringe, which he then used to draw blood from one of his vials and inject it into a preservative vial I provided. He got a second used syringe and did the same thing with the second vial. I never did tell Erdmann I knew he was not telling the truth about the California lab—especially in the second case—but simply took the blood to the police lab as I had been ordered. The chemists receiving the blood were not encouraging as to the possibility of accurate results because of the length of time the blood had been in the pathologist's refrigerator without any preservatives.

6

The Storm Hits

Storms that come across the plains of West Texas are among the most unique in the world. The land is so flat that when a frontal system moves through there is nothing in the way to slow it down. Days can start out clear and fair with what appear to be friendly clouds building on the horizon. However, as that front blitzes through, torrential rains and wind gusts whip up a frenzy, and the temperature drops as much as fifty degrees in just an hour.

Sometimes human beings and natural elements have much in common. So it was with Dr. Erdmann. By the end of January, the dark clouds around him were gaining force because of my investigation, as well as his sorry testimony on the witness stand in Canyon. Then the storm hit Hockley County just west of Lubbock where a body was about to be exhumed.

Family members had been going over Dr. Erdmann's autopsy report on their loved one, Craig Newman, who had died in what was believed by them to be either a natural death or an accident. In reading the report they noted that Dr. Erdmann had listed the weights of organs they knew Craig had had surgically removed years ago. Since the death was not a homicide, the odds that law enforcement personnel had been at the autopsy were slim to none. The people present would have been just the pathologist and the deceased. Suspicion was great over in Hockley County that no autopsy had been performed at all.

The media smelled a story and went to Erdmann, who said that he had done a "partial" autopsy on Newman, that he had a "very clear explanation of what happened" and that he "never cheated anyone."

However, a second autopsy was now ordered. It revealed that the standard Y-incision that is normally used to enter the chest to do an autopsy was never made. In fact, no incision at all was found, and all of this was quite contrary to Dr. Erdmann's written autopsy report.

Erdmann was up in arms. "I talked to Travis Ware today, and he told me we can't do anything until we know more. My conscience is clear." I found it interesting that, as the first heavy rain of the storm fell, Dr. Erdmann brought Ware into it and also used the term "we."

The ruling on the death was changed from "cocaine poisoning" in the Erdmann autopsy to "accidental" after the second autopsy. This made quite a difference to a family who had insisted from the start that their loved one was drug free. On February 24th, a Hockley County grand jury indicted Dr. Ralph Erdmann on felony charges of tampering with a government record (his autopsy report) and theft by a public servant (for receiving payment from the county after billing them for a full autopsy).

Now the storm which had first touched down in the county west of Lubbock was about to sweep the plains. The next week was one of gathering momentum as the Erdmann disturbance continued. Within two days of his indictment, the sons of the deceased Craig Newman in the Hockley County case sued Dr. Erdmann, for what they termed great distress, psychological trauma and embarrassment they suffered as a result of the initial autopsy report. Two days after that, Ector County, for which Erdmann had also done autopsies, informed him that his services were no longer needed. When Lubbock County commissioners announced they'd begun studying his employment record in early March, Dr. Erdmann resigned.

Even after the months of receiving information about Dr. Erdmann and the meeting that spelled it all out to him on February 5th, Travis Ware was still not willing to publicly acknowledge that we had major problems with Erdmann's practices. The excuse was shifted from incompetence to a heavy workload.

"Dr. Erdmann for the last year has been crying out for more help," Ware told the newspaper. "He was overworked, and we asked too much of him. He was trying to serve too many counties." To me this was ludicrous! Ware was willing to excuse Erdmann for writing an autopsy report on an autopsy he had never done, because Erdmann was overworked! I felt the greed factor must figure in somewhere.

Instead of cutting back, Erdmann took on more and more work because each additional county was willing to pay for his services. It got to be an impossible task to cover all that territory. Yet Erdmann apparently wanted the money so badly that he was willing to write reports without having done the work so he could get on to the next job and the next paycheck. Of all the things Dr. Erdmann "forgot" or intentionally neglected to do, I found out that billing for his services did not seem to be one of them.

Meanwhile, more bungled cases illustrating Erdmann's inadequacies caused lightning bursts of news. Three days after Ware's statement, a man was arrested in

Childress, Texas, for a May 1991 killing. Dr. Erdmann's original autopsy concluded at the time of death that the victim had died of natural causes. However, disputes arose after exhumation, and another autopsy by Amarillo's new forensic pathologist concluded that the death occurred as a result of smothering.

By March 13, 1992, Dr. Erdmann's services had been canceled in the counties of Dawson, Gaines and Garza. Rumors abounded that Castro and Lynn counties were expected to follow suit soon. Speculation was running rampant as to what other dark secrets might be buried on the panhandle plains of Texas. People wondered what kind of criminal behavior by Dr. Erdmann might be hidden in graves there, and if previous cases in which Erdmann had performed autopsies might be jeopardized in courtrooms or overturned on appeal. Guesses were made that "hundreds" of bodies might need to be exhumed in order to determine the extent of the problem.

Meanwhile, subpoenas were flying all over West Texas. They demanded court appearances, by mostly law enforcement officials, at the pretrial exhumation hearing on the capital murder case in Canyon. Not only had I received a subpoena but seven or eight other Lubbock officers and officials had been summoned as well, including the past two officers who held the position I now had. Largely due to the fact that we had been summoned by the defense, the City of Lubbock attorneys were contesting the subpoenas and the materials that we had been ordered to provide to the court. We were all briefed on the status of the city's motion to contest our appearances at a meeting in the chief's conference room on March 19th. In that meeting, I made no bones about the fact that I had documentation that led me to believe that Dr. Erdmann was a major misfit, and that under oath I intended to hold nothing back.

This did not appear to go over well with some at the

meeting. In the police world, there seems to be an unwritten code that demands silence in any matter that reflects poorly on the law enforcement community. I still find that code to be revolting, because I believe things that reflect poorly on the law enforcement community need to be confronted and corrected.

At the meeting I also detected some nervousness on the part of certain officers in attendance. They appeared to be worried that they might be made to look foolish on the witness stand, if it was brought to light that they, in fact, had some knowledge of problems with Dr. Erdmann but had failed to take steps to do anything about it. Some had not so much as even advised their superiors. As the meeting adjourned, I was mocked by one person for "stirring it up." This was the same person who had once told Pat Kelly to leave the problems about Erdmann to be worked out between Erdmann and Ware. The general advice was to keep a low profile. *Stay out of it. Don't get involved.*

Lubbock was not the only area that was getting hit with a rainstorm of subpoenas. Farther south in Odessa six detectives received summonses to appear in Canyon for April 2nd. This was after it was discovered that those detectives had written memos citing complaints about Dr. Erdmann back in February, on the very day my bosses and I had been in Travis Ware's office spelling the problem out to him.

In the Odessa detectives' memos the complaints about Dr. Erdmann included improper specimen collection procedures, reluctance to do cranials, asking detectives to assist or do portions of autopsies, confusion on wound identification, not weighing organs, failure to document during the autopsy, and splattering infected blood on detectives. All of the things detailed in Odessa sounded very familiar to me from my firsthand experience. It seemed to me that the lawyers for the defense in Canyon had done their homework and were laying the foundation for quite a courtroom scene on April 2nd.

Just when it looked like the dark, tumultuous cloud could hold no more before a tornado tore through Canyon, one more startling revelation came to light. Dr. Erdmann's wife had been receiving money from tissue harvesting firms in return for her giving tips to them concerning the names of decedents and how to contact families of potential donors. Who could be in a better position to receive such information than the wife of the only man doing autopsies in a forty-one county region? The legalities and possible unethical involvement of Dr. Erdmann in all of this was nauseating. It was revealed that even though the checks from the tissue firms were made out to Mrs. Erdmann, many of the checks had been endorsed by Erdmann himself and deposited into his personal bank account. The money ran into many thousands of dollars. Just when I thought that Erdmann had found every way possible to squeeze a few more dollars out of West Texas, I learned he had found yet another way. At $140,000 a year from Lubbock County alone, plus $650 to $750 per autopsy for other counties, plus $50 for an autopsy report, plus cash for information given to tissue firms about potential donors, it didn't take much skill in arithmetic to see that the Erdmann family was knocking down some major dollars.

Douglas Nathan Palmer, one of the six young men who had been accused of beating an elderly man to death, and who was facing capital murder charges in Canyon, had some big guns to assist in defending the case. One was a tall, lanky, Abraham Lincolnesque southern gentleman from Atlanta named Millard Farmer. Farmer was as smooth and mannerly as his partner, Steve Losch, was brusque. Losch came from New York, which was pretty much like scratching a blackboard to a Texan in the first place. But Losch and Farmer formed an incredible team together, kind of a "good cop/bad cop" duo. Just when Losch made everyone so angry they couldn't stand it, Farmer would soothe the courtroom and get what he wanted. Both were extremely intelligent and completely committed to the cause of defending capital murder suspects. They believed it was their job, their calling under the Constitution.

It was Losch and Farmer who stirred the pot in West Texas during those early spring weeks. If there was information out there that would help their case they would find it, they announced. Farmer and one of his investigators went so far as to drive one hundred miles to Lubbock for the sole purpose of meeting with the morgue manager, Woodson Rowan, to appeal for his assistance in asking Dr. Erdmann to come clean about his activities.

The morning before the hearing, Captain Wiley appeared at the door of my office with a rather seedy looking, Columbo-like individual. The guy looked more like a drug informant than anything, but my captain introduced him as Michael Rodhe, an investigator who was working on the Canyon case. Wiley had approved the investigator talking to me and left us alone.

Rodhe cut quickly to the chase and asked about my Erdmann file. I never thought to ask him how he knew about it, but since he did, I told him in general terms the kinds of materials it contained. He pulled out a pad and took notes. Lots of notes. When he left my office thirty minutes later, I am sure he felt he must have stumbled into the mother lode.

I was never contacted for a prehearing interview by the prosecutors of the Canyon case, the Randall County District Attorney's office or D.A. Randy Sherrod.

I was now uneasy enough about facing the Canyon hearing that I decided to ask Denette Vaughn to go there with me. I had absolutely no faith in the city attorney who was going along. I knew he was there to watch out for the City of Lubbock and couldn't care less about my interests. However, I was very aware of the bomb I carried in my briefcase in the form of the Erdmann file and knew launching it might cause a personal attack on me.

I am always self-conscious when I ask Denette for something extra because I know her time is at a premium. Now I was about to ask her to take a full day or two out of her incredibly busy schedule to come with me, and do what I felt she might think amounted to client hand holding. When I finally mustered the courage to make the request of her, she responded as she always did. It was pretty funny to watch her pull herself up to her full four feet eleven inches, kind of swagger and say, "Of course I'm going to Canyon with you! What are you, *nuts?* It's already on my calendar. If you think for one minute that I'm letting you go there by yourself, you gotta be crazy! Everybody up there will be looking out for their little pet interests, or the interest of the city. No one cares squat what happens to you. Of course I'm going to Canyon. You couldn't keep me away!"

She was the best. I was asking for special consideration in a matter for which there was no way on earth that I could pay her hourly fee for two full days, and here she was, acting as if she were volunteering to go. "And I'll go in my own car, rather than ride with you in a city vehicle and have someone accuse me of an impropriety," she announced.

On the evening before I was to travel to Canyon, I returned to my office to get some paperwork that I thought might be needed. While I was there, my pager went off, telling me to call home. When Debbie picked up the phone, she said, "Chief Bridgers called the house wanting to talk to you before you go to Canyon."

"This has to be important," I told her. "I have been working here for almost thirteen years and have never had a police chief call me at home." I turned to the police computer in my office and looked up Bridgers's home phone number.

When he answered, I said, "Chief, this is Bill Hubbard. You wanted to talk to me?"

"Yeah, Bill. I got a call from Travis Ware."

"Yes, sir?" I said as I took out a sheet of paper and began getting this down.

"Well, he . . . he expressed some concern that some of the things he said in the February meeting you attended in his office about Dr. Erdmann might be misconstrued by you when you testify in Canyon."

"No way, Chief. I know exactly what he said and what he meant. I wrote it all down right after I got back to my office."

"Good, but he was concerned. . . ."

This, to me, was classic Travis Ware. He had stepped in it. He knew it. He knew I knew it. And he knew I would not hesitate to tell the whole truth about it under oath. So here Travis Ware was the night before I was going to testify trying to institute damage control before any damage had actually occurred. I felt this was another sign Ware was not concerned with the truth nearly as much as protecting his image.

I assured the chief that everything I had to testify about was documentable fact and had little or no personal opinion attached to it. "I will stick to those documents unless specifically asked to state an opinion, at which time I will make it known to be just that, my opinion."

Despite my words, there was little doubt in my mind that the Erdmann situation was reaching a crisis point, and that my telling the whole truth, as I was committed to do, would bring the crisis to a combustible state.

It is roughly a two-hour drive from Lubbock to Canyon. The interstate the morning of April 2nd looked like a parade of Chevy Caprice detective cars. Almost all the officers under subpoena took separate cars because each would likely be finished at a different time and would be anxious to get back to work as soon as possible.

In Canyon, after having checked in with court officials to let them know I was there, the game became "hurry up and wait." The courthouse halls were lined with police officers from all over the area. In typical courtroom fashion, "The Rule" had been invoked, which requires that all witnesses remain outside the courtroom. We could not hear the testimony of the other witnesses or even discuss our testimony with other witnesses while we waited. Most cops have pretty well gotten used to this procedure since it is the common one encountered when we go to court.

This particular hearing's purpose was to introduce testimony about the original autopsy of the victim, so the judge could determine whether or not to grant a defense request to exhume the victim and allow a second autopsy. The victim had died as six suspects burglarized his home. The prosecution argued that the victim died as a result of the beating he received at the hands of the suspects during the burglary. The defense believed, and hoped to prove by a second autopsy that the victim had a bad heart and died of a heart attack and not from the beating. The difference could be a long prison sentence or the death penalty for each of the suspects.

Before hearing the testimony of any of us under subpoena, the court had a "housekeeping" chore, so we waited. Randall County assistant D.A. John Davis told the court that the tissue samples that Dr. Erdmann provided to prosecutors and represented as being the tissues of the deceased in this case were in fact not from this victim. County D.A. Randy Sherrod said he did not consider this to be an "honest mistake." It was revealed that when investigators went with Erdmann to recover the tissue slides for this case the doctor could not locate them. According to the report, Dr. Erdmann then simply picked up some slides at random and told the investigator that these were the correct slides and that he had just mislabeled them. Erdmann encouraged the investigator to relabel the slides with the current case number. When the investigator refused, Erdmann made the change himself. Prosecutors had the slides examined by another forensic pathologist, whose expert opinion was that the slides could not possibly belong to a person of the age of the victim in this case.

Even with this embarrassing revelation before the court, the district attorney proceeded with the hearing in order to fight the proposed exhumation. It seemed to me a bad position to be in, but I also understood that the victim's family had been through a lot and did not want their loved one dug up and autopsied again. Though D.A. Sherrod referred to Dr. Erdmann as a "kook" and a "nut," he continued to do his best to argue before the court that the exhumation would not have a bearing on the case. In light of all that had recently transpired, along with the most recent revelation about the tissue slides of the deceased, I felt it was a losing battle from the start.

Shortly before noon the trial began. Erdmann was in attendance with his attorney, Texas State Senator John Montford. Coincidence or not, Montford had been the district attorney in Lubbock several years before and was the mentor and former senior law partner to Travis Ware. Some speculated that when Erdmann got into trouble he turned to his friend Ware for help, who in turn went to Montford to keep it all neatly "in the family."

Dr. Ralph Erdmann took the stand, and the questioning by Millard Farmer began. Nearly all of the twenty or more witnesses who were there were police officers, and most of them were detectives. And they were all there under defense subpoenas, so that the defense team could extract from them what they knew of the alleged shortcomings of Ralph Erdmann. Cops don't usually care for defense attorneys, nor do defense attorneys usually care much for cops. However, willing or not, there they were. The situation was highly unusual and things were tense.

On top of that, though there were cops from Amarillo, Lubbock, Odessa and elsewhere, we could not talk to each other about what we knew or why we were there because of "The Rule." So most of us hung out in the halls or tried to get comfortable in a hard chair or on a window ledge. Some paced. Some thumbed through the well-worn magazines in the tiny witness room.

One lieutenant from Lubbock had the presence of mind to bring a book with him. I thought his choice of reading matter that day held a special irony. The title was *Buried Secrets.*

I fared a little better than most in finding a place to kill some time. The judge's outer office was open and empty, so along with a couple of other officers, we put the couch to good use while we waited. And waited. Denette Vaughn came in and out of the room, and since "The Rule" did not apply to attorney/client privilege, she and I were able to talk generally about what was going on.

"It's very tense in there," she said at one point. "Erdmann's lawyered up and is taking the Fifth. It's funny, though, because the defense attorneys aren't backing down. Millard Farmer keeps asking him question after question, and Erdmann pleads the Fifth over and over. This could go on for days. You'd think that after a few Fifth Amendment answers they'd stop the questioning. But not this Farmer guy. Farmer just keeps chipping away, hammering Erdmann with one question after another, hoping he'll break.

"Erdmann looks nervous up there, too. Instead of answering questions with something like, 'I invoke my Fifth Amendment rights,' he's saying, 'I plead my rights.' It's kind of funny in a pathetic sort of way."

That began a frustrating period for Mr. Farmer as he undauntedly questioned Dr. Erdmann. Each time, he was met with Erdmann invoking his constitutional rights. After the lunch break, Dr. Erdmann even pleaded the Fifth when Farmer asked him if he had a good lunch! Before Farmer finished his questioning, Dr. Erdmann had invoked his constitutional rights 237 times.

The minutes painfully turned into hours, the hours mounted, and the lunch break was a welcome relief. After a burger at a local steakhouse that turned into "lawyer and copville" on this particular day, we returned to the courthouse and began waiting again.

Suddenly there was a shuffling at the door of the courtroom, and a few reporters came out. Word filtered to us in the judge's office that Dr. Erdmann had been allowed to step down from the witness stand. Word also came that the next witness was Dr. Erdmann's wife. We all settled in for what we believed would be another long wait.

Denette popped in and sat down beside me. "She's started taking the Fifth, too," Denette told me. "We could be here awhile."

Mrs. Erdmann had answered five questions before being stopped by her attorney, Mike Thomas, who advised her to begin taking the Fifth. After that, Mrs. Erdmann answered with the Fifth Amendment sixteen times before Farmer gave up since this testimony was going to the same place his questioning of Erdmann had gone—nowhere. He allowed her to step down.

Expecting that the questioning of Mrs. Erdmann

would be as lengthy as that of her husband, I had gotten comfortable again. Then there was another shuffling at the courtroom door. This time it was a bailiff, and he called out to the cops lounging everywhere, "Bill Hubbard! Bill Hubbard to the witness stand!"

My chest contracted and I felt breathless. There were more than twenty people there to testify. Many of them had been dealing with Dr. Erdmann for years and had been homicide detectives even longer. It was April 2nd, and I'd only been a homicide investigator since the previous August. Why me first?

Denette got up from the couch where she had been sitting next to me. "Here we go," she said matter-of-factly.

"Why me first?" I asked and struggled to take a deep breath. Standing very still, trying to calm myself, I picked up my briefcase containing the Erdmann file and glanced at the clock. It was 2:30 P.M. I told myself I had to get moving because Denette was already headed toward the door. Those legs of hers weren't very long, but she was fast leaving me behind.

An impatient bailiff was holding the door for Denette when I caught up with her. I took another deep breath and exhaled louder than I intended. I was trying to do something to get my heart out of my throat. My loud exhale obviously attracted my lawyer's attention for she spun around abruptly.

"You have earned this day, Bill," she said. "You have done your homework. You've investigated all this Erdmann stuff and tried to make it right."

"I know," I said. "I had a job to do and I did it."

"Well," Denette whispered sternly, "this is your chance to make that known. I'll be right here and what happens, happens. You'll do fine." With that she turned and walked into the courtroom, toward the observers' seats.

It was zero hour.

A courtroom of any size never seems bigger than

when you are called as a witness. Everything stops as they await your arrival in the room, and all eyes are on you as you walk to the stand. It's awful, it's exciting, it's nerve-wracking and exhilarating, all at the same time. But the center aisle of the courtroom can also seem very long at the moment you walk down it.

Slowly, I made my way to the front, where I was sworn by the judge. Then I sat down on the witness stand and faced all the strange faces. When testifying in Lubbock, I knew the prosecutors, the defense, and the judge. Here in Canyon I knew very few of those present, and those I did were the media people from Lubbock seated in various places around the courtroom.

I scanned the faces until I saw Denette. Being able to keep eye contact with her was reassuring to me. Over the years I had known her as an excellent prosecutor, and through our years of friendship, I had gotten so I could read her glances. With a certain blink I could tell that everything was going okay, and I could relax. Another dart of the eye said to be cautious. A movement of her eyebrow would alert me to hold up for a second in order to allow for something such as an objection from the opposing side to be voiced.

The courtroom was packed. The media sensed this was a hot news story and occupied a significant portion of the seats. And attorneys from all over the region where Erdmann worked were either present or had sent representatives from their offices to see what was going on. In addition, eleven lawyers came who were involved either directly or indirectly in the proceedings, including attorneys for the defense in the murder case under question, prosecutors from Randall County, Dennis McGill representing the City of Lubbock, and Senator John T. Montford and George L. Thompson, attorneys for Ralph Erdmann.

As I shifted in my seat, tall and lanky Millard Farmer

stood up to begin the questioning in his slow Georgia drawl. In fact, he asked not one question from a seated position. This was unique, something else I had not experienced previously from the witness stand, either from prosecutors or defense attorneys. Then, instead of being inattentive as he prepared his next question, he *listened* carefully to each of my answers before moving on.

Farmer's first task was to establish my credentials and background so I could be questioned as an expert witness. After I stated that I was a police officer employed by the City of Lubbock, Texas, Farmer asked the crucial question, "Do you have an area that you specialize in within the detective division?"

"Yes, sir."

"And would you please tell me what that area is?"

I nodded at him. "My current rank is that of sergeant, and I am the supervisor who is assigned as the first-line supervisor of the identification section of the detective division."

"And will you tell me, what does that job entail?"

"The job that I do, as well as the officers who are under my command," I looked him in the eyes, "entails processing evidence of major crimes mostly and fingerprint testimony, some forensic type work. We also gather and preserve the evidence from major crime scenes, most of them being homicides."

"Sergeant Hubbard, when you say you process information, would you explain that in a little more detail for me?"

"Yes, sir. When a major crime occurs where the identification section is needed, a patrol supervisor would approve calling out the I.D. officers under my command. I would arrive at the scene shortly thereafter and I would make the calls as to which one of the officers under my command is assigned to do what tasks in retrieving evidence, taking photographs, making videotapes at the scene.

"Once we have recovered the evidence from the scene, the evidence normally stays in the custody of the identification officers because we are all qualified to process those things by chemical means and other means to retrieve latent fingerprints and to do laser tests. Those are the sorts of things that we are trained to do."

"Would you give me a background of your education, if you would?"

"Yes, Mr. Farmer. I was born and raised in Albuquerque, New Mexico, and graduated from high school there in nineteen seventy-two. I hold a bachelor's degree with a double major in English and theology from McMurry College in Abilene, Texas. I completed some sixty to sixty-five hours of work on my Master of Divinity degree at Oral Roberts University in Tulsa, Oklahoma, and then pastored two churches. I completed fifteen or sixteen weeks of training at the Lubbock Police Academy when I was first hired there, and have had several in-service schools since then. I've also had additional training by the FBI in fingerprint technology and things of that nature."

"In addition to the information that you gather and test there within your department and people working under you gather and test, do you find it necessary from time to time to use consultants to help you in analyzing certain evidence that you gather?"

"Yes, sir. We do."

"And if you will, if you could just give us a little sketch of the type of consultants that you may work with in the course of your work."

"The identification section itself does not have a chemistry department, for example. The regional Department of Public Safety lab is located in Lubbock, so any blood type work or DNA testing, semen analysis, things of that nature, we act merely as the agents who gather and preserve evidence like that, so that it is submitted to the Department of Public Safety. Some of that is done locally at the D.P.S. lab there, others they ship to the main office in Austin.

"For example, firearms and ballistic comparison—we do not have the facility to test-fire a gun to see if the bullet that we retrieved at the scene was fired from a particular gun. And all of that is done out on a consultant basis. Occasionally, on fiber comparisons and things of that nature, we have used the Forensic Institute of the Southwest, located in Dallas, Texas. They are currently working on some things for us at this time."

"What about forensic pathology? Do you have consultants in that area?"

"Yes, sir."

"And what does your department's duty consist of as deals with the evidence of a deceased person in a homicide case, or when that deceased person becomes the subject of evidence?"

I felt more at ease now discussing my own duties. "We are subject at that point to the orders of the Justice of the Peace, who would order an autopsy to be done. The person who is designated to do that autopsy is employed by the County of Lubbock, and it's an agreement between the City of Lubbock and the County of Lubbock. And we are, at that point, observers or coworkers with the person who's actually doing the autopsy."

"So as I understand what you're saying, Sergeant Hubbard, you do not select the person to do forensic pathology, but you participate with the individual as far as identification and retention of evidence. Is that correct, or would you explain it better?"

I sat back and looked at him. "I think that's pretty accurate. Mostly, we're observers and gatherers of evidence at, say an autopsy."

"And is part of your duties that you perform for the Lubbock Police office, is it keeping such things as lawyers talk about—chain of custody, knowing who had the evidence and making sure that the evidence is not mixed up or making sure that the evidence would be properly admissible in court? And if so, explain those duties to me."

"In regard to general evidence that's recovered at the scene of the crime, the officers who are assigned to the identification section demonstrate a high level of knowledge in the area of chain of custody and admissibility of evidence by the very nature of their work and the success that they have had in getting the evidence that they have recovered admitted into evidence.

"In the case of an autopsy, we would be present. For example, if a bullet was recovered from a body at an autopsy that we attended, then the identification officer, either myself or one of the men under my command who was present at the autopsy, would immediately take a photographic record of that, as well as actually receive the physical evidence from the forensic pathologist, and it would be tagged and labeled at that point and we would handle the piece of evidence further from there, as far as logging it into the property room or submitting it for further testing in a firearms examination to the Department of Public Safety in Austin."

Farmer nodded. "So that if some evidence was retrieved during the autopsy or some evidence was going to be necessary to be preserved, it would be the duty of your department to see that it was properly preserved and retained?"

"Provided that we are present at that autopsy, yes, sir."

"And by virtue of that duty and obligation, have people in your department been present during autopsies?"

"Yes, sir."

"Have you ever been present, or someone under your

supervision been present, during autopsies which Dr. Ralph Erdmann performed?"

"Yes, sir."

"What period of time have you known Dr. Ralph Erdmann?"

"Personally known him?"

"Yes, or known him by reputation, either one."

Murmurs in the courtroom which had begun at the mention of Erdmann's name, ceased. Silence reigned. Beads of sweat broke out on my forehead. I took a deep breath and seized the moment. "I've known for some time—years—that he was the forensic pathologist who did autopsies in Lubbock. I was not assigned to the identification section, and I had been working first in a property crimes detective capacity, and later in a patrol officer capacity before I went to the identification section in August of nineteen ninety-one. And it was at that time, shortly after that, that I had personal dealings with Dr. Erdmann and got to know him personally."

"And I believe that you told me you've had special training in addition to experience in working in this section."

"Yes, sir."

Farmer addressed the judge. "Your honor, we would like to tender Sergeant Hubbard as an expert in this particular area."

Judge Pirtle, who looked as if he wished this were not happening in his courtroom, declined, and prosecutors Sherrod and Davis objected as well. After a brief discussion, the judge agreed that he would rule on individual questions rather than accept me as an expert witness generally.

Mr. Farmer then zeroed in on the briefing I had received from Thomas Esparza when I first went to the identification section and the one-page Erdmann file I had received from him.

Sherrod spoke from the prosecutors' table. "Your

Honor, I object to it on the basis of relevancy and also on the basis of I think it would be calling for hearsay from the standpoint of what that gentleman told the witness."

The judge turned to the defense table. "Response, counsel?"

Steven Losch spoke for the first time, quoting from memory statutes that sent the lawyers at the prosecution's table as well as the judge himself flipping through their law books. Mr. Losch then expounded on how those statutes were related to the subject at hand. The objection was overruled. I had never seen anything like this Losch/Farmer team in a live courtroom. On television maybe, but not in real life!

From there Mr. Farmer inquired about the one page in the file as I received it and its content. There had been some concern that the entire Erdmann file might not be accepted as evidence. Farmer now had a delicate job. He had to direct the questioning in such a way that the first page of the file became tied to every other page. Thus, the whole file would become a package of evidence.

Farmer queried, "I'm asking you if, in fact, you received a complaint. If you did, did you document it? And what was the complaint?"

Determination flowed through my body and I reached for the truth. "Yes, there was a complaint. The complaint came verbally, and it was a complaint about the completeness of the autopsy of a homicide victim named Barbara Hinojosa."

"Explain that to me."

I maintained eye contact as I replied. "Barbara Hinojosa was murdered in Lubbock on or about October twelfth of ninety-one. There has still been no one filed on for her murder. But suffice to say that, during the course of focusing on a suspect, the contents of the stomach of Barbara Hinojosa came to be critical."

"Can you explain that a little bit?"

"I must be very cautious because of the continuing investigation in this case, sir."

"Yes. I won't ask you to divulge anything that would—"

I broke in, my eagerness to get it all out in the open palpable. "But it was learned that a suspect had alleged that he had taken Barbara Hinojosa to a certain place at a certain time shortly before her death and had consumed a certain food."

"Identifiable food that could be determined in the stomach. Is that what you're saying?"

"Yes, sir. And it was learned by detectives that the contents of the stomach during the course of the autopsy on her had not been examined."

Farmer accelerated the pace. "Would that be part of the normal autopsy protocol that the contents of the stomach be examined?"

My thoughts flashed back. "At that time, I had no idea. And it put a barrier in our investigation because of that. And the detective who voiced that complaint was quite angry about it."

"And came to you with the complaint?"

I felt my own voice strengthen, reflecting my inner resolve. "He came to the whole chain of command in the homicide division, yes, sir. Myself was included in that."

"And the person performing that autopsy was Dr. Erdmann?"

"Yes, sir."

"All right. Was there another occasion which you received complaints about his, Dr. Erdmann's, performance?"

More arguments from the attorneys.

Finally, I was allowed to go on, and Mr. Farmer said, "Go ahead, tell us about the next one."

"When the complaint about the Barbara Hinojosa situation came to my attention, I discussed it with my superior and was assigned as part of my duty, a task by my captain, Captain Frank Wiley. He assigned me to do some research on autopsies, specifically to talk to some medical examiners' offices and such to determine, if I could, if the contents of the stomach are normally examined during the course of a homicide autopsy and to gather some information for him. And I did that."

"And did you take any action after you did this research? And if so, tell me what you did."

Mr. Davis stood up. "Your Honor, now, this is not as to his people in his department, so I would object to backdoor hearsay here on what actions he took as a result of contacting, I believe it was the medical examiners' offices."

The judge responded, "Objection will be sustained. Counsel, if you can be more specific in your question."

Farmer nodded. "Did you personally take any action as a result?"

"Yes, sir."

"What action did you personally take?"

"On October—"

"Excuse me. Same objection, Your Honor."

The judge looked weary of this endless bickering. "Objection will be overruled. You may proceed," the judge said perfunctorily.

I picked up where I had left off. "On October twenty-second, nineteen ninety-one, I personally wrote a memo to my captain, Captain Frank Wiley, concerning some information that I had gathered."

"And what information had you gathered?"

"My memo tells of calls that I placed to the—to certain individuals at the Tarrant County Medical Examiner's office and to the Bexar County Medical Examiner's office. It names the individuals that I spoke to at those places and what I learned from them concerning autopsies."

"And what else did you do other than make that documentation? You made notice to your superior?"

"I personally delivered this memo to Captain Wiley."

"And was the determination that the autopsies were not being performed correctly?"

Sherrod objected on the basis of the hearsay rule. He and Losch argued back and forth once again while I grew increasingly frustrated at the mechanisms which kept me from revealing the facts I'd come here to state.

Davis struck, "Your Honor, I believe that, again, in addition to hearsay, backdoor hearsay, he's asking him for a conclusion as a medical expert as to whether or not autopsies were being performed properly, and I don't think Hubbard's been qualified as an expert in the field of pathology."

Losch delayed replying while silence permeated the room, then suddenly lunging hard, he made his point. "We are not offering Sergeant Hubbard as an expert to determine whether or not Dr. Erdmann performed each of these autopsies properly. What we are trying to do is to make a record of what he did and the actions that Sergeant Hubbard took and how, what he felt about it as a police officer, with his experience."

Finally, the judge ruled. "Counsel, I'll sustain the hearsay objection to the question for the witness."

"Exception under Rule One Hundred Four A, Sixth and Fourteenth Amendments of the United States Constitution," Losch replied.

"Exception noted." The judge nodded.

"May we make a bill on this particular question, Your Honor?" Farmer asked.

"You may."

Farmer drawled, "All right," and his voice betrayed his own dismay with the interruptions. "Would you tell us what—we'll go back to the question that, if you remember the question we were trying to ask you before. We were trying to say, once you obtained this autopsy information, what did you learn from this autopsy information in discussion with other pathologists?"

Caught off guard at finally being allowed to speak, I stammered, "I was not able—I did not draw a conclusion concerning the Barbara Hinojosa autopsy, if that's what you're getting at."

"Did you draw a conclusion as to future protocol of what would take place in future autopsies? That's what I really wanted to get to."

"Yes, sir."

"If you will, tell me that, then."

Farmer raised one hand. "I think that kind of cures what we're doing with the bill, Your Honor. We'll go direct to the questions now."

"All right." The judge nodded.

Farmer emitted a deep breath. It was self-explanatory. "Go ahead and tell me," he said.

Finally, I did. "In this memo of October twenty-second that I wrote to my captain, it tells what the Tarrant County office, Medical Examiner's office, and the Bexar County Medical Examiner's offices do in autopsies in the case of a homicide."

"Now, after you learned what they did, was there some effort to enact or see that that procedure was followed in part or entirely in Lubbock?"

"I was assigned additional work by my captain."

Farmer nodded. "All right. Tell us what that work was."

"I was assigned to research and write a rough draft for a homicide autopsy protocol."

"And did you do that?"

"Over a period of time, yes, sir."

"All right. During this period of time, did you observe or did you have someone working for you report to you things about Dr. Erdmann in performance of autopsies?"

"Not at this time, no, sir."

"When did you next have contact or next gain information about Dr. Erdmann?"

"Just a second."

"Yes, you may refer to—" Farmer said, pointing to my notes.

"Specifically information about Dr. Erdmann would have been on November thirteenth of nineteen ninety-one."

"All right. Tell me about that. Was that nineteen ninety-one?"

"Yes, sir. Officer Pat Kelly—who is the rank of patrolman, and he is assigned as an accident investigator for the police department—he goes to the scene of traffic fatalities and investigates those. He contacted me because the identification section, of which I am the supervisor, is the custodian of the records that Lieutenant Esparza had familiarized me with. This includes the photographic evidence of crime scenes. And Pat Kelly contacted me in my capacity as the custodian of those photographic records because of a problem with Dr. Erdmann."

"What was that problem?"

"The case was apparently a traffic fatality. Dr. Erdmann was going to court in reference to that case, and he had contacted Pat Kelly for copies of the pictures that Pat Kelly had taken at the autopsy because he, Dr. Erdmann, said that he hadn't taken any pictures at the autopsy. I pulled the pictures, kept the negatives, as required by me as the custodian of those records, to give to Officer Kelly. And in those pictures were pictures of Dr. Erdmann with his camera up taking pictures."

"In other words, the pictures that he had taken were not available?"

I twisted in the hard chair and shrugged. "I guess."

"Or he didn't know where they were?"

"I don't know," I said and bit my lip, reflecting.

"When is the next contact you had about Dr. Erdmann?"

"During this time—well, it would have been two days later, on the fifteenth of November nineteen ninety-one. I was still at my ongoing task at the orders of my captain to be writing a homicide autopsy protocol, and I had occasion to place a phone call and have a conversation with a Lieutenant Smith of the Potter County Sheriff's office."

"What did that conversation of November fifteenth, nineteen ninety-one, consist of?"

"I inquired specifically why Dr. Erdmann was no longer doing autopsies for them."

"All right. What was that?"

"He gave me three reasons."

Attorney Davis stood up. "Your Honor, at this time, I'm going to object because this is outside of his—people under his supervision. Object to hearsay on that."

"Objection will be sustained."

Once again, frustration as the lawyers played a ping pong game of words. Finally the judge said, "The request will be denied. Counsel, you will be permitted to make your bill at this time."

Farmer continued, "What were the three things that Lieutenant Smith told were problems with Dr. Erdmann?"

"He said that Dr. Erdmann was released because of one, trouble with accessibility, finding him and running him down when they had an autopsy to do. They had trouble getting copies of his reports. And they believed—or Lieutenant Smith believed—that his autopsies were not complete."

"Did Lieutenant Smith tell you anything about Dr. Erdmann resisting opening the head of a deceased?"

"Yes, sir."

"And what was that?"

"He said that in almost all situations where there was not a head wound that was part of the cause of death, that they had a lot of trouble getting Erdmann to do a cranial examination, or to open the head and examine the inside of the head."

"Now, did you take action pursuant to the information that you obtained from Lieutenant Smith? And if so, what was that action?"

"Same objection. Backdoor hearsay, Your Honor."

"Counsel, if you'll rephrase the question, please," the judge said.

"Yes. What happened after you talked to Lieutenant Smith next relating to Dr. Erdmann?"

"I made a note of the conversation and filed it, and I made my superiors aware."

"Now, what was the next contact you had with Dr. Erdmann, or what next complaint you had from someone working under you regarding Dr. Erdmann?"

"During this time, I was continuing to do my task that had been assigned to me by my captain, gathering information, that was why we had conversations. But we had then a homicide that occurred in Lubbock on Saturday, November sixteenth, nineteen ninety-one."

"What happened regarding that homicide and Dr. Erdmann?"

My mind raced backward as I sorted out the tangle of images flooding it. "I attended my first autopsy for me to personally witness that was performed by Dr. Erdmann."

"What did you observe?"

"After I had assisted in working that homicide scene with Detective Wesley Shields, who is under my command, Detective Shields and I, at fourteen hundred hours, two P.M., on November eighteenth of nineteen ninety-one, attended the autopsy."

The critical juncture for which I had prepared myself had arrived. I felt totally alone. Some could, of course, have avoided it by pretending they saw nothing. But for me, there was no choice. Taking a deep breath, I seized the moment, and I began to tell the whole truth as I had witnessed it about Ralph Erdmann, and ultimately his connection to Travis Ware.

"Dr. Erdmann performed the autopsy. Detective Shields fingerprinted the body of the victim for identification, and I was present as Detective Shields took photographs of the autopsy in progress. I was also present during the retrieval of the bullet slug from the victim's chest cavity, and also was present when a blood serum sample was retrieved."

"And did you observe anything unusual during this autopsy?" Farmer's steady prodding fleshed out the past.

"Yes, sir."

"Tell me what you observed."

"Dr. Erdmann appeared to be through and a cranial examination had not been done."

"Was that relevant as to the homicide that had occurred?"

"We didn't know."

"And what happened at that time?"

My heart skipped a beat. "I questioned him."

"And what did he do?"

"He wanted to know where I had received my training."

"In other words, he felt affronted?"

I spoke slowly, deliberately. "He was angry."

Farmer leaned towards me, and his voice rose. "Did he do it? Did he do the cranial examination?"

"Yes, sir."

"After you insisted?"

"Yes, sir."

"What did he do with the tissue samples during the autopsy?"

"The . . . Which ones, sir?"

"In that particular autopsy. Do you remember what he did with the tissue samples?" Farmer's voice had an edge now. He was meticulously building the case with a relentless accretion of fact upon fact.

I was silent for a moment. Then I said, "Yes, sir. The samples that were taken from the organs in the chest, he cut a wedge out of each of the major organs and put them in a plastic container."

"Did he separate them?"

"No, sir. All the samples went into one container."

"All samples of all the organs went into one container. Is that correct?"

"Yes, sir."

"Does that differ from anything that you had learned up until that time as far as proper protocol was concerned?"

"I didn't know at that time."

"You didn't know at that time?"

"No, sir." I breathed a heavy sigh.

"All right. Is there anything else that happened relating to that autopsy?"

"Yes, sir."

"Tell me what else happened."

"On November nineteenth of ninety-one, I wrote a memo to my superiors because of that autopsy."

"And what happened as a result of that memo? Did you document what had occurred?"

"I documented—quite frankly Dr. Erdmann had had an argument during the course of the autopsy and there had been a heated exchange."

"And what was that exchange about?"

"About who I was to be questioning him about how an autopsy is to be done."

"All right."

I felt the same whiplash of emotions that I had experienced that day, and I could not keep the bitter tone from my voice. "After all—and this was the first autopsy I had ever attended in my life. I felt it necessary to let my superiors know about this exchange before they got wind of it someplace else, so I detailed the confrontation between Dr. Erdmann and myself and what procedures I had observed at the autopsy and weighed that against what limited knowledge I had at that time concerning autopsy procedure."

"At that time, did you see him weighing any of the organs of the body?"

"No, sir."

"Did he record in the autopsy report weights of organs of the body?"

"I have not seen the autopsy report in this case, sir."

"Did he take out the— Were you there during the entire autopsy?"

"Yes, sir."

"From the beginning to the end?"

"Yes, sir." Looking into Farmer's eyes, I read approval. He obviously thought I was making the kind of direct, methodical, concerned impression a good small town cop should make.

"And at any point did he put any of the organs in that particular autopsy in that case that you're talking about on the scales?"

"No, sir."

"All right. Let's go to the next time that you had any contact with Dr. Erdmann."

"Officer Gaylon Lewis, who is assigned to my command, voiced a complaint to me concerning Dr. Erdmann on November twenty-fifth of nineteen ninety-one."

"And what was the basis of that?"

I made my voice slow and quite deliberate. "Detective Lewis had attended this autopsy for the purpose of photographing and recovering evidence of what we do. And he expressed to me at that time that, while samples were taken of the major organs, that none of them were actually physically removed from the body, examined and weighed. And," I went on, "Detective George White, who is a homicide detective for the Lubbock Police Department, who had also been present at that autopsy—that the cranial examination was only done at Detective White's insistence."

Farmer inclined his head. "He was not going to do it, according to Detective White, if he hadn't insisted. Is that correct?"

I returned his gaze. "Yes, sir."

"And do you know if the autopsy report contained the weight of the organs?"

"I don't know."

"Did you report that also to your superiors?"

"Yes, sir."

"And were these timely reports? Did you make these reports in a relatively short period of time to these events happening?"

I nodded and framed my answer with care. "My superior's office is right across the hall from my office, and we had communication daily on several occasions."

"So this is nothing that's been delayed until the last week or so to report?"

"No, sir."

"This has been reported on an ongoing basis?"

"Yes, sir."

Farmer paused a moment, letting the jury absorb this. Then he went on. "All right. When is the next time you had some contact with Dr. Erdmann, either through yourself or your people working with you?"

"There was a homicide occurred on Thanksgiving Day of ninety-one, which was November twenty-eighth."

"Excuse me just a second." Farmer became more relaxed, discursive. "Who was the J.P. that ordered the two previous autopsies? Do you have that?"

"Sir, I couldn't tell you."

"You don't know if any of them . . ."

"I don't know."

"All right. Go ahead." Farmer waved me on.

Earnestly, I picked up the tale. "Detective Shields and

I worked the scene of this homicide and made calls to the normal answering service and all that we do when we notify Dr. Erdmann's office that there is a homicide autopsy to do. And we were not notified by Dr. Erdmann or his office that the autopsy was going to be done and we knew nothing about the autopsy being done until it had already been completed."

"And did that present a problem?"

Blood pounded in my temples. There was no turning back. "Yes, sir."

"And what kind of problem did that present?" Farmer raised his head and looked at me directly.

I held his gaze. "It violated accepted procedure, which at that time was not a written procedure, but it violated the accepted standard that we had, the working agreement that we had with Dr. Erdmann up to that point." I paused and felt my face harden. "And I made my superiors aware."

"Was there someone available to attend that from the identification section, had they been needed?"

"Yes, sir."

"Or had the procedure been followed?"

"Yes, sir."

"And is there someone on call all the time from your section?"

"Yes, sir."

"All right. Go to the next time you had contact with him." He gave me the measured, unhurried look of a person who sought every detail.

"Lubbock was busy, and on December thirteenth of ninety-one we had a double homicide. And I personally attended both of those autopsies."

"Did anything unusual or out of the ordinary occur at those autopsies?"

"Yes, sir."

"What?"

My mind was razor-sharp clear about the incidents and Erdmann's incompetence. With flickering quickness I glanced at the judge and began my truthful yet lethal answer. "Both of the homicide victims, we had strong reason to believe, were HIV positive. During the course of those autopsies, the procedures that—or lack of procedures that were followed by Dr. Erdmann—put not only himself but myself and Detective Gaylon Lewis at health risk."

"Did the organs that were removed, or the tissue samples removed in those autopsies, were they placed in one container, also?"

"Yes, sir."

"Were they removed and weighed in that instance?"

"No, sir."

"Have you seen the autopsy report since then?"

"No, sir."

"And so you do not know if, in fact, they contain any weights at all?"

"I don't know, sir." I shook my head.

A few questions on Erdmann's system of numbering his autopsies passed quickly. Then Farmer said, "Go ahead with your next instance in which Dr. Erdmann was involved."

"As a result of those two autopsies, I wrote a memo to my superiors."

"What happened about the memo?"

"It was dated December sixteenth, nineteen ninety-one, and it detailed the procedures that were used in that autopsy and the contamination risks that both myself and Detective Lewis were placed in."

"All right. Are there any more instances which involve Dr. Erdmann?"

"Yes, sir."

"Tell me about them."

"Detective George White contacted me because it was

common knowledge in the detective division that I was the custodian of information concerning Dr. Erdmann, and he brought me a memo that he had written to himself and kept a copy of that was dated back in nineteen ninety. It was dated November twenty-first."

"And what information did you gain from this memo?"

"It concerned the problems and the cause of death of an earlier homicide before I had been assigned to the detective division. The name is Terry Nathan. N-A-T-H-A-N."

"And what happened in the Nathan case?"

"George White expressed to me from this writing that he gave to me problems concerning the cause of death in this homicide. And it also details what steps he took to correct the problem."

"Were they able to be corrected?"

"According to the memo, they were corrected."

"Perspectively or for that case?"

"I don't understand your question."

"In the future—was it corrected for the future or was it corrected for that particular case?"

"*That*," I emphasized the word, "case was corrected."

"Would it be revealing confidential information to tell me how it was? Can you tell me without revealing something that's confidential? I don't want to ask you if it was confidential."

"This was not given to me in confidentiality."

Skillfully, Farmer was directing me from point to point. He made few comments as if he was holding back his opinion to serve as a mirror to my thoughts. "All right. Tell me how it was corrected and what the problem was."

"The detectives that attended the autopsy, who were Jimmie Riemer and Gaylon Lewis, who were assigned to the identification section at that time under a different sergeant than myself, brought the problem with the cause of death to Dr. Erdmann's attention and made an appointment to see Justice of the Peace Blalack, who had ordered the autopsy. And at the time and place designated for the meeting, Jimmie Riemer and Gaylon Lewis and George White met with Judge Blalack, and Dr. Erdmann missed that appointment and, according to this, Judge Blalack handled the situation."

"How did he handle it?"

I looked at Farmer. "Can I read two sentences from this?" I said with grim intensity.

"Yes, go ahead."

"This is George White writing. 'Blalack told me that all Erdmann would do to correct his autopsy report was to take the incorrect pages out and replace them with corrected pages. Blalack said that Erdmann has done this in the past.'"

"Was that memorandum turned over to your superior?"

"I don't know. I kept a copy of this because I was the custodian of the compilation of this information concerning Dr. Erdmann."

"And how far back did that go with Dr. Erdmann's performance?"

"The date on this that George White gave me is November twenty-first of nineteen ninety."

"What was wrong with that particular autopsy? You told us the cause of death, but specifically what was wrong?"

"According to this document, the original cause of death had to do with suffocation with a plastic bag, and the investigators and the identification officers who were assigned to work the case had absolutely no knowledge of any involvement of a plastic bag at all."

The judge's face bore a stunned look.

Farmer pressed on. "What was the next instance in which you were involved with Dr. Erdmann?"

"On December seventeenth of nineteen ninety-one, which was a homicide/suicide that occurred in Lubbock. And, at my direction, Detective Shields attended the autopsies there and he informed me that both of these, the homicide victim and the suicide victim, were gunshot wounds to the head, that the autopsy had been limited strictly to a cranial examination to determine cause of death, and that Dr. Erdmann had said that this had been so ordered by the justice of the peace in the case."

"Was that true?"

"I believe so."

"That the justice of the peace had limited—"

"Had ordered the limited autopsy."

"All right. What else was unusual about that autopsy?"

"Nothing in particular, other than the fact that Shields had made it a point to bring it to my attention that the chest cavities were not opened. And I have not reviewed the autopsy reports on these."

"So if there were weights of body organs, they couldn't have been obtained from the autopsy. Is that correct?"

"Not according to what Shields told me. I have no idea what the autopsy report says."

"All right. Have you ever in any of the time that you have known Dr. Erdmann or any of the people observed, have you ever seen him weigh any of the organs?"

"Yes, sir."

"And on what occasions were those?"

"I attended an autopsy on February eighth of nineteen ninety-two."

"And is that the first time you saw him weigh any of the organs?"

"He weighed one organ that day."

"What organ was that?"

"The heart."

"And did he—you didn't see the autopsy in that case?"

"I attended the autopsy there."

"Did you see the report?"

"No, sir."

"And did he take out any of the other organs?"

Images and memories rushed through my mind. "He brought them to the surface of the chest cavity in order to obtain a sample. But the heart was the only organ that he actually physically removed from the body, examined outside of the body and placed on a scale."

"Did he also take the samples from that and put it in one container?"

"Yes, sir."

"Go ahead and tell me what other . . . What was your next contact with Dr. Erdmann?"

"You broke my chronology there by asking. . . ." I joked.

"I'm sorry. I apologize." Farmer made a sweeping gesture in return.

"I'm back into December now. Dr. Erdmann contacted me. On December twenty-third, nineteen ninety-one, Dr. Erdmann contacted me by telephone and he asked me to write a letter and direct it to him as a result of our phone conversation.

"What he expressed to me was that he had drawn some criticism due to how clean the University Medical Center Lab was or was not left when the two suspected HIV positive autopsies were done. And he asked me to write him a letter that he could take to the U.M.C. officials to reasonably show that he left the lab in a clean— more or less clean—manner."

"Okay. Did he leave it clean?"

I could not quench my disgust. "He cleaned up what blood he saw. He missed some."

"Did you write the letter?"

"Yes, sir." I didn't go into the candid comments I'd made.

"All right. And what was the next contact you had with him?"

"Detective Wesley Shields wrote a memo to me—I

am his supervisor—in reference to the autopsy that had occurred on Thanksgiving, for the murder that occurred on Thanksgiving, and it details Dr. Erdmann's explanation as to why police officials had not been contacted to attend that autopsy."

"And what was that?"

"He said that he wasn't clear that we wanted to be contacted on autopsy—all homicide autopsies—and have a police officer present."

"What was the next contact you had with him?"

"On January sixth of nineteen ninety-two, as custodian of these records, Detective Doug Sutton gave me a copy to put into this file of a memo that he wrote to Captain Wiley, who is our division commander, in reference to a problem in getting back a toxicology report on an autopsy Dr. Erdmann had performed."

"Tell us about that one," Farmer said, not letting up.

"It concerns an individual named Michelle Haidacher, H-A-I-D-A-C-H-E-R, who was found dead in Lubbock on December twenty-third, nineteen ninety-one, and it details conversations that Dr. Erdmann had said he had had with the deceased's psychologist and some question was raised as to the cause of death."

"From the psychologist?"

"Yes, sir. Basically, she appears to be disputing the information that was received from Dr. Erdmann."

"And what happened as a result of that?"

"I discussed it with Captain Wiley, who is our division commander, made him aware that a copy of this was in this file that I was the custodian of."

"And what was the information that she had regarding dispute of cause of death?"

"Dr. Erdmann had apparently said that it appeared to be an overdose of medication, but there was some confusion as to concerning some bruises and wounds that the deceased had on her. And Dr. Lim, L-I-M, who was the psychiatrist who had the ongoing care of the deceased, had—there was a mix up of communication or something—was not getting the information that she thought she needed from Dr. Erdmann."

"What was the next contact you had with him?"

"On February fourth of nineteen ninety-two, Detective Wesley Shields, who was assigned under my command, presented me a supplement report to a homicide that occurred Thanksgiving morning back in November. And Shields had been contacted by the Department of Public Safety Lab, who was doing the blood analysis and toxicology from that homicide. And they needed—you have to recall this was the homicide autopsy that no peace officers had been present."

"Right."

"During the course of that, Cathy McCord of the D.P.S. Lab told Wesley Shields that she needed a sample of the victim's blood to use as a constant in the analysis that they were doing on the murder weapon and other blood evidence that had been received—recovered at the scene by myself and Detective Shields.

"Shields contacted Erdmann for the requested blood. Dr. Erdmann couldn't locate it and told Shields that he would call him back. Shields made at least two additional tries at getting in touch with Dr. Erdmann. Dr. Erdmann didn't return his calls. So he informed me of the situation. As his supervisor, I contacted Dr. Erdmann, I got a hold of him, and I requested the blood. He told me that he would have given that blood to the police officer who was present at the autopsy. I told him that this was the autopsy that there wasn't a police officer present at. He told me that that blood must be at the toxicology laboratory and that he would find it and call me back.

"And as of February fourth—let's see. On February fourth, we contacted one of the investigators from the district attorney's office, Tom Loper. Dr. Erdmann called Tom Loper back and Dr. Erdmann had told Tom Loper that the blood had been submitted to an independent toxicology laboratory and that all of the blood had been used, so that there was no additional blood from that victim available to use as a constant.

"As a result of that, we contacted the D.P.S. Lab and told them that the blood that they retrieved from the victim's clothing would be the best that they would be able to get to use as a constant in their further blood testing."

"All right. What was the next contact you had with Dr. Erdmann?"

"On February fifth, which was a Wednesday, I attended a meeting at the district attorney's office."

"Tell me what happened at that meeting, who was the district attorney, and who else was present."

My mind raced. For a split second I thought about what I was going to have to say and what it might cost me. Then I spoke as sincerely as I could. "District Attorney Travis Ware, investigators from the D.A.'s office, Dewayne Haney and Tom Loper—Colonel George Ewing was the assistant—one of the assistant chiefs of police who is assigned over detective division; Captain Frank Wiley, who is my division commander; Lieutenant Dean Summerlin, who is my immediate superior; and myself. We all had a meeting."

"What happened at that meeting?"

"The protocol for a homicide autopsy that I had been working on for several months and a protocol for a call-out to a homicide scene and what the responsibilities of the C.D.A.'s office investigators . . . Excuse me. What the C.D.A.'s office investigators would be responsible for at a scene, what me and my people and the detectives of the Lubbock Police Department would be responsible for at the scene.

"Basically, the protocols were put together, the ones that they had put together and the ones that I had made at the direction of my division commanders were examined together to see if they had any conflicts. The protocol was adopted, and specifics were discussed concerning Dr. Erdmann."

"What were those specifics?"

"I expressed concern about attending autopsies having to ask for certain procedures to be done, that I was not a forensic pathologist, and I just . . ." I paused and tried to capture the exact needs I'd had. "I wanted him to do his job.

"We discussed the difficulty we had getting cranial examinations done when it did not immediately appear that the contents of the head may or may not be important to the cause of death or any other related matters. Organ weights were discussed and . . ."

Farmer directed me back. "And what about organ weights was discussed?"

"It was discussed in the meeting that, whether or not an autopsy report had an estimated weight or an actual weight of a liver or a heart, probably didn't have much to do with what the cause of death was.

"Mr. Ware expressed that if the victim had been—had received—a shotgun blast to the face, probably died of a shotgun blast to the face, and it didn't necessarily matter what his organs weighed."

"Was there a discussion indicating if it was estimated or if it was just put down as an absolute? Was that discussed?"

"Yes, sir."

"Tell us about that."

"Mr. Ware said that he had checked around. He did not say specifically where, but he had said that the accepted standard in the industry in autopsies was that an estimated weight of each of the organs was not unusual at all according to what he had found out."

"That's what he told you?"

"Yes, sir."

"All right. Go ahead. Had it been—was it discussed that the organs were never removed from the body at the time the estimates were made? Was that discussed?"

"Yes."

"And was it also discussed that that was an acceptable procedure, also, just look and guess?"

"Mr. Ware expressed somewhat of the expertise of Dr. Erdmann, and he said some very complimentary things about Dr. Erdmann personally."

"For instance?"

"He said that Dr. Erdmann works very hard. He said that Dr. Erdmann is always there when we need him. He said that Dr. Erdmann performs lots of autopsies and is able to perform under lots of pressure. And he also said that Dr. Erdmann is a very good witness on the witness stand."

"Meaning when he's testifying in court to a jury?"

"That's what I took it to mean. Yes, sir."

"And how did you," he paused and rephrased the question. "What else happened after that at that meeting?"

"Mr. Ware expressed that if we had problems with Dr. Erdmann, whatever they are, whether it be punctuality or a procedure or a lack of a procedure, that we should come to him." My sense of right was palpable now and my voice rose. "And Travis Ware said that he would straighten Erdmann out. And we expressed concern that the homicide autopsy protocol was quite detailed and Step A, B, C, D, all the way through. And Mr. Ware said, 'He'll either comply or I'll fucking fire his ass.'"

Farmer's next question had an indefinable edge. "Was any other direction given to you regarding—from Mr. Ware at this time?"

"Yes, sir."

"Tell me what that direction was."

"A day or two before this meeting took place, there was an article in the *Lubbock Avalanche-Journal*, the newspaper in Lubbock, concerning Dr. Erdmann being on the witness stand in reference to a subject by the name of Rey, being on trial."

"And how do you spell that last name?"

"R-E-Y, I believe."

"And is that the co-indictee in this case or do you know?"

"I believe so."

"All right. Go ahead."

"As our meeting came to a close and we had discussed all this stuff—the meeting lasted twenty or thirty minutes—Mr. Ware made direct reference to the trial in Amarillo and the problems that had been voiced in the media concerning Dr. Erdmann, and he enjoined all of us there to keep that meeting quiet."

"To not mention the content of the meeting?"

"Yes, sir."

"And did you take that as an order from him?"

"Mr. Ware knows that we are not—that we don't work for him, and he knows that we're not in his chain of command. It was not expressed as an order. It was a strong suggestion." My words had a bitter ring.

"Did he tell you why to keep it quiet?"

I gathered myself to answer. My tone was quiet, sincere. "Yes, sir."

"What did he tell you?"

There was a stricken silence.

"He said, 'Because if this gets out, the defense attorneys will have a field day with it.'"

"How many autopsies did you attend, approximately, or someone from your department attend, that Dr. Erdmann did?"

The judge intervened. "Counsel, the court reporter needs to change paper, the witness is looking up an answer, and I've had enough coffee—I need a break. Why don't we take about ten minutes at this time."

Walking out for a breath of air, the taste of freedom was welcome. But, before I knew it, the break was over and I was back on the stand.

"Sergeant Hubbard," Farmer said, "your counsel came up to me during the break and said if I didn't ask you this question that I was going to have trouble with her for the rest of her life. Were you subpoenaed to come here today?"

"Yes, sir."

"And did you voluntarily come here?"

"I came here because of the subpoena and for no other reason."

"All right, sir. And the documents and things you're bringing, you're bringing pursuant to a subpoena, also?"

"Yes, sir."

"All right, sir. I think I've satisfied counsel. She's giving me a nod of approval at this point." Farmer smiled, then got serious again. "During the time that you have observed Dr. Erdmann performing autopsies, what percent of the time have you seen him take notes?"

"Every time he began an autopsy, before he actually got into the body, he would open a notebook, and he would make some notes concerning the beginning of the autopsy, who was present, the time and date, what the victim's name was. Only in about half the time did he add to those notes during the course of the autopsy."

"As far as weighing organs are concerned or anything like that, did you—you know you saw him weigh one organ, I think you told me one time?"

"Yes, sir."

"Did he stop and write that down or do you remember?"

"I remember we both went over to the scale and I watched him put it on the scale and I don't remember whether he went over and wrote it down then or not. I have not seen the autopsy report."

"Does he use any type—have you ever seen him use

any type of recording device to talk into while he's doing the autopsies?"

"Never."

"So, while he's actually doing the work, you've never seen him talking into a recording device or having someone there to take notes for him in any way?"

"I've never seen him do that, no, sir."

"And generally, how many autopsies have you seen him perform?"

"Counting that before we took a break, I think I've actually been to four autopsies."

"And have you ever seen him take X-rays?"

"Yes, sir."

"And what about—do photographs for purposes of slides or making slides from part of the tissue, have you ever seen that?"

"Of the tissue?"

"Yes."

"I haven't seen that. I've seen him take thirty-five millimeter photographs during the course of the autopsy using his camera, as we were with our camera equipment. I have never—having not seen an autopsy report, I have never seen the results of his photography."

"Have you ever been present when he's taken organs with him out of the autopsy room?"

"I've never seen him do that, no, sir."

"Or any kind of bone tissue or any parts of the body?"

"I've never seen that."

"Have you ever been present when he made calls to solicit donation of tissue from the family of the victim?"

"No, sir."

"If I could have just a second," Farmer said. There was a pause while he consulted his notes.

Then he went on. "Any other acts that we haven't discussed relating to Dr. Erdmann that are relevant to his conduct, if you would tell me."

"Two others," I said calmly.

"All right. Tell me."

"Both of these occurred on the same day, which was February seventeenth, nineteen ninety-two. Let me qualify that, please. It would be three others."

"All right."

"Chronologically, the first being February eighth of nineteen ninety-two, was a suicide, suspected suicide death investigation. I attended the autopsy that Dr. Erdmann performed. This was the one where he actually took the heart out of the body and weighed it. The problem here," now it was I who paused, but only for a moment to scan the judge's face. He was watching me intently. I went on, my thoughts gathering momentum. "The problem was that this autopsy occurred after my chain of command and myself had had the meeting at the district attorney's office and the protocol had been adopted.

"I had knowledge that on the date of that meeting, that Travis Ware had met with Dr. Erdmann. I don't know the content of their conversation, of course—I was not present. But this autopsy occurred after we had met with the D.A.'s people and the protocol had been adopted. The autopsy that I observed that day was a better autopsy, in my opinion, than I had seen previously, but it still did not satisfy the concept, if you will, of the protocol."

"The next incident?" Farmer interjected, pressing me on.

My heartbeat accelerated as I thought of what I had to reveal next. "These two occurred on February seventeenth. Both of these deaths were believed to be at the time to be either naturals or chemically induced, not homicides. And the toxicology—these occurred about the third week—both of them occurred about the third week of December of ninety-one. And since they were not believed to be homicides at the time, it was not required, according to our procedures between Dr. Erdmann and my office, that a police officer be present."

Suddenly, I caught Denette's gaze on me from the courtroom, and she smiled encouragingly. Determinedly, I went on. "The detectives who were assigned the case both came to me—excuse me. Detective Doug Sutton, was the detective that was assigned to both of these cases, and he had not had any toxicology reports come back yet as a result of these autopsies. And he had contacted Dr. Erdmann and had been told that the blood samples in each of these cases that had been submitted for toxicology had been lost by the lab that they had been submitted to.

"Acting under order, I brought this immediately to the attention of my division commander, Captain Wiley. And acting on his orders, I personally contacted Dr. Erdmann and discussed it. Dr. Erdmann told me that he still had blood on file from these two autopsies and that a lab that he had sent these to in California for toxicology had lost both of them. Since he did have blood left over from those autopsies, he and I agreed that I would come to his office with the proper vials for submission of these two blood samples for toxicology to the Department of Public Safety Lab."

I heard the reaction of those watching, bodies twisting in their chairs, whispers, the sounds of nervous attentiveness. I heard them, but all I cared about was telling the facts about how Erdmann acted.

"Prior to going with these vials to receive the blood from Dr. Erdmann, I read the case reports that were already in existence, the previous reports that the field officers had written at the scene and subsequent. And I learned that at the time when that autopsy had occurred, since it was not a homicide, it was not necessary that a peace officer be present. But a detective under my command, Detective Corporal Jimmie Riemer, had been present in the lab on December twenty-third of nineteen

ninety-one when Dr. Erdmann removed a blood specimen from this victim.

"Mostly as a matter of convenience, Detective Riemer
received this blood specimen from Dr. Erdmann and
submitted it to our Department of Public Safety Lab for
toxicology testing. That was back in December. And now
on February seventeenth, I had Dr. Erdmann telling me
on the telephone that the blood that he had removed
from the victim that day, he had submitted to a toxicology lab in California and they had lost it, along with this
other case that occurred the same week.

"I suspected that Dr. Erdmann either had his facts
wrong or that he was lying to me."

"Did you confront him and tell him that?"

"I went to meet with him."

"What resulted from that meeting?"

"I went to his office in the basement of the University
Medical Center in Lubbock. He had a refrigerator. This
one had his lunch in it, as well as blood samples. They
were in tubes with numbers on them. He found the corresponding numbers that went with the victims in these
cases. And with the specified tubes that were required by
the Department of Public Safety Laboratory, we took
those two tubes over to the lab and Dr. Erdmann got a
syringe and withdrew a sample from the victim in one of
the cases and put it into the specified tube, and then
used a different syringe, removed a blood sample from
the other tube, and put it into the specified tube for
D.P.S., and I retained custody. I labeled both of those
as I would evidence and retained custody of them."

I pushed on. I wasn't about to stop. Weary now, I
wanted to tell it all before someone objected to something. "I pressed Dr. Erdmann for the name of the lab in
California that he had sent the blood—the original
blood samples—to, that had been lost. I expressed to
him that I wanted to be able to write a letter to that lab

to protest their procedures for handling our important evidence. Dr. Erdmann could not provide me the name or address and became angry when I pressed him, so I dropped it.

"I took the blood sample from the one case where I didn't know where the first blood sample had gone to, submitted it to D.P.S. Lab, and I took the second blood sample to the D.P.S. Lab, knowing that they had already received from Jimmie Riemer a blood sample from that same victim, and I told that to the head chemist there, Mr. Jim Thomas, and I told him that I wished to go on and submit this second blood sample in order that tests could be made to see if they were the same because by this time—we're talking the middle of February—I was highly suspect of Dr. Erdmann's procedures.

"The D.P.S. Lab's, Jim Thomas, received that second blood sample. They told me that in reference to both of these blood samples, that they would be very limited in what they could do because the blood had not been, according to Mr. Thomas, properly preserved. There were no anticoagulants or preservatives that are normally put in blood that is going to be stored. The blood had been put into a tube with a lid on it and had been refrigerated since the third week of December, and now it was the second week of February.

"And I took those to the Department of Public Safety Lab and returned to the police department to write my supplement reports to each of those cases, documenting this, and submitted these reports to my superior, Lieutenant Summerlin, who approves them. I have not received back news of the toxicology reports or seen the autopsy reports in either of these cases."

"Are there any more instances?"

"No, sir."

Though there were a few more questions followed by

a few more objections, I had done my duty as I saw it. The interrogation was over.

Court ended abruptly. The prosecutors seemed to have convinced the victim's family that the granting of the exhumation order was inevitable after my testimony, and that prolonging the process by allowing the defense to present additional witnesses could only further hurt their chances of obtaining a conviction. The prosecution stipulated to the exhumation.

Of all the twenty or so witnesses who came from all over the area to testify, I was the only one who had actually been called to the stand. But the repercussions of my few hours as a whistle-blower would keep rolling in for a long time to come.

The aftermath of this trial was peculiar. The Randall County D.A.'s office decided that they should curtail Dr. Erdmann's ability to do things such as change case numbers on tissue slides and lose other samples, notes and reports. Officials prepared search warrants that would allow searches of Dr. Erdmann's home, laboratory and office. Even more strange was that upon the group's arrival in Lubbock to execute the search warrants, "as a courtesy" they notified Erdmann's attorney, John T. Montford. They did this before officials went to the sites to execute the warrants. Afterward, the D.A.'s office voiced surprise when very little was found except a pile of ashes in the fireplace as a reward for their effort. To me, it was almost as if they didn't want to find anything. Never in all my time of policing had I heard of agents notifying the suspect's attorney that they were coming to conduct a search!

Lubbock officers who were present to assist the Randall County officers also noted that many of Erdmann's assets, such as an expensive gun collection he had boasted about, had been moved out. They had wanted to seize some infamous lampshades that had purportedly been made by Nazis from the skins of Jewish concentration camp prisoners. Even the most callused officers considered keeping memorabilia like that to be sick. However, those items had also been moved to an unknown place along with whatever else Dr. Erdmann considered valuable.

7

Damage Control

Widespread media reports alleged that the seeds of conspiracy to have Bill Hubbard indicted were planted the very evening after he testified in Canyon.

News of Hubbard's testimony was the number one story on all three network television stations. According to later reports, the assistant Criminal District Attorney, Rebecca Atchley, and her husband Randy, were watching in their home. A picture of Hubbard flashed on the screen and the voice-over told of his testimony. "Why didn't y'all get that son of a bitch when you had your shot?" was said to be Randy's first question.

Of course, he referred to the internal investigation of Hubbard in the summer of 1991. In truth, the C.D.A.'s office really didn't have a shot at Hubbard because it was strictly an internal investigation brought on by the complaint of a disgruntled member of Hubbard's Street Crimes Unit, of which Randy Atchley was a member. And very surely, both Rebecca and Randy knew, or should have known, it had ended with Hubbard's being cleared of any criminal acts by an exhaustive nine-week command level investigation with which the prosecutor's office was not involved.

Nevertheless, the two apparently believed the Ware office should have acted back then to get Hubbard removed from his job.

The best bet to offset the damage Hubbard's testimony had done to the D.A.'s office and to Ware himself was to now discredit the discreditor! If Hubbard could be made out to be a liar on anything else, maybe a shadow could be cast on all of his testimony concerning Erdmann and Ware. Even Steve Losch had said of Hubbard, "He is either a courageous whistleblower—a man who has opened up a can of worms in Lubbock County—or he is a liar."

Most believed the former, but Ware appeared to be struggling to provide another explanation for my testimony. He had his back to the wall. To claim that I had lied on the stand would mean that an elected prosecutor was making an accusation of a felony, because lying under oath in court is aggravated perjury. Ware evidently did not want to go that far. One of his attorneys had been in the courtroom as an observer when I testified; so he had gotten a firsthand account of all I had said. The D.A. obviously knew that the repercussions from publicly calling me a liar would be swift and sure, since he also knew I was represented by counsel in the matter.

Joe Gulick, who covered the courts for the *Avalanche-Journal,* asked Ware point blank, "Did Bill Hubbard lie on the witness stand in Canyon?"

"No," Ware told Gulick. "Hubbard didn't lie, but he grossly distorted the truth." What sort of response was this? Ware couldn't have it both ways. Either I had lied or I hadn't.

In reality, I'd had no opportunity to distort anything. I had testified to documents in my file and conversations I'd had with others in the law enforcement community concerning the procedures of Dr. Erdmann. I had given them the horrifying facts. These were conclusive enough. Meanwhile, more tactics targeting my reputation were being tried.

The day after Hubbard's testimony, it was reported that Ware called Captain Frank Wiley to meet with him to discuss the February 5th meeting. Wiley refused to meet with Ware alone. It had gotten to the point that many police officers were hesitant about meeting alone with Ware, because many felt he had a way of reinterpreting any topic of discussion after the meeting was over. So Wiley asked Chief Don Bridgers to go with him to Ware's office. The meeting started at 11:00 A.M. and continued for almost two hours. During that time Ware tried to "refresh" Wiley's memory about what had occurred at the February meeting in his office. Not all of the "refreshing" coincided with the way Wiley remembered the discussion.

Ware asked Bridgers to participate in a joint press conference to announce that no cover-up had occurred, but Bridgers declined to be a participant.

Frustrated, Ware's next move was to go to the other police officials who had been in attendance at the February 5th meeting and ask for sworn, notarized statements refuting Hubbard's testimony and saying that no cover-up had been hinted at in the meeting. All three of those command level officers—Colonel Ewing, Captain Wiley, and Lieutenant Summerlin—declined to give Ware such statements.

The next attempt at damage control had to do with old capital murder cases in which Erdmann had done the autopsies. Within two weeks after my Canyon testimony, Ware hired two outside pathologists to review Erdmann's autopsy reports in those cases. Without having the bodies present to compare with what Erdmann had written in his reports, it was almost certain that no discrepancies would be discovered. Cosmetically, however, it would look good to have two reputable pathologists agree in a press release that the capital cases all looked okay. If a body were to be exhumed and compared with Erdmann's report, real trouble would begin. And it was obvious Ware didn't want that to happen. The reports from the pathologists, however, fooled no one.

"I think he is knocking down a straw man," said Steve Losch, one of the defense attorneys who had participated in the Canyon hearing. "He is responding to an argument no one has made," Losch told reporters.

"Are the doctors going to endorse everything the man (Erdmann) said?" asked Lubbock defense attorney Floyd Holder, in a public statement. "I don't think anyone worth his salt would endorse his testimony."

Meanwhile, despite the findings of the internal police investigation on Hubbard, Rebecca and Randy Atchley were said to be investigating the possibility of bringing surprise criminal charges against Hubbard, even if it was well-known that those old charges were not supported by probable cause.

To simply go to the chief of police or the internal affairs lieutenant who was the custodian of the investigation records on Hubbard would not be prudent. That road would certainly lead to being confronted by all the facts of the investigation that had cleared Hubbard. Moreover, it also would have signaled the police department that a new investigation was going on. Secrecy was paramount. In reality, raw accusations without any reports of the subsequent investigation and the findings that led to Hubbard's exoneration were needed. The best sources of those accusations was the Street Crimes Unit, of which Randy Atchley was still a member.

This unit had been a stepping stone for several dedicated officers who wanted to advance in their field. Several of those who had worked under Hubbard's leadership had transferred out to the prestigious narcotics unit of L.P.D., and three had been given promotions in rank. Some who were left were grumblers who could not compete successfully for openings in other desirable units. David Hagler, who had instigated the internal affairs investigation, and who was a good friend of Randy Atchley, had passed a promotional test. But it looked for a time as if he were not high enough on the list to be promoted unless another unexpected sergeant's opening occurred. Certainly, if Hubbard were removed from his position there would be an opening for sergeant and Hagler would be a step closer to his promotion.

Without taking a single new or more recently dated statement, Rebecca Atchley solicited old sworn statements Hagler and others made at the time of the original investigation. The original signed and sworn statements were in the Internal Affairs files, so copies of the copies that the complainants had been given would have to suffice. Three other officers' statements were obtained. It is logical that the statement of Travis Sanders, a member of the unit whose statement supported Hubbard, was not sought. Not only would Sanders have resisted turning over his statement, but, if his suspicions were raised, the secrecy needed might also be compromised.

After these personal files were gathered, there apparently was no attempt to contact the police administration or to seek out the investigative files or even to interview the police commanders who conducted the investigation. The accusations, and not the investigation's findings or outcome, were wanted. Once these documents were in hand, any appearance of impropriety had to be avoided.

Why were police officers willing to risk their personal integrity and possibly their jobs by sneaking around behind the back of every supervisory officer in the entire police administration and participating in this attack against Hubbard? It is a question never answered. If their complaints had merit and if Hubbard was a criminal, that would have come to light

during the original investigation. If the complaints were valid,
they did not have to be made confidentially.

Nevertheless, the secretive plan against Hubbard began to
take shape.

Meanwhile, not suspecting anything, I was focusing on
my work and handling the aftermath of Erdmann's actions. I had expected after I returned from Canyon that
additional investigations into the cases about which I
had testified would begin. Nine days later, I came to the
conclusion that nothing was going to happen. It appeared that everything I had brought out on the stand
was going to be ignored. Apparently, the hope was that
the problems with Erdmann would solve themselves,
even though those problems might have a huge negative
effect on many of our cases.

Because I felt my own responsibility to the public su-
perseded any other, I began an investigative move of my
own. In my testimony I had brought up the case of a
murder/suicide that happened in Lubbock in mid-
December of 1991, approximately four months earlier.
An estranged husband had shown up at the home where
his wife was staying, and had been invited to the breakfast table by the occupants of the house, so he could
have a conversation with his wife in the presence of witnesses. At the table, the husband had abruptly pulled a
pistol, shot his wife in the head and then shot himself
as the others at the table watched helplessly in horror.

Because there were witnesses and both the victim and
only suspect were dead, the police involvement in the
case was fairly open and shut. However, routines had to
be followed and a proper investigation conducted, even
though we believed we knew from the start where it
would end. In light of this, when Justice of the Peace Jim
Hansen came to the scene and ordered autopsies, he

showed proper discretion and concern for taxpayer money by ordering that only bullet retrieval autopsies be performed. Since these were head shots, the chests would not need to be opened at all, according to the judge's order.

In my testimony I had expressed my concern that, knowing Erdmann's lack of organization the way I did, he had possibly made a report on a full autopsy even though only bullet retrieval had been ordered by the judge. Now it was mid-April, and so far as I could tell, nothing had been done by anyone to check out my suspicions, so I paid a visit to Jim Hansen's office myself. Detective Shields and I had attended the procedures, so I would know on sight if the autopsy report fit what I had seen done at the morgue.

Sure enough, the autopsy report on the wife reflected a full autopsy with a Y-incision at the chest, internal examination, weights and condition of major organs and the like. Worried, I returned to my office to double check the photos we had taken during the procedure and to talk to Shields about it. All of this was consistent with the fact that even though the J.P. had ordered only a limited autopsy and relieved Erdmann from having to do a full autopsy, Erdmann was so used to being asked for reports on full autopsies that he had not performed, he did not realize that this was one that he did not have to lie about! I notified Hansen and my supervisor, Lieutenant Summerlin, of my findings.

Next, I drafted a memo to my bosses that detailed the suspicions I had raised at that hearing, and my belief that the police department should begin looking into some of these matters lest the public believe that we were taking a head-in-the-sand position. I asked Captain Wiley to look at my first draft. He seemed somewhat irritated by it, so I did not officially sign the memo on Erdmann's falsification nor present it to the chain of command.

However, the following morning I discussed its contents with Lieutenant Summerlin, who advised me not to destroy the note but to give it a few days. It was his feeling that a little time was needed for the autopsy report of the murder/suicide to reach the D.A.'s office. At that point, we would see if Ware's office would bring criminal charges against Dr. Erdmann. Summerlin told me that if the C.D.A. was not willing to file anything on Erdmann, this would probably dictate the direction the police department needed to take.

As I left Lieutenant Summerlin's office, I ran into my senior officer in I.D., Corporal Jimmie Riemer. Very matter of factly, he told me that the autopsy report on another recent murder case said that a cranial examination had been done at an autopsy he had attended, when he knew it had not been done. I notified the other sergeant in homicide about this, since his officers were in charge of the actual investigation. I was beginning to feel as if the dam had broken and the flood of indiscretions by Dr. Erdmann would never stop.

That evening, shortly after I got home from work, the doorbell rang. At the door stood Carrie McClain, an investigator in the district attorney's office. I had known Carrie since she was twelve years old, and Debbie also knew both Carrie and her family. After Carrie completed her degree in Criminal Justice, she had been called away to reserve duty in the Gulf War. Upon her return from four months at the battlefield, she had no home or job, so she moved into our spare bedroom while she attended the area's law enforcement academy. She graduated first in her class, got a job as an investigator in the Ware office, and bought a house. For a time, it seemed things were really going her way.

Tonight, however, she was extremely upset. She fell into

my arms, sobbing. I knew that our almost-family relationship had made things uncomfortable for her at her office, but I could not imagine what was going on now.

When she composed herself, she said, "Travis Ware called me into his office, along with the chief investigator, just before closing time. Ware began by complimenting my work and then launched into a tirade against you. He threw photos of homicide victims into my lap and said, 'The people who do this sort of thing are the ones Bill Hubbard is trying to get off.'" According to Ware, Ralph Erdmann wasn't the problem. Bill Hubbard was.

Carrie said, "Ware used one particular derogatory term (motherfucker) to refer to you over and over." He claimed to have initiated the 1991 internal investigation of me. He claimed I should have been fired as a result of that investigation. He said I had lied on the witness stand in several cases. He even told Carrie that he had gone to all of the county and district judges to warn them that I had no credibility. And, he said I had psychological problems and needed help. "Not one word was said about what an incompetent Ralph Erdmann was. The problem was Bill Hubbard."

I think Carrie's tears were more from anger than from hurt. She was angry at Ware because she knew the things he had said were not true. Carrie wasn't about to let Ware see her cry, however, and she managed to hold back the tears until she left his office. "After his tirade against you," Carrie said, "Ware asked me to attend a function at Reese Air Force Base, just west of Lubbock, and accept an award for him." She could take a guest, he told her, "but not Bill Hubbard."

Despite Ware's ignoring the subject of Ralph Erdmann, others were centering their attention on the pathologist. On

April 18th the local newspaper reported that a new trial had been requested in a murder that had occurred back in late 1986 before I joined the I.D. unit. In that trial, the whereabouts of the victim prior to her murder had been a key issue. Whether she had been at a certain place drinking for some time prior to her death was critical to the defense. Therefore, the toxicology report on her blood content was of vital importance. Dr. Erdmann had done the autopsy.

Unlike prior cases about Erdmann's incompetence I had encountered, the blood had not been lost or simply untested. There was definitely a toxicology report. And another toxicology report. And yet another toxicology report. Three reports written on two different dates with different results by different laboratories. Toxicology reports dated December 19, 1986, and July 8, 1987, had surfaced from the Ralph Erdmann Laboratories. They showed no toxic substances in the blood of the victim. However, another report dated December 19, 1986, from the Amarillo Medical Laboratories showed significant levels of alcohol and cannaboids. Ware's office was to contend that the report from Amarillo was in error. That would have to mean, however, that Dr. Erdmann had sent mislabeled blood from another case to Amarillo. On the other hand, no one was really surprised that the Ware office was ready to utilize the Erdmann reports, because they provided a better fit with the prosecution's theory.

Though I could not get my mind off Erdmann, the next few days at the office were routine. However, just when I thought things had calmed down a bit for me, I was served a subpoena on April 20th. The attorney who represented the suspect in the case in November of the previous year—involving the first Erdmann autopsy I had attended—was not giving up. Not by a long shot. The subpoena ordered me to provide the defense with a copy of my Erdmann file. This was no big deal since the entire file had been admitted into evidence in Canyon and was now a public record. As a courtesy, though, I notified the felony prosecutor in the district attorney's office that I had received the subpoena. The prosecutor told me to comply with it, but to deliver the file copy to her office so they could formally hand it over to the defense attorney.

I figured that the real reason for this request had to be because Travis Ware wanted a copy of the file. All he had to do was ask, because it was already a public record. Anyhow, I had the file delivered to the prosecutor. Imagine my shock twenty-five days later when I was informed by the defense attorney that he had not received my file! This meant I was in contempt of the subpoena! I contacted the D.A.'s office, where one of the investigators told me that their office had reviewed the file and had decided to challenge, in court, turning it over to the defense. They had not notified me of this development, and I was the one who had been ordered by subpoena to comply.

Immediately, I notified Captain Wiley of the situation and he called Travis Ware. They must have gotten the situation resolved because nothing came of it. Captain Wiley would not tell me the content of his conversation with Ware, other than to say that we needed a new C.D.A.

Soon afterward, I received a letter from a different prosecutor in Ware's office, saying that this was a misunderstanding. They "thought I had sent over a courtesy copy for their files." This was not what the first prosecutor and I had agreed upon, and it certainly was not what their own investigator had told me earlier.

It appeared as though enough attention was being drawn to all of the Erdmann problems that the police department was finally on the verge of investigating some of the cases for possible criminal conduct on the part of the pathologist. Justice of the Peace Jim Hansen had made specific calls to the police department, bringing to their attention what he felt were possible violations by Erdmann. Then on May 19th, Captain Wiley came to me and asked for the memo I had written on April 14th, outlining the problems and questions that had been brought to light by my testimony in Canyon. The next day I wrote a supplemental memo to him, detailing additional documentation that had become available for the twelve sections outlined in my memo from the month before. Though these two memos spelled out at least a dozen starting points that would lead the police straight to what other counties were calling "Erdmann's criminal behavior," nothing was done.

Tempers were running hot and emotions were high. By now Dr. Erdmann was under indictment or being investigated for criminal violations by several counties on the south plains. Dozens of cases in the Lubbock County Criminal District Attorney's office were being brought into question and were in danger of being overturned. In trying to convince the public that their office was completely ignorant of any wrongdoing on Erdmann's part, the D.A.'s office did not appear to be at all interested in initiating a rigorous investigation of Erdmann's practices in Lubbock County.

At the police department, even though there were rumblings that an investigation needed to be conducted, there was much foot dragging. L.P.D. brass seemed to be waiting to see what the D.A.'s office would do. The operating rationale appeared to be that it would be pointless to spend time and manpower conducting a thorough investigation if the D.A. would not prosecute.

The defense attorneys' association also appeared to be waiting. In their case, the impotence stemmed from trying to see what was going to happen at the police department and at the D.A.'s office. These attorneys were eager to find out, before taking any action, what effect all of this might have on clients they represented, with regard to either pending cases or those where the defendants had been tried and convicted.

Despite the atmosphere of inertia which prevailed, verbal criticism flew back and forth. Defense attorney Floyd Holder was especially critical of the situation. He had long been an open critic not only of the C.D.A.'s office but of Travis Ware personally. Mr. Holder had begun to represent families who had been victimized one way or another by Dr. Erdmann. Now he got word that Ware was making malicious and slanderous remarks about him. Holder felt Ware had crossed the line one too many times. He wrote a strong letter to Ware, and then breaking the paralysis the others were held by, he hand-delivered it to the D.A.'s office. In the letter, the contents of which leaked out, Holder conceded that Ware was a powerful man, but if he persisted in his smearing and "retaliation," Holder promised to make Travis Ware his life's work. The final paragraph of the letter consisted of two words: "Back off!"

8

Stories, Accusations
and Lawsuits

By April and May, rain was flooding a great deal of West Texas, including a deluge which fell directly on Dr. Ralph Erdmann. The stories, accusations and lawsuits against Erdmann were pouring in. Each day the newspaper headlined additional developments in existing cases, or gave word of a new lawsuit or the discovery of yet another indiscretion by the pathologist.

One of the most bizarre reports concerned the remains of an unidentified headless woman, which had been found in a ditch north of Lubbock in Hale County in 1982. Ten years later, on the day after the Canyon hearing on April 2nd, Erdmann turned over to Hale County authorities what he claimed were the bones of this woman. There was only one problem. Among those bones was now found an unidentified skull containing a bullet hole.

Hale County investigators working with the Texas Rangers—the investigative branch of the state police—

began comparing the skull to autopsy reports. They believed the skull could be that of a fourteen-year-old boy who had died in Terry County, south of Lubbock. Hale County opened a criminal investigation into possible wrongdoing by Erdmann in their county, trying to determine if he had tampered with government records by falsifying autopsy reports there. The district attorney in Hale County declined to identify the child they believed the skull belonged to, because they thought he had been buried in Missouri and were afraid his family might not know that he was buried without a head.

The tragicomedy of errors continued.

Meanwhile, the *Dallas Morning News* reported that Odessa police were still trying to determine what Erdmann had done with the head of a homicide victim from 1990. The victim had been found dead in a Lubbock Dumpster. The body had been set afire to hamper efforts to make a positive identification, but the head was still attached to the rest of the body at that time. Erdmann received the body for autopsy purposes, and he was also to assist with identification efforts. Shortly thereafter, a suspect was located driving the dead man's car. The suspect told police he had nothing to do with a bullet hole in the man's head. Suddenly, the autopsy results—specifically relating to the man's head—became vitally important. When police contacted Erdmann about it, the head was nowhere to be found. Erdmann said he had shipped it to the state police lab in Austin, but the laboratory had no record of it.

A member of the C.D.A.'s office in Ector County, where Odessa is located, told Lee Hancock of the *Dallas Morning News*, "It's been a running sick joke around here for a couple of years. All I can tell you is that the Hale County head is not our head. Our head is a much older head, and our head is still out there somewhere."

It isn't easy to charge someone with killing another

person when the part of the victim's body that received the death wound cannot be located.

A reporter for the *Avalanche-Journal* asked Erdmann about the Odessa head. "I'm not going to keep heads in my closet," he protested. "Why would I keep a head? Texas Tech disposed of it. Who would bring this up? Someone who wants to discredit me."

Erdmann said he had not kept that particular head, but he obviously had kept other bodies and possibly heads and bones, or else he could not have delivered a skeleton to Hale County almost ten years after he had received it.

About the same time, Lubbock County learned that a man living in Lamesa, about an hour's drive south of Lubbock, could have been wrongfully jailed on child abuse charges because of a possibly botched autopsy Erdmann did on the man's infant son. Erdmann's autopsy, in January 1992, had indicated the cause of death to be pneumonia resulting from blunt force trauma to the abdomen. A second autopsy in April showed the child had died of accidental drowning. The father was released from jail and a grand jury was to look at the case. Erdmann continued to defend his original autopsy findings to the press. Meanwhile, the justice of the peace who had the case changed his death ruling to accidental. The tragic loss of a child because of an accident had been turned into a double tragedy for the wrongly accused father.

Back in Hockley County where the first indictments on Dr. Erdmann had been handed down, officials had begun investigating two autopsies Erdmann was supposed to have done in July 1991. The case concerned two persons who had been killed in Big Bend National Park. So far as Hockley County District Attorney Gary Goff could determine, no one who had handled the bodies after Erdmann could recall seeing any evidence of autopsies having been done. The case as to who committed the murders was still unsolved. The problem of ever solving the crime was compounded by Dr. Erdmann's actions.

Every day, more bizarre claims of Erdmann's inadequacies or worse surfaced. An *Avalanche-Journal* headline screamed, "Man Says Erdmann Stole His Daughter's Brain." The twenty-one-year-old woman had been killed in a Lubbock traffic accident in April of 1991. After the father had adamantly told Erdmann that none of his daughter's organs were to be kept, he learned that the pathologist had sent the body to its grave without the brain. Now the father was suing Erdmann.

In another case, a nineteen-year-old man had been found in his apartment dead from a gunshot wound to the head in August of 1991. Justice of the Peace Jim Hansen had ordered an autopsy. Erdmann had submitted a full autopsy report and Hansen subsequently ruled the death a suicide. D.A. Gary Goff from Hockley County now turned over to Lubbock D.A. Travis Ware statements from funeral home employees who had prepared the body for burial. The statements indicated that the body did not show evidence of having had an autopsy.

The Lubbock newspaper, meanwhile, persuaded Erdmann to talk about the "referrals," long rumored about, that his wife was making to bone and tissue harvesting companies. "I just didn't want to do it," Erdmann said. "I felt it was best if I stayed out of that. She would answer the phone. She would get the information for the recovery institutions, and then I think she got paid."

Mrs. Erdmann did, indeed, get paid for her referrals. And at least some of her checks were endorsed by her husband and deposited to his personal account.

* * *

Louder rumbles sounded that District Attorney Ware was in a bind. If he pursued criminal charges against Ralph Erdmann, he could be jeopardizing many past and pending criminal cases in which the pathologist had been involved. If Ware did not pursue charges against Erdmann, Lubbock County voters were going to find out that he had knowledge of Erdmann's "problems" and had done nothing about them. There was no doubt it was going to be difficult to find a pathway through all of this that would not trash many cases and that would not reflect poorly on his office.

In late April, Ware told the press that he would request a special prosecutor if any criminal cases developed against Erdmann in Lubbock County. Evidently Ware had not been reading any of the newspapers or paying attention at meetings where Erdmann's behavior was loudly discussed. Specific allegations of conduct by Erdmann that would constitute crimes were being made public. Other officials said they had personally informed Ware of them. If, at the time he received the information, Ware was unclear as to whether or not the behavior was criminal, by now other counties had demonstrated that they believed Erdmann's actions constituted felonies.

Even though Erdmann had exercised his Fifth Amendment rights 237 times on the witness stand in Canyon in April, and even though he was under indictment on felony charges and was represented by counsel, he was far from silent. He was granting interviews and, some supposed, still trying to talk his way out of his situation.

Erdmann told Lee Hancock of the *Dallas Morning News*, "I don't think I've done anything serious to anyone. I think that my efforts at all times were to see that justice was served. The only thing I can emphasize: I don't think that I have done anything at all with intent to falsify. I will claim that I am human. Yes, I did do mistakes. None of them was intentionally trying to cover up nothing."

He went on, "People don't understand forensic pathology—that's ninety percent of it. I don't think there are very many people around here that have my education," he told Hancock. "I don't think any other people have the track record I have." Hancock's readers fervently hoped he was correct in that statement!

Of the head he had sent to Hale County with the bones of the headless woman, he said, "I should have kept the head and buried it the way I bury everything—dispose of it." That was a chilling idea. He made no mention of trying to keep track of what head belongs to which body or that each body be given to the next of kin for proper burial.

Of the tissue slides that Erdmann renumbered to fit the Randall County case when he could not locate the correct samples, he said simply, "It was dumb."

And of the two victims found dead in Big Bend where funeral home authorities told the Hockley County D.A. that the bodies showed no signs of having had autopsies, Erdmann claimed, "They have a vendetta against me."

Dr. Erdmann maintained that he expected to be vindicated completely. When his legal problems were put to rest, he said he would move to Mexico City where he grew up and attended school and would continue to practice medicine there. If there was any blame, though, Erdmann said that the prosecutors who accepted him as an expert witness and the defense lawyers should have to shoulder some of it.

Those defense lawyers, according to Erdmann, had achieved their goal of destroying his credibility. There was no hint that Dr. Erdmann blamed any of his own actions for the loss of his reputation. However, it was not only defense attorneys who were causing him trouble. By this time, he had almost as many West Texas prosecutors on his trail as he did defense lawyers, who wanted fair treatment for their clients as guaranteed by the United States Constitution.

Nevertheless, a cocky Erdmann protested to the *Avalanche-Journal*, "I pray that the authorities can see through and see what's behind all this." However, one authority, the Texas Society of Pathologists, now wanted to discuss the allegations with Erdmann, as did the State Board of Medical Examiners. He said he would fight hard to retain his credentials. On the other hand, he reiterated, as soon as he had cleared his name, he was headed for Mexico.

Though Erdmann's presence in Lubbock and right to practice had seemed, in the early years, to be accepted without question, as the Erdmann controversy burgeoned, there was increased curiosity about the doctor himself. Who was this strange little man with the thick German accent? Where did he come from? How did someone with an obvious German heritage come to live in Mexico? Where was he educated? What educational degrees did he have? And how did he wind up in West Texas?

Attorneys for the defense at the Canyon hearing had sought to answer those same questions. They had become frustrated, however, as they tried to discover exactly what Erdmann's background and qualifications were. The more they researched, the more frustrated they became. The few solid items of evidence they could lay their hands on often contrasted starkly with what Erdmann himself contended his background was. And because of time constraints, a thorough investigation was not undertaken. The pathologist was shrouded in mystery on many levels.

Now, however, more enigmas were revealed. Erdmann's Texas medical license said he was born in Mexico. However, in 1988, he filed an education summary that claimed he was born August 8, 1926, in

Brownsville, Texas. From the beginning of Erdmann's troubles, people were wondering if he was a citizen of the United States, a resident alien, a naturalized citizen, or even if he was an illegal alien.

Erdmann had testified in previous cases that he was educated in German schools and that he had a bachelor of arts degree, though he was not specific as to where he had received the degree. At another time, Erdmann had testified that the bachelor's degree was from a school called Dutchover, which he said was located in Mexico City. Erdmann said the school was for children of German colonies in the Americas.

The curriculum summary by Dr. Erdmann identified the source of his elementary, junior, and senior high education as being Alexander von Humboldt School, but did not give its location. It also stated that he received his "Bachelor in Sciences" from Alexander von Humboldt College in 1944, but that would have made him eighteen years old at the time of his graduation.

The summary then jumped to when Erdmann supposedly received his doctor of medicine degree. Court motions claimed Erdmann maintained he got his medical degree under the name of Rafaelo Meliton Rodriquez from the University of Mexico Medical College in April of 1952. But Erdmann's Texas driver's license showed his name as Ralph Rodney Erdmann.

The summary also stated that Erdmann received a master's degree in forensic sciences from George Washington University in Washington, D.C., and that he completed a fellowship in forensic pathology in 1979 at the Armed Forces Institute of Pathology. Erdmann maintained he was board certified in forensic pathology in 1980 and that for the next ten years he practiced pathology part-time in the army as he worked on a contract basis for forty-one Texas counties.

However, no one seemed to be able to verify the facts.

Whether he was Rafaelo Meliton Rodriquez or Ralph Rodney Erdmann, whether he was a United States citizen or not, he had definitely gotten a great deal of mileage out of his cloudy educational history. An Oklahoma investigator who went to Mexico to check out Erdmann's history and education reported that all of the education Erdmann received in Mexico was about the equivalent of a high school education in the United States.

With so many questions about Erdmann's past remaining unanswered—for instance, how he got from Mexico to be chief of West Texas forensic pathology in a few short years—even more doubts crept up.

However, even though evidence about Erdmann's background and education was still lacking, there was much proof that his practice of pathology was filled with incompetence or worse. With all the information already at hand, Travis Ware still had not requested a special prosecutor and was still telling everyone that he felt Dr. Erdmann would be vindicated.

Rumors abounded that Ware knew of Erdmann's incompetence well before the 1992 confrontation in which I participated. However, Erdmann's testimony satisfied prosecution theories. Ware continued to use Erdmann's services as a pathologist and as the star witness for the prosecution in many cases.

For example, on November 10, 1988, the court of appeals of Texas had overturned the murder conviction of Zane Lee Ham. Ham's conviction had been based largely on the testimony of Ralph Erdmann. Represented to the trial court as an expert, Erdmann had told the jury that the injuries to the victim, a child, had been inflicted approximately fifty-five hours before her death. The prosecutor who argued before the court for it to uphold the conviction was none other than Travis Ware himself.

Why was it important that the injuries be fifty-five hours old? Because that would fit perfectly into the prosecution's theory that the victim was in the sole custody of Ham at the time the injuries were received. The only problem was, other forensic experts had stated that it was not possible to determine the exact age of the child's injuries. Those injuries might have been inflicted two days before death but to pinpoint them to approximately fifty-five hours was, as one forensic expert put it, "medical nonsense."

In overturning the conviction, the appeals court chastised the prosecution for putting on Erdmann's testimony as medical fact when they knew it was controverted by other medical experts.

So, not only was the murder conviction overturned, the Ware office received an emphatic slap from the court that rendered the decision. That was documented fact he could not deny.

More questions were inevitable. If cases were being overturned because of Erdmann's incompetence as far back as 1988, why was Ralph Erdmann still doing autopsies for Lubbock County in 1992? How did Erdmann manage to negotiate a new contract with a significant salary increase in 1990? Why was the county still keeping him on the payroll? And why was Travis Ware now dragging his feet in moving toward a definitive investigation into Erdmann's wrongdoing in Lubbock County?

Public perception, as well as the perception of people around the courthouse, was that Ware was not doing anything about Erdmann. Some said he would not ever do anything. John R. McFall, judge of the 237th District Court, got tired of waiting for the Ware office to act. McFall, long known to be anything but a fan of Travis Ware, used an obscure Texas statute to convene the first court of inquiry that Lubbock County had seen in thirty years.

Judge McFall signed a brief affidavit on April 26, 1992, which said that forensic pathologist Ralph Erdmann had committed felony and misdemeanor offenses, including perjury, tampering with government records, and theft. The affidavit went on to say that it was time for the judicial system to get into the situation because of all the rumors and innuendo about Erdmann.

Next, McFall prevented the prosecutor's office from getting the case by appointing Tommy Turner, a private practice attorney in Lubbock with previous experience as a prosecutor, to act as attorney pro tem, the equivalent of a special prosecutor. The court of inquiry had the power to file a complaint with the Lubbock County grand jury for further action if it was deemed appropriate.

In his affidavit, McFall stipulated that Ware and members of his office would be barred from participating in the investigation because members of his staff might become potential witnesses before the court. The judge also noted but did not specify "other circumstances" that would prevent Ware's office from conducting or participating in the probe. It appeared to many interested onlookers that Judge McFall was telling the district attorney he'd had plenty of time to investigate Erdmann and, since he had failed to do so, he and his entire office could just sit on the sidelines while someone else was called on to see that the job finally got done.

Ware responded by reminding the media that he had already indicated his intention to ask for a special prosecutor if any criminal cases against Erdmann developed in Lubbock. From where did he think reports on those cases would come if his office did not conduct an investigation, I wondered. Would they magically appear or fall from the sky? Obviously not. But now there was no doubt they would be forthcoming from the sixth floor of the county courthouse where the court of inquiry was beginning to hear testimony.

Another Ware roadblock had been bypassed.

9

Mustard, Jelly, Picante Sauce—and Blood

Meanwhile, although Dr. Erdmann was under indictment on felony charges and was facing trial in nearby counties, he could not seem to stop talking to the media, whose attention to the bizarre commotion in Lubbock, Texas was rapidly expanding. When *60 Minutes* arrived on the scene with investigative reporter Ed Bradley, Erdmann granted a full interview, complete with a tour of the laboratory he had set up in his kitchen. He even opened the refrigerator and showed the astonished Bradley that, housed next to the mustard, jelly and picante sauce, were blood and urine samples.

A host of newspapers now began covering the Erdmann attraction, from the *New York Times* to the *Los Angeles Times* to the *Houston Chronicle* to the *Lubbock Avalanche-Journal*. Then AP and UPI jumped into the fray. Lee Hancock of the *Dallas Morning News* seemed especially intrigued by the weird unfolding tales of misplaced heads, body parts and identities, and Erdmann's prosecutions in other parts of Texas.

In mid-May, when Erdmann talked extensively to Lee Hancock about his autopsies, his testimony and the criminal cases pending against him, people were astonished that Erdmann's attorneys were still letting him spout off to the media. On the other hand, maybe they had tried but just could not get Erdmann to keep quiet.

Hancock also interviewed other forensic experts as well as prosecutors who had used Erdmann's services and testimony. One medical examiner from Georgia told her, "I don't know how anyone could read one of his reports and trust anything he had to say."

In spite of this outcry, Ware was, as Hancock's story reported, "one of the few West Texas prosecutors still willing to publicly defend Dr. Erdmann."

The Childress County D.A. commented, "This has really given the criminal justice system in West Texas a black eye. Ralph's philosophy was, 'Maybe in error, never in doubt.' He was never going to admit there was something he didn't know."

But Erdmann's story was different. "I think the D.A.s were real happy that they had someone who knew what they were talking about. I know how to talk to a jury."

He acknowledged to Hancock that his time estimate for the injury that led to the death of the child in the Zane Ham case was not exactly scientific. Erdmann admitted that he would often find out the police theory and then prove it for them.

"I could have never come up with that unless I got that information from the sheriff's deputies. How would I know otherwise? I like to work as a team. Working as a team, I can't challenge what (police) say unless it's out of context. I accept what they say unless it's way out of line. I don't think it's bad pathology. It is the way I was trained."

When asked directly about the case in which there were three different toxicology reports on blood samples, one of which showed a widely varying result from the other two, Erdmann said, "Oh my God. I have no idea. I think this is wrong. Isn't that helpful to the defendant? I don't know how all of these things occurred.

"I was not really aware that there were all these things," Erdmann went on to tell Hancock. "It was the details that obviously escaped my close attention."

In the interview, Dr. Erdmann insisted that any wrong he did amounted to "clerical errors." Reading about it, I wondered if he really meant that he had not sufficiently covered his tracks with piles of paperwork.

With an indicted client still giving interviews to the press and making statements such as these, Erdmann's attorney, Senator Montford, certainly had his work cut out for him.

Apart from the Erdmann case, and because I, as yet, didn't know of the rising tide against me, the spring and early summer months of 1992 were some of the best yet for me in the homicide identification section. The police department allowed me to attend some excellent training courses in crime scene processing, especially in fingerprint technology. So now I was trained and certified in latent fingerprint techniques, not only by the Texas Department of Public Safety, but also by the Federal Bureau of Investigation. Whatever had to be done at a crime scene to develop, photograph and recover latent fingerprints, I could do, and I had ample opportunity to put my knowledge into practice.

I had come on board the I.D. section just as two new computerized photography outfits arrived. In addition to still photography, we also were getting into video taping. Two of us had been able to attend a police video school, so the quality of what we were producing was steadily increasing. Four complete new video outfits had been purchased so that tapes could be made of crime scenes. We found it extremely valuable being able to get back to the police station and immediately taking any detective who had the need on a complete video walk-through of the scene.

As time passed, my areas of expertise included processing for gunshot residues, chemical processing for fingerprints and laser recovery of trace evidence, as well as recovery of blood and body fluid evidence for use in DNA analysis and suspect identification. I felt I had come a long way in a comparatively short time, and apparently my supervisors agreed. Lieutenant Summerlin and Captain Wiley frequently commended me on how quickly I had gotten a grasp on my job and how well the unit was running. Gone were the suspicions that had accompanied my arrival in homicide. What a great feeling that was!

The I.D. section had a terrific working relationship with the people in the local state police laboratory, and we had a very good reputation with area law enforcement agencies for really knowing our stuff. We were called on regularly to give smaller agencies advice on puzzling cases and even directly assisted those agencies with their investigations. In addition to all this, we were making plans to introduce in early 1993 a new type of technology to the area by hosting an AFIS terminal.

AFIS stands for Automated Fingerprint Identification System. Our unit wanted to host a terminal that would be linked to a database in Austin. At that time, fingerprint matching was done on a one-to-one basis. Latent prints from a scene would sit in our files until a suspect's name came up whose prints we had on file or until that suspect was brought in to be fingerprinted. By acquiring AFIS, we would have in the database the fingerprints of almost everyone who had been arrested and fingerprinted in Texas. For the first time, we would be able to feed a fingerprint from a crime scene into this computer. Then the computer would give us a list of the twenty fingerprints in the database that were closest to the one entered. In most cases, the match would be the top name on the list. We were proud that our unit would finally be bringing this technology to West Texas.

Another sense of pride came when I was certified as an expert in these areas, first in state district court, then in federal court.

Soon I was using my expert certification in 137th District Court. The arrest I was asked to testify about had occurred on the first day after I had gone back on patrol. I had stopped by the place where one of the young patrol officers in my squad was investigating a house burglary. We went to work on the case, and within an hour made an arrest and recovered part of the victim's property.

But we didn't stop there. Footprints photographed at the scene matched the shoes the arrestee wore when we bagged him, and fingerprints lifted at the window that had been broken to gain entry were matched to that same criminal. Now, ten months later, the case was finally being tried. I not only got to testify about my involvement in the arrest, but I also was able to offer expert testimony about the fingerprint match.

When we were finished, and the man we had arrested was convicted, the prosecutor who tried the case commended me on the quality of my fingerprint testimony. "I'll bet you don't have the guts to tell your boss what you just said!" I joked with him. I knew that after all that had happened during the previous winter and spring, I was not one of Travis Ware's favorite people, and I commented, "I am probably off his Christmas card list."

The prosecutor told me a few days later that he had braved the odds by telling Ware and other prosecutors of my testimony. Within months, that prosecutor would watch a three-time convicted dope dealer walk out of the courtroom after negotiating a plea bargain with Ware for a two-year sentence. The dealer could—and should—have been facing twenty-five years to ninety-nine years, but at the time of his plea he was employed by the automobile dealership where Ware had purchased his last new car. That prosecutor later took a job as an assistant D.A. in Smith County and left Lubbock, Texas, in his rearview mirror.

Next, I was certified to give expert testimony in federal court on a cop killer. In 1953, this individual had gunned down Detective Ralph White as he responded to a burglary-in-progress call. Ralph was the brother of George White, an L.P.D. homicide detective. White's killer had been convicted and did time but had been able to avoid the death penalty when it was set aside for a time by the Supreme Court. Eventually, the killer was paroled.

After his parole, he went back to his old life of crime, progressing from a common burglar to a drug dealer. When our narcs busted him and brought him to trial in federal court, I got to go along to testify concerning his "pen packet."

A pen packet is a compilation of an individual's convictions. At the time of each new conviction the person is fingerprinted again, and those prints become part of the conviction file. As a fingerprint expert, I testified that the person who was convicted of killing Ralph White in 1953 was, without a doubt, the person on trial for dealing drugs in 1992. He was convicted and is now doing federal time. I felt good that I had a part in putting a cop killer away.

Now that Erdmann was no longer plying his trade in Lubbock, the city was in need of a pathologist. David Hoblit, a pathologist—although not certified in forensics—who lived in Lubbock, approached the county commissioners with a plan to at least be a stopgap measure until a permanent appointee could be found. The justices of the peace who were ordering the autopsies began appointing Hoblit to do examinations of bodies on a per-autopsy basis.

This gave me an opportunity to see for the first time an autopsy done by someone other than Dr. Erdmann. Up to that point I had only read about what procedures a real autopsy should include.

At the first autopsy by Dr. Hoblit which I attended, I was relieved to find the pathologist taking notes, dictating portions of his report and having sufficient assistance on hand to see that the job was done right by professionals. An assistant and a medical photographer were present. Though Dr. Hoblit had not had the specialized training afforded a forensic pathologist, my unit found him to be conscientious and personable. In addition, Hoblit had connections to good forensic pathologists in the state that he could call for advice or assistance as needed. The situation was not ideal, but it was made to work and it was a vast improvement over the way things had been done. David Hoblit was doing his very best to make a contribution to his community.

Hoblit and his staff were cordial to officers who attended his examinations, and he made quick friendships with all of us. Every time we got together to work a new case, he showed sensitivity to the officers by participating in conversation with them about what was going on in their families and their lives. For Hoblit, questions about an autopsy were received as genuine requests for information rather than suspicions that the procedures in the autopsy were being questioned. We all worked very well together. This friendly, professional relationship was soon to be appreciated in a way I would never forget.

* * *

On June 18, 1992, I was called about a crime scene where an officer had been shot. Whether he was alive or not was unclear. My heart leaped into my throat when I heard the police officer's name: Sergeant K. D. Fowler, an officer whom we all loved and respected. I rushed to the scene silently praying he would be okay.

When I arrived at the site, I was updated by a police officer who had been summoned there. James Haliburton, a part-time service aide for the Lubbock Regional Mental Health & Mental Retardation Center, accompanied a patient, James Kevin Voyles, to a doctor's appointment. Haliburton and Voyles returned to the latter's dilapidated apartment complex between 9:00 and 9:30 A.M. Shortly afterward, one of Voyles's neighbors heard the sound of six quick shots, and when he went outside, he found Haliburton's body in a breezeway between two of the barracks-like apartments. A maintenance worker at the complex called 9-1-1 at 9:30.

Lubbock police patrol officers Jimmy Cornelius and George Arce were first on the scene, and according to standard operating procedure, called for a supervisor. Sgt. Kenneth Fowler responded and the three began processing the scene as if it were a routine homicide, with no idea the gunman was still in the vicinity.

They began taping off and securing the crime scene, keeping the crowd of curious neighbors and television news cameras at a distance. Fowler knelt beside the body of 48-year-old Haliburton, which paramedics had covered with a yellow plastic sheet. Suddenly, Voyles slipped his hand out the partially open door of his apartment and fired from four to six rounds, several of which struck Fowler. The crowd was stunned. When they had collected their wits, everyone, including Officers Arce and Cornelius, scurried for cover. Voyles continued shooting sporadically through the thin walls of his duplex apartment, preventing Arce and Cornelius from going to

Fowler's aid. They had no idea whether he was alive or not. They called for backup—the call I received.

I and another detective were the first backups to arrive. We set up a perimeter and tried to make verbal contact with the gunman. Our attempt was answered with gunfire. For a half hour, Fowler's body lay in sight of his fellow officers, who had no way to take care of him. A SWAT team arrived, got set up and created a diversion by setting off two explosives near the apartment and firing their weapons high. This distraction allowed officers to retrieve Fowler's body, which was placed in a waiting EMS ambulance and whisked away to the University Medical Center.

At 11:30 A.M., hostage negotiators threatened Voyles with tear gas, and a short time later, he surrendered.

While I worked the crime scene, about thirty grim-faced police officers, both on-duty and off, congregated in the halls outside the emergency room at the University Medical Center for word of Fowler's condition. A shock wave spread through the silent group when it came. Fowler had been pronounced dead on arrival. They all consoled each other in hushed voices. Some officers shed silent tears. Others hid their grief behind stony visages. By early afternoon, every officer wore a black strip across his or her badge, honoring their slain comrade.

From a supervisor's standpoint, I knew that the autopsy of Sergeant K. D. Fowler—much beloved by his fellow police officers—would have to be attended by a detective to gather evidence and keep the necessary records. It was a responsibility I could not delegate. That sad duty went along with my sergeant's stripes. Later that afternoon, I met Hoblit and his staff at the morgue. Hoblit had called in area forensic pathologist Dr. Sparks Veasey to be the lead pathologist on the case, since

Veasey was better qualified and because this case potentially involved a death penalty for the suspect.

Sergeant Fowler had been sort of a "father of sergeants" to the rest of us who had gotten our stripes at young ages. Just that morning, I had walked through the police department lobby and heard his familiar gruff voice, "G'morning, Bill!" Now, I was attending his autopsy. It was almost more than I could handle. But it was my job.

Hoblit, Veasey, and their staff members earned a great deal of my loyalty that day, as they treated Sergeant Fowler with the greatest respect and were extremely compassionate to me. Removing Sarge's badge from his bullet-riddled uniform shirt was one of the most difficult acts of my career. I was completely overcome, yet everyone there set aside their professional duties to simply be kind human beings and help me regain my composure. As soon as I was able to get it together, we continued and completed what we had to do.

Early in July, Travis Ware gave an interview to the Lubbock newspaper, expounding on all that *he* was doing to bring a medical examiner's system to Lubbock. I felt Ware had continued to be a roadblock in shedding light on the Erdmann situation, and now he was publicly taking credit for David Hoblit's hard work to make the situation right. Ware did not so much as mention Hoblit's name in the interview with the reporter.

It had been Dr. Hoblit's plan to form a pathology group in Lubbock that would include at least two highly qualified forensic pathologists. They hoped to win the contract from the county, with the intent of working toward eventually establishing a medical examiner's system that would be large enough to serve the entire area. It could be a lucrative business deal for Hoblit, who intended to be the medical director of the group, but it also would fill a crying need. This had the potential for making something very right come out of what had been very wrong. Hoblit was recruiting diligently to bring some good forensic people to Lubbock.

At first I felt chagrined, then incensed at Ware's duplicity. So, sitting down at the typewriter as a citizen, I wrote a letter to the editor of the *Avalanche-Journal* to try to set the record straight. "I read with great interest the Joe Hughes editorial in the July 2, 1992 *A-J* in which District Attorney Travis Ware expounded on all that he is doing to bring about a medical examiner's system in Lubbock. It seems to me that it has been only a couple of weeks since the *A-J* ran an article telling of Dr. David Hoblit's personal efforts to get us some qualified forensic pathologists for Lubbock. As the Ralph Erdmann situation continues to be a hot topic and criminal charges against him in Lubbock at this point seem inevitable, could it be that Mr. Ware is trying to distance himself from a problem that many believe he helped create? And is he doing this even to the point of taking credit for other people's work—a concept with which Mr. Ware apparently has been familiar since his days in law school?"

The last question was in reference to information that had become public recently. Ware had been thrown out of law school because of plagiarism. He had to stay out for an entire year before he was allowed to complete his law degree.

A day or two later, my letter ran on the "Letters to the Editor" page, but the sentence referring to Ware's law school difficulties was edited out. Nevertheless, I felt the point still came across loud and clear. In fact, I was sure of that because, when I got to work the morning my letter appeared, my bosses all hovered around back in the chief's reception area. And I got plenty of cold

shoulders from command-level personnel who did not
seem to like my doing anything to set Ware off. However, they also knew that since I had not represented
myself in the letter as a Lubbock police officer, there was
nothing they could do about it. As any citizen, my right
to speak was protected by the First Amendment.

With the pot boiling on many fronts, the court of inquiry created by Judge McFall on April 28, 1992, was
bubbling. Two police department detectives had been
assigned to assist the prosecutor pro tem, Mr. Turner.
My superiors did not allow me to be one of those detectives. Sergeant Randy McGuire and Detective Doug Davenport were given the chore of assisting Turner.

On Monday, June 29th, testimony began in McFall's
courtroom. Opening testimony indicated that in two
months, investigators had found at least forty-two Lubbock County cases where discrepancies existed between
Erdmann's autopsy reports and funeral home records.
Dr. Erdmann did not show up for the hearing but was
represented by a new attorney. Senator Montford had
suddenly become too busy with state affairs to represent
Erdmann. The pathologist's new attorney, Travis Shelton, had been a Lubbock district attorney several years
earlier.

Detective Davenport told Judge McFall that twenty-
nine of the forty-two cases involved cranial exams. Erdmann's reports, which were considered government
records, showed that he conducted the procedures, but
embalming reports from the funeral homes indicated
no evidence that he had.

In six other cases Erdmann's reports told of opening
the bodies with Y-incisions, but the funeral home
records did not confirm Erdmann's accounts.

Obviously, the purpose of the court was to establish
probable cause to move ahead, because there hadn't
been enough time to allow a complete investigation into

all these cases which could end up in the court. This would require exhumation of each of the bodies to determine if Erdmann was right or if the funeral home records would prevail.

Mr. Shelton was not happy with the court of inquiry and openly criticized it. At one point, he told Judge McFall that it was a mockery of the justice system. He made motions to have the court of inquiry disbanded and to recuse McFall from presiding over it. Neither motion was granted by the judge.

On the second day of the court of inquiry, Sergeant McGuire told of the case of a Lubbock man whose Erdmann autopsy report conflicted with the records of the funeral home. In that case, the subject's body had been exhumed in Las Vegas, Nevada. The Nevada exhumation report showed that no autopsy had been performed, even though Erdmann's report gave many specific details about the examination he supposedly conducted of the head and internal organs.

The new pathologist, David Hoblit, was to be called to the stand. I went to the 237th courtroom to listen to some of the testimony and heard Hoblit's report. He described a local case where he had done the exhumation autopsy, and found no evidence of the complete autopsy Erdmann had reported. When Hoblit finished, Judge McFall declared a recess for lunch. Dr. Hoblit invited me to join him, and we rode down on the elevator with Shelton.

After we got in the elevator, Hoblit suddenly snapped his fingers and looked at me. With a straight face he remarked, "You know, I forgot to mention that the reason that body didn't have a Y-incision on it could have been from postmortem healing!" Shelton's eyes widened.

I clamped my jaws together to keep from guffawing, knowing there's no such thing as postmortem healing. Shelton, realizing that Hoblit was playing a joke at his expense, quickly averted his eyes and spent the rest of the elevator ride staring at the doors.

Initially, it was thought that the court of inquiry might go on for as long as two weeks. The court had convened on Monday, and by Wednesday afternoon Turner had established nine felony violations that Erdmann had committed in Lubbock County. Turner began to summarize his findings. It was then up to the judge to determine if he believed Erdmann had committed crimes. If so, he said he would appoint the Texas Attorney General's office as special prosecutor to see that the Erdmann case was taken before a grand jury.

Though the purpose of the court of inquiry had been to give a cursory look at possible crimes by Erdmann and to establish probable cause, Travis Ware downplayed it all and said he was "somewhat surprised" that so few cases had been presented. It appeared he wanted to make it sound as if an exhaustive effort to look into Erdmann allegations had turned up only nine violations. However, these nine alleged felonies represented only the seven cases that had been given a thorough examination.

Tommy Turner said that when their investigation had "seven for seven," he thought they had a pretty good grasp on the nature of the Erdmann problem and where those other 100 or so cases might be headed.

Turner told the *Avalanche-Journal* that whether more cases developed on Erdmann "depends on how much more the police are going to be able to follow up their investigation."

The next grand jury was scheduled to meet beginning the following Monday, July 6th. Indications from both Turner and McFall were that they expected the grand jury to begin looking at the Erdmann situation, and the attorney general's people would come in as special prosecutors. It wasn't until mid-July, however, that assistant State Attorney General Shane Phelps arrived on the

scene. He told the press that it could be the end of July
before those possible violations by Erdmann made it
before a grand jury.

More foot dragging.

To most observers, it seemed significant that when
Ware allegedly requested his "investigation," it was done
quietly in early June. At that time, Shane Phelps was relatively unknown in the Lubbock area. In the five weeks
that went by after the initial Ware request to the attorney
general's office, the court of inquiry had presented its
findings in a public hearing, and Judge McFall, hoping
for an impartial special prosecutor, had passed the
mantle on to the office of the attorney general. By July
14th, Shane Phelps was firmly in control of the findings
of the court of inquiry.

Lubbock citizens became dubious about the Phelps
appointment when, on July 17th, Ware made public a
letter addressed to him that had been written by Phelps.
It stated that on June 10th, Ware had formally requested
the attorney general's office to look into allegations that
Ware and his office had acted improperly in handling information brought to him concerning Ralph Erdmann.

Phelps was the attorney who received the information
from the court of inquiry, and Phelps was also the one
whom Ware had contacted in June and who, five weeks
later, was clearing Ware of any wrongdoing in connection with Ralph Erdmann.

Rumors flew that either Phelps was a bad choice, or
the situation smelled of an unholy alliance, especially in
light of the fact that it was virtually unheard of for an attorney general's investigation to be requested, conducted, and the results issued in only five weeks. Months,
maybe. Weeks, no.

One paragraph of Phelps's letter fairly leapt off the
page at those who were familiar with the chronology
of events. It said, "It appears that concerns about Dr.

Erdmann were first communicated to you (Ware) in January 1992 during a meeting with members of the Lubbock Police Department."

How could an investigation not uncover the fact that Travis Ware had been the prosecutor who had argued unsuccessfully for the court of appeals to uphold the Zane Ham conviction? Huge problems with Erdmann and his testimony had been specifically pointed out by the court as it threw out Ham's conviction. That had been in November 1988.

The Phelps letter continued. "We find no evidence that anything you said was intended in any way to 'cover up' the Dr. Erdmann situation, nor were your comments even remotely construed that way by persons at the meetings of January and February 1992 with the one notable exception."

So now I and my sworn testimony were relegated to being a "notable exception." As Ware waved this letter before the local media, the police officers who had been present at the meetings mentioned in the letter indicated that Phelps and his people had not conducted many interviews about the matter in the police building. Perhaps a quick talk with the two Ware staffers who had also been in the meeting was the basis for Phelps's "findings."

The last sentence of the Phelps letter seemed to be revealing as well. "If we may be of any further service to you, please do not hesitate to call."

10

Summer's End

Auspicious developments were quickly piling atop each other during the latter part of July in the hot, cotton-growing summer of 1992. I was aware of only a few of the things that were occurring. These mostly concerned Ralph Erdmann and the cases mounting against him.

After the mid-July letter from Assistant Attorney General Shane Phelps, Lubbock County Criminal District Attorney Travis Ware acted energized. It was as though he felt the entire stink had passed over him without leaving even the faintest of scents malingering in the still summer air.

Some in Ware's office who attended a July 23rd clerical staff meeting reported that he had gone off on one of his "typical tangents," had shown off the Phelps letter and continued to maintain Ralph Erdmann's innocence. The most astonishing statement to come out of the meeting was Ware's reported prediction that Gary Goff, the Hockley County D.A. whose office originally brought charges against Erdmann, would end up resigning in disgrace and would be disbarred once Erdmann was exonerated.

Assistant D.A. Rebecca Atchley, with the help of her police officer husband, Randy, one of those who had made disgruntled complaints about Bill Hubbard, had by this time contacted the few Street Crimes Unit members who still felt they had an ax to grind concerning Hubbard. It is difficult to understand what was going on in their minds. How could anyone have convinced them, and how could they have convinced themselves, that acting clandestinely was the correct thing to do?

Whatever they were thinking, individual files were copied which contained statements which had been made during the internal investigation of 1991 and were then given to Mrs. Atchley. She, in turn, gave them to her boss, Travis Ware.

Atchley and Ware were not ignorant people. It is difficult to conceive that they did not know what they had in their hands were old statements, authored by disgruntled subordinates about a supervisor who had been cleared of wrongdoing after a thorough investigation by L.P.D. commanders. Updates of the investigation had made the local newspaper seven times. How could they say truthfully that they had no knowledge of the investigation and its outcome? After all, Rebecca Atchley was married to one of the complainers, and he had firsthand knowledge of the outcome of the investigation.

Add to that the fact that Ware and Atchley, as two prosecutors in the Criminal District Attorney's office, had to be aware, probably better than anyone in the county, of a prosecutor's legal and ethical obligation to pursue exculpatory or exonerating evidence if it is known to exist. And there was no denying that the investigative file in L.P.D.'s internal affairs office was known to exist.

Meanwhile, I watched Erdmann's problems compounding. Not only was he facing charges in Hockley County and the findings of Lubbock County's court of inquiry, but now Dickens County was bringing charges against him as well. The county had exhumed the victim of a hit-and-run accident, and two forensic pathologists, Linda Norton of Dallas and Sparks Veasey of Ector County, conducted a second autopsy. The two found that Erdmann's autopsy report showed him doing procedures he had not in fact done, and they also disagreed with Erdmann's finding as to the cause of death. Erdmann had ruled that the victim had died of a "broken neck." Norton and Veasey said the cause of death was a closed head injury. It seemed evident that Erdmann missed the closed head injury because he had not done a head examination, even though his report said that he had.

Felony warrants were issued for Dr. Erdmann's arrest. Two days later, a Lubbock County sheriff's deputy recognized Erdmann's Cadillac coming into Lubbock and pulled it over, arresting the pathologist who was driving. He was taken to jail and booked, then released after he posted bail.

By the middle of August, Erdmann had surrendered his medical license to the State Board of Medical Examiners. The executive director of the board expressed his opinion that he doubted Erdmann would ever again practice medicine in Texas, or in any other state.

Ralph Erdmann still faced a huge legal battle, and the penalties of his alleged crimes might include lengthy penitentiary time. Now he would face those charges not as Dr. Erdmann, but as Mr. Erdmann.

About this time, less than a month after Ware produced his letter from Shane Phelps exonerating him from offenses connected to Ralph Erdmann, the defense attorneys in the capital murder case in Canyon were heard from again. Those lawyers—Millard Farmer, Steve Losch and V. G. Kolius—had heard the news of Ware's exoneration and asked Phelps to reopen his probe of Ware.

"We intend to find out why these two prosecutors (Ware and Randy Sherrod) are not prosecuting Erdmann," Losch told the *Avalanche-Journal.* "Millard had to call Phelps, because Phelps' letter says in effect that Hubbard committed perjury. If Hubbard committed perjury, then we have to present that to Judge Pirtle."

These attorneys were sure I had not committed perjury. Ware himself had told the press immediately after my testimony that I had not lied on the stand. But Phelps's letter essentially said that I was the only one who held Ware responsible, and that Phelps's investigation had found no one who had construed anything Ware had said in the February meeting to represent a suggestion to keep quiet about Erdmann's problems. Like the attorney, I felt that the Phelps's letter did, in fact, sound like an accusation of perjury against me. Losch wanted him to put up or shut up.

Losch continued, "Ware is trying to confuse the issue of whether Erdmann committed crimes with whether the crime resulted in wrong conclusions in causes of death. What really matters is whether Erdmann committed crimes.

"Phelps is saying that everybody in the February fifth meeting agreed with Hubbard, but that the disagreement was over the interpretation of the meeting. If Phelps agrees that Hubbard's notes (of the meeting) are accurate, how could anyone misinterpret what went on in that meeting?"

Losch concluded, "Hubbard's version of the meeting will be corroborated as true in (the Canyon trial)."

Five days later, Shane Phelps revealed that he did not plan to reopen his investigation of Ware. It was a decision that precipitated much discussion and more rumors among the increasingly suspicious public and press.

In August, Phil Wischkaemper, the defense attorney who had subpoenaed a copy of my Erdmann file, visited me. He was defending the suspect who had been charged with murdering Jesse Flores, the victim on whom I watched Erdmann perform the first autopsy I had ever seen. Phil was interested in the results of the toxicology on blood taken at the autopsy. I reviewed my report and that of Shields, who had been in attendance also, and told Phil, "No blood was drawn at the autopsy." I recalled discussing this while the body was open during the autopsy.

On the night the victim was brought into the hospital, emergency room personnel had performed surgery on him in an effort to save his life. During that effort, the victim had received about thirty units of blood, which was about the equivalent of a complete transfusion. At the autopsy, Detective Shields and I had agreed that, because of the transfusions, drawing blood at this time for toxicology purposes would be a worthless effort. Shields's report reflected that Erdmann had given us one vial of blood serum that had been drawn in the emergency room. That was all we had, all we received, and all we took to the D.P.S.

Phil then showed me Erdmann's autopsy report, which showed exact organ weights, although no organs were removed while we were present. It also stated that Erdmann drew blood from the thoracic aorta during the autopsy, gave it to "the authorities," and the results would come through the D.P.S. That just hadn't happened.

I notified the case detective of this as well as Lieutenant Summerlin and the prosecutor assigned to the case. We had multiple witnesses to the offense. Patrol officers had arrested the suspect with the gun within minutes of the crime, but now it looked like a deal would have to be cut for the suspect because of Erdmann's involvement.

In spite of the fact that we brought this to the attention of the prosecutor, she made no mention of pursuing criminal charges against Erdmann for submitting a false report. In September the suspect would accept a plea bargain, which sentenced him to ten years for involuntary manslaughter. I was disgusted by the result. All our efforts to bring a guilty man to justice were for nothing. The plea bargain documents included no mention that a deadly weapon was used in the crime. The "no deadly weapon" stipulation would make the subject a candidate for early parole. With the time he had served awaiting trial, he was almost due to be released as the deal was done.

Ralph Erdmann's autopsy was the kiss of death to a case into which we had put almost a year's work.

On August 31st, pursuing other police matters, I went to the courthouse for a meeting and learned that the person with whom I had an appointment would not be available for half an hour. Knowing the 137th District Court was listening to testimony in a hearing about the case that had produced three different toxicology reports, I walked over. While I was there, Travis Ware was called to the stand.

Surprisingly, because he had been maintaining Erdmann's competency, Ware testified that, going back to 1987, Erdmann was extremely difficult. He said he could never find the pathologist and that when he was on the witness stand, he never knew what would come out of Erdmann's mouth.

This was in stark contrast to calling Erdmann a "hell of a witness who has gotten us lots of convictions" in the statement Ware had made on February 5th.

Ware also testified that at the time of the original trial in this case, Erdmann had been away on military duty and had resisted returning to testify. The D.A. said he'd had to threaten Erdmann with a writ of attachment and arrest if he did not return voluntarily for the trial.

Ware's testimony under oath seemed to contradict all his previous statements and raised some interesting questions. If Ware had suspected Erdmann of lying as far back as 1987, why then was the pathologist still doing autopsies for Lubbock in 1992, to the tune of $140,000 a year? Shouldn't the pathologist—who had done the procedures on the victim but would not cooperate for a trial, and whose testimony was anybody's guess—have been fired a long time ago?

Mr. Ware must not have appreciated my sitting in the courtroom listening to his sworn testimony and taking notes. A day or so later, Lieutenant Summerlin and Captain Wiley came into my office and closed the door. Bad sign, I thought, and took a deep breath.

"I understand you were in court the other day and heard Ware testify," Wiley said.

I explained that I'd gone to the D.A.'s office to meet with the administrator, Steve Holmes, on a computer matter. "Since he was not in, I went up to the One Hundred Thirty-Seventh to hear some of the testimony. Tanya Northrup, an attorney in the D.A.'s office, was on the stand when I went in. Then Travis was called. I did not stay for his whole testimony but did hear some of it."

Ware had called Chief Bridgers and complained that my presence in the courtroom caused him some concern that I was not using my paid duty time effectively.

Since Wiley and Summerlin were interrogating me about the Ware/Erdmann situation, I decided to let them in on a few things. "Investigator Carrie McClain at the D.A.'s office is being pressured by her superiors not to be seen in public with Debbie and me," I told them reprovingly. "The same pressure is being exerted on my best friend, Bill Kerns, an editor at the *Avalanche-Journal.*

"Also," I went on, "Dr. Hoblit has spoken to his new forensic pathologist, Dr. Jody Nielsen, about Ware's having told him that it was not good for pathologists to associate with police investigators." When Nielsen, who had been hired from Dr. DiMaio's office in San Antonio, had moved alone to Lubbock, Debbie and I befriended her and took her out to dinner a few times. As far as I know, the only "police investigator" Nielsen had socialized with was Bill Hubbard.

To my relief, both Wiley and Summerlin were understanding—kind, even. "Remember, though, that whatever run-ins you have with Ware will have implications on the whole police department," Wiley reminded me. "Please, Bill, don't do anything intentionally to set Travis off."

"Captain, short of stopping breathing, I don't know what that would be," I replied, shaking my head.

According to a source, Travis Ware had twice contacted City Manager Larry Cunningham by telephone. He told Cunningham he was concerned that Hubbard's job performance was deficient, and indicated to the city manager that "we" needed to do something in regard to Hubbard.

Ware told Cunningham he had talked to Chief Bridgers, but Ware felt he needed to bring all of this straight to Cunningham to see if Cunningham could "help in dealing with some of the problems" that involved Hubbard. Ware told Cunningham that Hubbard was not performing well and that he was not respected by his fellow officers. When Cunningham informed Ware that the matter was one to be taken up with the chief, the D.A. told Cunningham that he at least wanted the city manager to reassign Hubbard to a "less sensitive" area in the department. It was Cunningham's understanding that what Ware really wanted was for Hubbard to be moved out of homicide where he would no longer have contact with the pathology end of investigations.

A few days later, according to the same report, Ware paid a personal visit to Cunningham's office. He told Cunningham he had just come from lunch with Rebecca Atchley and

that if Cunningham did not "do something about Hubbard,"
they would dredge up some of the old allegations from the in-
ternal affairs investigation of 1991 and take them to a grand
jury "in hopes of getting some kind of indictment." Ware told
Cunningham that he and Atchley had come up with this
"plan," but Cunningham was not to tell anyone about it.
Then, in a thinly veiled threat, Ware told Cunningham that
if there was a leak concerning the "plan," he "would know
where it came from."

Despite this, Cunningham did not help Ware "do something
about Hubbard," which left it up to Ware and Atchley to move
ahead with their plan.

On September 3rd, a thirty-five-year-old woman was
found dead in her central Lubbock home by her
teenage son. The woman had a history of drug abuse
and had a fresh needle mark at the crook of her right
elbow. It was learned, however, that she was right-
handed, and right-handed people tend to shoot up in
the left arm. As the detective of my unit and I worked the
scene, we suspected that someone had injected her with
a "hot load," or overdose.

The investigation focused on a man named Ray, a
recent parolee with a history of forgery, property crimes
and dope. When I had been assigned to the Street
Crimes Unit, I had been instrumental in sending this
man on his latest trip to the pen. As he was led away, he
vowed that he would be out soon and then, when he got
out, he would get me.

That was the kind of garbage that a cop learns to cope
with. You don't completely blow off the threat, but you
don't get paranoid about it, either. Most of us just tend
to pack a gun every time we venture out of the house
and stay reasonably alert all the time. But you learn not
to look for the bogeyman behind every tree.

I was aware that this creep was out of the joint, and I will admit I wasn't too sorry when his name popped up as the likely suspect in this homicide. The case had been assigned for investigation to Ronnie Goolsby, one of the "suits" in our division.

By the weekend after the death, Ray, the parolee, was lighting up the phone lines at the police department asking to talk to me. It seems that some friends of the dead woman were hot on his tail wanting to do him in.

The desk sergeant on duty called me at home, saying, "He's driving us nuts wanting to talk to you." I told the sergeant, "Tell the suspect I will be in my office at eight o'clock Monday morning."

At 8:05 A.M. Monday, my phone rang. A familiar but frantic voice was saying, "Please, I want to meet with you away from the police department." I grimaced. Did he think I was stupid enough to go out on my own to meet a prime murder suspect who was desperate and who had previously threatened my life?

"You come here, Ray," I said. He resisted, but finally agreed to come to police headquarters. Within ten minutes he was in my office.

"Mr. Hubbard, ya gotta help me!"

"Why should I help you, Ray?" I snapped.

"Because I didn't do it and they are out to kill me!"

"Speaking of 'out to kill me,' I haven't forgotten the threats you made to me when you went to jail," I reminded him.

"Aw, Mr. Hubbard, that was the drugs talkin'. Ya gotta help me now!"

I waited, stretching the tension almost to the breaking point. "You make me sick," I said finally. "But I'm going to do you a small favor. I'll introduce you to Detective Goolsby who's working this case and you can see if he wants to talk to you." In reality I was laying the foundation for the good cop/bad cop scenario so the suspect would be inclined to see Goolsby as his last resort and would cooperate.

I took Ray around and introduced him to Ronnie Goolsby. I told Detective Goolsby a little about how I knew Ray from years past. "I'm not inclined to do anything on his behalf, but since the case is yours, you can do with Ray as you please." Great act. As the detective engaged the suspect in conversation, I went on about my other duties.

I found out later that Goolsby eased into conversation with the suspect, just talking to him about things in general. The detective asked Ray general questions about the drug trade in Lubbock and who was doing what, remaining very relaxed, just throwing out questions and conversing with Ray. The detective already knew the answers to some of the questions. These he was able to use as a gauge to know if Ray was inclined to lie.

Goolsby queried Ray about what he knew about the dope racket in the jail. Short answer. He asked about who was moving most of the heroin in Lubbock. A few names were forthcoming. He asked what Ray knew about certain well-known citizens and their involvement in drugs. Some Ray knew a little about, some nothing at all. And then pausing a little, he questioned what Ray knew about Travis Ware and a cocaine investigation. Rumors of an investigation of some sort on the federal level had been tossed around a few years earlier, but nothing specific was known. And, frankly, rumors of that sort are common about public figures.

To Goolsby's question about Ware, the parolee replied, "Nothing."

Goolsby eased on to the next subject. No big deal. The conversation ended with no startling revelations about anything, much less our dead overdose victim.

The next morning Goolsby answered his office phone and was greeted in a casual way by Jeff Creager, the chief investigator at the Ware office, who requested that Goolsby "stop by" when he had a minute, so they could discuss a case. Nothing more specific.

When Goolsby walked into Creager's office, he found Rebecca Atchley there. Creager picked up the phone, punched four numbers, said, "He's here," and hung up. In a few moments, Travis Ware walked into the room and closed the door behind him.

It quickly became apparent to Goolsby that Ray had been playing double agent to his own advantage. The question Goolsby had asked Ray had gone straight to Ware. Ronnie Goolsby sat and took all they could dish out for the next three and a half hours.

During the course of the meeting, Ware repeatedly used the very uncomplimentary noun he reserved to refer to me, which Goolsby came to refer to as Ware's favorite word. Ware warned the detective that he was about to follow in my footsteps if he did not mend his ways.

Ware then told Goolsby something that did not get back to me for months but, when it did, was a startling revelation just the same. He said I was "about to be indicted" and that Goolsby was coming precariously close to going along with me. I am sure Goolsby thought at the time that this was simply a scare tactic Ware was using.

The same afternoon, according to the recipient, Ware left a message at the office of Lubbock's new forensic pathologist, Dr. Jody Nielsen, saying he wished to talk to her. Already suspicious, since Nielsen was cognizant to the fact that Ware disapproved of her seeing Bill and Debbie Hubbard socially, she decided to record the conversation when she returned his call. This practice is perfectly legal, if one party consents to the recording, and Dr. Nielsen was that one party.

During this conversation, Ware told Nielsen that he really wanted her to come to his office so that he and Rebecca Atchley

Denette Vaughn speaks to reporters about Bill's indictment, while Bill Hubbard listens solemnly. (*Courtesy of* Lubbock Avalanche-Journal, 1992)

Bill Hubbard's mug shot taken October 21, 1992, the day he was booked into the Lubbock County Jail.

Bill and Debbie Hubbard keep their spirits up during the holidays in 1992. (*Photo courtesy of JQT Visual Productions, Lubbock, Texas*)

Ralph Erdmann is led to court in handcuffs by two deputies. *(Courtesy of Lubbock Avalanche-Journal)*

As criminal district attorney for Lubbock County, Travis Ware, a staunch supporter of Ralph Erdmann, helped to bring about the indictment of Bill Hubbard after Hubbard publicly revealed Erdmann's indiscretions and unethical behavior. *(Courtesy of Lubbock Avalanche-Journal, 1990)*

Reporters at a press conference in Seattle, Washington with the over 120 guns that were seized from the home of Ralph Erdmann in 1995. *(Courtesy of Chuck Hallas, Journal American)*

While defending a capital murder suspect in Canyon, Texas, Millard Farmer was indicted on charges of tampering with a witness by Randall County DA Randy Sherrod. Attorneys from all over the country were outraged by his indictment and offered their help. *(Courtesy of Millard Farmer)*

Renowned and respected attorneys came to the aid of Bill Hubbard, Pat Kelly, and Millard Farmer.

Gerald Goldstein of San Antonio, Texas. *(Courtesy of Gerald Goldstein)*

Richard "Racehorse" Haynes of Houston, Texas. *(Courtesy of Richard Haynes)*

Dan Hurley of Lubbock, Texas. *(Courtesy of Weldon Holcomb, Esq., Tyler, Texas)*

Pat Kelly *(left)* and Bill Hubbard smile after learning the judge ruled in their favor in the RICO suit.
(Courtesy of Lubbock Avalanche-Journal, 1993)

Bill Hubbard on duty as deputy marshal of Red River, New Mexico in 1997.
(Courtesy of The Taos News, Taos, New Mexico)

Law Enforcement Officer Courage and Integrity award presented to Bill Hubbard at the MacArthur Justice Center in Washington, D.C.

could personally and fully fill her in on the situation. Ware said he was going to Austin the next day because of some legislation he was working on and he wanted to meet with Nielsen before he left. The doctor pressed Ware to tell her what the meeting was to be about.

"I've just been hearing some reports that you and Hubbard are pretty tight. We're having a lot of problems with Hubbard." He said he wanted Nielsen to meet with him and Atchley to get an "objective viewpoint."

Ware then took credit for being involved in the police department's old investigation of Hubbard and told Nielsen that Hubbard was trying to get even with the police department and with his office. "This guy's screwing around trying to defame or slander this office," he said. "I want you to be clued in as to what the true facts are."

He also told Nielsen she needed to be careful for the sake of appearances, that defense lawyers might start chucking rocks at the state's cases by making an issue of a friendship between Dr. Nielsen and the Hubbards.

"And the rest of the department hates him," Ware went on. "They don't trust him. And I don't spend my life running around trying to make a big issue out of it. And I don't spend my life running around trying to find something criminal in what he did or didn't do. I guess I could but I haven't seen fit to do so."

Taking a different tack, Ware commented, "You know, I've always liked Bill Hubbard, until he started acting kind of crazy over the last six or eight months. Despite the fact that we've had our differences, I've always thought he should be and could be a superior police officer."

Crazy for the last six or eight months? Eight months prior to this conversation, I had been sitting in Ware's office trying to get him to comprehend the kinds of problems Erdmann was creating. Six months before this conversation, I had been on the witness stand in Canyon testifying about not only that, but the rest of the bizarre Erdmann matters.

Commenting again that he wanted Atchley in on the discussion because she would be more objective, Ware said to Dr. Nielsen, "I'm too pissed off right now at Hubbard over some stuff he's done over the years that I am just now finding out about. So it had better come from Rebecca," he decreed.

According to Ware, it was extremely urgent that the matter they were discussing on the phone got settled that afternoon of September 8th. Ostensibly, the reason was Ware and Atchley's meeting the next day. But the real reason was not the one Ware had given Nielsen.

11

An Unholy Alliance

The day following the conversations with Detective Goolsby and Dr. Nielsen, according to the sources, Travis Ware and Rebecca Atchley traveled to Austin. There the old and settled but now readdressed information from selected Street Crimes Unit members was given to the Texas Attorney General's office.

It was important that the D.A.'s office not personally prosecute the potential cases against Hubbard. The problem was not a conflict of interest so much as it was appearance. Thus, with the Texas A.G.'s office prosecuting, there was no appearance of impropriety which surely would have been forthcoming, if the exonerating file on Hubbard known to be over at the internal affairs office at the police department was made public.

Moreover, Ware and Atchley turned to the assistant attorney general who had written the letter absolving Ware of wrongdoing in the Erdmann matter back in July: Shane Phelps.

Ware and Atchley would both say later that when the "information" came to their attention they had three choices: ignore it and violate their ethical code, prosecute it themselves and be accused of vindictiveness, or pass it on to another prosecutor. A fourth and more reasonable option seemed conveniently left out: investigate to see if the Street Crimes officers' allegations had any validity. In police matters, once a person has made an allegation, an investigation is always conducted before charges are filed.

The case that was building against Hubbard was not to be afforded that important double-checking. Instead, the documented findings of Hubbard's innocence by the police department were ignored, and the allegations with the worst possible reflection on Hubbard were submitted. Thus, indictments could be obtained.

City Manager Larry Cunningham was later to state his understanding that the goal was not necessarily to convict Hubbard but simply to win an indictment. The thinking must have been that an indictment would get Hubbard fired from his "sensitive" position at the police department, discredit the allegations he had made about Erdmann and Ware, and ruin him financially. All of this was possible, even if he were to be found innocent at a trial.

Exactly what words were said that day will probably never be known except to the three people involved. But Phelps took the file from Ware and Atchley and forwarded it to another assistant attorney general, Ned Butler. Butler sent it to still another assistant attorney general and former Harris County D.A. who worked out of the Houston A.G.'s office, Frank Briscoe.

As the file got farther and farther from Lubbock, the less likely it became that charges of impropriety would come back on Ware, Atchley, and now, Phelps. And although the attorney general's office was known for complete and thorough investigations, none was done. The allegations against Hubbard began to spiral toward a grand jury without a shred of investigation being done to try to support or disprove them.

Shane Phelps was not finished with Lubbock's justice system, however. There was still the Ralph Erdmann matter to which he had been assigned as special prosecutor. When Phelps had occasion to be in Lubbock on business about the Erdmann case, Ware had opportunity to express his thanks to Phelps for all of his help by treating the assistant A.G. and his staff who accompanied him to a barbecue and memberships in the Lubbock County Peace Officer's Association. The treat was paid for with a check drawn on Lubbock County taxpayers.

Finally, in September, the Erdmann cases seemed about ready to be presented to a grand jury. Phelps was back in Lubbock and busy. A rumor started circulating that Phelps was negotiating a plea bargain with Erdmann's attorneys before the grand jury even had a chance to announce its returns. That rumor was confirmed by an article run on September 19th in the *Lubbock Avalanche-Journal.*

This was the ultimate insult to all who had worked so hard and put their careers on the line to put the light of day on the deeds of Dr. Ralph Erdmann. A plea bargain of any kind would prevent any public testimony being given. It would be desirable for Ware, for his name would not be dragged into the Erdmann mess again. Judge McFall had said that Ware and some of his staff were expected to be called as witnesses.

Talk of a single plea agreement being negotiated for charges that existed against Erdmann in three different counties sparked rebuke from the people and the legal profession. Rod Hobson, president of the Lubbock Criminal Defense Lawyers Association, lashed out, "It's outrageous and suspicious that a matter of this importance to the integrity of the judicial system is being settled behind closed doors by an unholy alliance of prosecutors, allied with one former prosecutor who is now a defense attorney."

Speculation was rampant that the prosecutors involved in the negotiating of the plea bargain were doing so not only to protect their criminal cases in which Erdmann was a witness, but were road-blocking the possibility of it coming out that any of them had prior knowledge that Erdmann was irresponsible. This would put their respective counties at risk of huge civil suits.

In a startling allegation, Hobson said he firmly believed that "people have been executed on his (Erdmann's) word alone. We're not opposed to probation in a case like this because of his age and his knowledge of wrongdoing by others. But before probation should be considered, Erdmann should agree to a complete disclosure of his perjured testimony and relationships with prosecutors in West Texas."

The "unholy alliance" to which Hobson referred won out. On September 21, 1992, Ralph Erdmann was allowed to plead no contest, rather than having to actually admit guilt, to seven felonies for which he received probation and a fine that amounted to about 10 percent of his yearly salary as Lubbock's pathologist.

Shane Phelps said the pleas effectively ended the prosecutions in Lubbock. That turned out to be an understatement. Detective Doug Davenport tried to move ahead with one of the Erdmann cases he had uncovered during the course of the court of inquiry but which was not one of the cases Erdmann pled to in the agreement. Davenport soon found out that the agreement apparently gave Erdmann some sort of immunity from prosecution on the other hundred or so known Lubbock County cases pending against him.

The television news coverage of the event that evening showed a jovial Ralph Erdmann, smiling widely. When he was asked by the *Avalanche-Journal* if he was guilty, he laughed and said, "No comment."

Rod Hobson had hoped for full disclosure of Erdmann's activities as part of the agreement. Of course, those hopes were dashed. Hobson disgustedly told the

Dallas Morning News, "With this sentence, he doesn't have to do anything."

Shane Phelps, meanwhile, told the same newspaper that he believed prosecutors had obtained "a stiff sentence."

Lubbock Justice of the Peace Jim Hansen disagreed. "Anybody who had any relation, any connection, to the case is probably going to be angry with this sentence. The general public, I imagine that they'll be angry, too."

Rod Hobson, however, who had already been critical of the verdict and of Phelps, didn't let Phelps get out of town without a parting shot. With all of the local news media looking on, Hobson and Phelps squared off in a hallway of the Lubbock County Courthouse.

"Your comments are unprofessional," Phelps charged.

"Your investigation was sloppy," Hobson snapped, then turned his back on the assistant attorney general and walked away in disgust.

Jim Hansen was right. The families who had been affected by Erdmann's misdeeds as well as the general public were not happy.

The editorial staff of the *Avalanche-Journal* concurred. Their lead editorial on September 23rd was titled, "Mr. Erdmann's Justice: Why the Lenience?"

The editorial said that justice came up with a dirty face in this matter, and they could only conclude that the system was light on "one of the boys" who was part of it.

"That (the plea agreement), ladies and gentlemen, is less than a slap on the wrist for someone whose forensic pathology activities were key components of court files."

The editorial concluded, "Justice was tarnished in the first instance by the disclosures of Mr. Erdmann's alleged mishandling of autopsies. The walk he got Monday smeared the notion of justice even more."

In a letter to the same newspaper, printed four days after the editorial, Rod Hobson charged that "the attorney general was derelict in his duty by not requiring Mr.

Erdmann to make restitution to the real victim in this
case and tell the truth—regardless of whom it might
hurt. The goddess of justice must be weeping with shame
at what happened."

Shane Phelps had come and gone. Those who had
run the risk of having their knowledge about Erdmann
and their relationships to him exposed undoubtedly
breathed heavy sighs of relief.

Meanwhile, in Canyon, the pot was boiling again. The
"fire in the belly" defense attorneys who had originally
brought me there by subpoena and put me on the stand
in April were gearing up to place another set of pretrial
motions before the court in the same case, the death of
Hilton Raymond Merriman Sr. The scheduled date was
October 14th.

Along with the approaching court date came another
swarm of subpoenas. Among those they hit were Travis
Ware and at least eight Lubbock police officers. Some of
those officers had been in the meeting in February when
Ware had told us to keep the Erdmann problems quiet;
so I was looking forward to the outcome of the hearings
as well. I anticipated that my testimony would be corroborated in a way that would get the truth about the Ware
and Phelps connection out.

The day before the hearing was set to begin, the prosecutors from Randall County gave the matter a nasty
twist. They presented information to a grand jury there
and had Atlanta defense attorney Millard Farmer indicted on a charge of tampering with a witness. Rumors
spread that the thinking seemed to be that if the opposition couldn't be beaten, maybe he could be thrown in
jail.

It was the way the indictments on Farmer were
brought about, however, that smelled the worst of all.

Back in March, Randall County D.A. Randy Sherrod had received information from Senator John Montford, who at that time was Erdmann's attorney, that Farmer and one of Farmer's investigators had paid a visit to Lubbock to morgue manager Woodson Rowan. Farmer and his associate had tried to enlist Rowan, who was believed to have a relatively good working relationship with Erdmann, to assist them by confronting Erdmann and encouraging Erdmann to get the real information on his past autopsies out in the open and tell the truth.

According to the reports, there was no doubt Sherrod and his associates had this information at the time of the hearing in April, when I had testified. However, from late March until October the information wasn't made public. Then, without presenting live testimony from Rowan or demanding Farmer's presence before the grand jury to explain himself, a rendition of the events was presented to a Randall County grand jury by the Sherrod office the day before the October hearing was scheduled to begin. An indictment was obtained against Farmer for "tampering with a witness."

Cries of "Foul!" rose from the Farmer camp. In the first place, Sherrod had the information that was used to obtain the indictment for some six months before he acted on it. That appeared to be at least somewhat suspicious. A member of Sherrod's staff would later say that the reason the information had not been acted on sooner was because they had been "really busy."

Second, Farmer had never spoken to Erdmann. He had spoken to Rowan and asked him to impart information.

Third, no live testimony had been placed before the grand jury. Woodson did not testify to what he knew. Neither did Millard Farmer, nor the investigator who had been present. The grand jury took no action against that investigator. It appeared as if the grand jury had been told only what those presenting the information wanted it to know.

Fourth, there was a constitutional problem. Was the defendant in the murder case losing his right to a fair trial when prosecutors had summarily indicted his attorney and were trying to get that attorney removed from the case?

And fifth, if an offense had in fact occurred, it had happened in Lubbock, when Farmer visited Rowan. How could a Randall County grand jury return an indictment for an offense that allegedly happened in Lubbock County?

The timing and motivation for seeking the indictment certainly caused a lot of questions. The matter was set aside temporarily, however, so the scheduled hearing could go on, and Millard Farmer was allowed to continue as counsel for the defendant, at least for the present.

When testimony finally got underway, Lubbock police officer Pat Kelly took the stand and was asked about his knowledge, as a traffic accident investigator, of the incidents surrounding the death of Darlene Hall. Hall had been struck and killed in April of 1990 by a prosecutor from the Ware office, who was intoxicated at the time.

Kelly testified that he had attended the autopsy of the victim, and that he and Erdmann had examined and sniffed the contents of Ms. Hall's stomach. Kelly testified that Dr. Erdmann said, "Well, she wasn't drunk."

Millard Farmer asked, "Was there any indication on the report at that time that Mrs. Hall was intoxicated?"

"No sir, there was not. We cannot know if a person is intoxicated until a blood test was run or a urine test. However, in this particular case, we did not get any blood from the body."

"Did anything later come up about this autopsy?"

Kelly testified that he later learned that Ralph Erdmann had entered into his autopsy report on Darlene

Hall that the victim had been intoxicated at the time of her death. He further testified that it would have been impossible to have taken an uncontaminated sample from Darlene Hall's body, because "the blood was just not there" in any of the parts of the body from which an uncontaminated sample might be taken. He stated that Erdmann had not taken any blood from Darlene Hall's body.

Kelly then testified that he had received a telephone call from the secretary of a justice of the peace, who told him that Erdmann had met with the J.P., Travis Ware, and a close friend of Ware's who reportedly witnessed the accident. After that meeting, the news media were told that the victim was intoxicated at the time she was killed.

Ware's office had removed itself from the case, which was then being investigated by the Texas Rangers, because one of Ware's prosecutors was the driver who had killed the woman. In spite of that, Kelly testified that Ware and investigators from his office continued to call the accident investigation office to "pass along" information about the dead woman's personal life, such as her alcohol use and spousal abuse.

Kelly explained his response to these repeated phone calls to Millard Farmer, "I told them that it was irrelevant to our investigation of involuntary manslaughter and that I thought it was improper for them to be trying to direct our investigation to Darlene Hall, when, in fact, we were just simply trying to investigate a traffic fatality itself and not her background."

Again, as if serendipitously, Ware produced a letter that exonerated him and his office from claims of any interference in this investigation. This time, the letter clearing him came from the Texas Rangers.

Kelly's testimony was barely out of his mouth before members of the D.A.'s office went to see the J.P.'s secretary and took a sworn statement from her. In that statement, the woman said she never told Kelly that a meeting had taken place between the J.P., Ware, Erdmann, and the accident witness. Eventually, the secretary would be indicted by a grand jury for giving two conflicting statements about the same incident.

Now, however, it was reported that, with her statement in hand, Ware and his associates paid a visit to Police Chief Don Bridgers. They demanded that Pat Kelly be investigated for aggravated perjury, contending he had lied under oath.

12

An Old Can of Worms

It seemed inconceivable that an assistant attorney general would move forward on allegations against Bill Hubbard without a thorough and complete investigation to see if the allegations had merit. However, Houston Assistant Attorney General Frank Briscoe, before going to Lubbock to host a grand jury, did, by his own admission, "very little" investigating of matters such as these, but simply looked over the materials that had been sent to him and planned for the grand jury.

Court records show that Briscoe did not even subpoena the Lubbock Police Department's internal affairs file to learn of its content and the result of the 1991 investigation on Hubbard until two weeks after the grand jury met.

Some observers commented, if indictments are to be gained merely by going before a grand jury and making accusations without backing them up with the results of an investigation, attorneys would be lined up waiting to go before the panel and get all sorts of people indicted on charges that would never stand up in court. Incredibly, that was now the situation.

Frank Briscoe called Rebecca Atchley and told her to arrange for a grand jury to hear the matter. A 72nd District Court grand jury was recalled. This court, it so happens, was presided over by Blair Cherry, who was not only a former Lubbock D.A., but also the former felony chief in the Ware office. The grand jury was resworn, and handed up indictments once again favorable to Ware.

Briscoe came to Lubbock and issued only three subpoenas, all to Street Crimes officers critical of Hubbard. Interestingly enough, one of the most active instigators of the proceedings, Rebecca's husband, Randy, was not one of the three whose presence would be required at the grand jury.

It was unusual in such circumstances for official subpoenas to be issued. In the normal course of police business, a phone call will get a police officer to court. Thus, the officers involved in this case would be able to assert they were not there by choice but were under subpoena and were compelled to testify. Also unusual was that those subpoenas did not come through normal police channels. They were sent "special delivery" in order to keep the police administration and Hubbard himself in the dark. Secrecy was an essential element in making the plan work.

When the three subpoenaed officers showed up at the courthouse shortly before their scheduled appearance at the grand jury, the prosecutors' case hit a snag. Among the documents provided by the Street Crimes officers was one which, it was suddenly discovered, agreed in almost every respect with Hubbard's written report of the incident. And the officer who wrote that document agreeing with Hubbard was one of the three who was there to offer testimony. If jurors got a chance, perused his document and questioned him about it, the chances of gaining an indictment would be greatly diminished.

A decision had to be made, and quickly, because the grand jury was waiting. Prosecutors hurriedly met behind closed doors and, when they emerged, the officer whose testimony might exonerate Hubbard was released from his subpoena and sent home. The grand jury would hear only the two remaining witnesses from the Street Crimes Unit. The two who were most antagonistic to Hubbard.

13

The Good Guys
vs. The Bad Guys

As a young cop on the streets of Lubbock in the late seventies, I thought the moral lines seemed clearly drawn. There were the good guys: the cops, the prosecutors and the judges. And there were the bad guys: the perpetrators who were committing crimes and the lawyers who defended them.

Theoretically and idealistically, that's how it should be. However, I learned that the elements of personality, personal agenda, hatred and human emotion enter in. Those clear-cut lines of good guys/bad guys, cops/robbers, and victim/suspect begin to cloud.

As I left the jail on October 21, 1992, the day of my indictment, I felt that my view of justice and the ideals to which I had dedicated my life were vanishing. Everything I believed in was under siege. Though I knew the truth, I also knew the perception of the public, whose knowledge was confined to what they saw on the television news or read in the newspaper, could be quite different.

I wondered, what would the average citizen think? What would my pastor think? What would my friends think? What would Debbie's business associates think? She was active in the community with United Way and the local battered women's shelter as well as being past president of the Advertising Federation. What would those we didn't know believe? Would the truth come out?

Ever since I had quit "playing church" as a teenager and truly become a Christian, I had been a student of the Bible. I turned to it for guidance, not only in the tough times but in the good times as well. I really believe the Bible is the Owner's Manual. When I get a new power tool or appliance, I am prone to plug it right in and try to make it work without reading the instructions that came with it. I know it is more typical of men than of women, but we try things and try them again, and only after repeated failure do we read the manual. We're the same men who tend not to ask directions when we are lost but will drive on, just knowing we will eventually be able to figure out where we are. So it is with studying the Bible. Most of us try to live our lives without reading the Book that comes with it. Fortunately, I got over my phobia about studying spiritual matters long ago. So now, in the midst of turmoil, I opened my Owner's Manual looking for directions.

I immediately turned to the Psalms. The history of David had long seemed to me a model to follow. For God had raised David up for special work, only to have David mess up big time. But that did not stop him from setting things straight again and forging ahead. And Goliath. David had been the young shepherd who had bravely stepped to the fore, fought the giant and won. I was certainly feeling as though I was facing my own Goliath.

Psalm Ninety-one had always been especially meaningful to me. It was read when I had a special honor from a fraternal organization I had belonged to as a teenager.

When I was a seminary student at Oral Roberts University, I remember that we had some lively, admittedly lighthearted remarks about verse four, where we are "covered with feathers."

On this particular night, however, Psalm Ninety-one spoke to me as never before. The psalm tells us to make the Lord our refuge and fortress. If we do that, it says, we do not need to fear the terror of the night or whatever else men may throw at us. God promises His protection to those who seek Him. The last three verses sum up for me the meaning of the passage. " 'Because he loves Me,' saith the Lord, 'I will rescue him. I will protect him, for he acknowledges My name. He will call upon Me, and I will answer him. I will be with him in trouble, I will deliver him and honor him. With long life I will satisfy him and show him My salvation.' "

In my despair at the present situation, I was struck anew with the words' relevance to my now troubled future. I got a three-by-five card and wrote on it, "Psalm 91." Taking a magnet, I stuck the card on the freezer door where I would see it all the time. Then I took my Bible, found Debbie in the back part of the house and read the whole psalm to her. "I know we have a long legal and emotional battle ahead of us," I told her, "but I believe if we see this as not simply a legal problem but a spiritual problem, too, we will know where to seek guidance and comfort from the very beginning."

Debbie agreed with me, as I knew she would. I was so thankful I had her beside me as I faced one of the most trying times of my life. Adversity was no stranger to her. She always met it head-on with her usual determination and optimistic spirit. She is self-made, smart, attractive, sexy—everything a man could want in a wife. One of five children, she grew up living in a trailer in South Dakota. As a young adult, she went to West Texas in hopes of establishing residency and going to Texas Tech University, but the money was never there.

Her first job in Lubbock was as the "puff" at the lobby desk of a television station, answering the phone. She observed the production end of the television game and said to herself, "I can do that." She learned it, and she did it. Then Debbie became an account executive for an advertising agency, then continuity director for a television station, then production director of a radio station. From there, she became marketing director at South Plains Mall.

I was privileged to be there to see this self-made woman buy her first new car (the first one in her family ever to own a new car) and then become a homeowner. Inside and out, Debbie is beautiful. Sometimes I have felt that it is I who have held her back. However, Debbie tells me she is drawn to my character qualities—what few I've been blessed with.

As the ordeal unfolded, my wife never once had the "why me?" attitude, nor did she blame me. "We can get through this, we can fight this together" is the attitude which came shining through. There was never even a hint of doubt cast toward me. Debbie became my strength during the times when I had none of my own.

The Bible teaches of friends who stick closer than a brother and of one man shaping another. Debbie helped gather such a group of friends at my favorite barbecue joint the night of my indictment. There were cops, doctors, lawyers, journalists, college students and their spouses. At times during the evening, this cheerleading crowd showed that they really enjoyed each other's company. They expressed their support and affection for Debbie and me loudly and vociferously. And they were indignant toward those who they felt were dishonorable, the ones who had brought this horrible charge against me.

These wonderful friends willingly came along with us down our dark thorn-strewn path and voluntarily shouldered part of the burden. Like Debbie, they never doubted me, and we bonded together to overcome what they believed to be a common obstacle. The miracle was this did not involve them directly, but they took it on as if it did.

Their support was great medicine for Debbie and me. I knew by that gathering that whatever I might have to face, I would not have to face it alone.

In the group that night were Pat Kelly and his wife, Yolanda. Pat was the detective who had also been rebuked and threatened for his criticism of Erdmann's incompetence. Until now, Pat and I had never been particularly close, but this new bond plus the many common circumstances at work brought about a mutual understanding and friendship. With outspoken Erdmann critic Millard Farmer under indictment in Randall County, and now my getting slapped with felony charges a week later in Lubbock, Pat felt it was just a matter of time before he, too, was attacked.

"Hang in there, bud," he said. "You won't be the lone cop long. I'll be next."

I had to acknowledge, "There does seem to be a pattern."

His face serious, he nodded.

When Debbie and I went home that evening, in spite of everything that had happened, I got a good eight hours of sleep. I needed the rest because, even as tough as this day had been, I knew the next was going to be even rougher.

The next morning, the ringing of the bedside telephone jump-started my day. After many years of being a cop, the ringing of the phone when I am asleep always gives me a shot of adrenaline and brings me instantly wide awake.

"Hello?"

"Hi. It's me. Denette."

"Hi, Dee."

"Well, are you ready to go get this thing done?"

"Not really. Can't I just stay in bed and think for a while?"

"No, come on now. We'll go do this and you'll be fine."

"You know, Dee," I said, "I was kind of hoping I'd wake up today and find out it was all a bad dream."

"No such luck, Bill," she said slowly and sadly. Then Denette quickly moved on to business. "I want us to get there early before the media have a chance to get all set up to spring on us. Why don't you drive your car down, park it on the front lot, and I'll meet you there in about an hour."

My mind heavy and plodding, I somehow got moving, and I showered and shaved. I dressed as I normally would for work, putting on a blue plaid shirt that was one of my favorites.

The exception that morning was that I did not put my pistol in a holster on my hip. In anticipation that I would be relinquishing that gun at the meeting with the chief, I put it in a carrying case instead. My thoughts about the scenario that would take place in the chief's office within an hour or so played over and over. I saw myself placing my gun and badge on his desk. The mental image depressed me even further.

Mechanically, I drove my jet black unmarked detective car to the police station and parked in the lot. As I locked it and walked away, I saw a familiar white Grand Am parked at the curb in front of the main entrance of the station. Denette was already out of her car, pacing up and down the sidewalk as she waited for me, a pile of folders in her arms.

"Hi, Dee," I muttered.

"Head up!" she coached. "This won't be that bad. I talked to them last night. It's just a matter of signing some papers and then we can go. You'll be fine."

Denette, ever the optimist, was always one to minimize a bad situation and maximize a positive one. I knew that her telling me, "This won't be that bad" and "You'll be fine" were for my benefit. I have always believed I could do whatever the job called for. I was ready to get this over with and to do it as a professional. But I was *not* enjoying any of it nor was I going to pretend I was. I didn't even try to come up with a platitude in response.

Keeping my eyes straight ahead, we walked side by side to the second floor where the chief's office was, using a back stairway that is mostly an employees-only route.

"Taking this way makes it less likely we'll be ambushed by TV cameras," Denette said. "Nevertheless, keep your head up and a smile on your face. You've done nothing wrong. You're a really good cop and no one knows it better than me."

I nodded but couldn't manage the smile. I fingered my badge discouraged. Denette patted my shoulder. Even with all her cheerleading and encouragement, she knew how proud I was of wearing it. Getting through this day was going to be a very difficult task.

When we arrived upstairs in the chief's office complex, Chief Bridgers was in the lobby, leaning against a wall sipping coffee from a Styrofoam cup.

"Morning, Don," Denette said in a friendly tone. The chief had to be glad to see that he was not again facing the same rampaging woman who had invaded his office the previous day.

"Hi, Denette. Bill," Bridgers said quietly. "Come on back." He turned and led the way down the hallway to his office. Assistant Chief Carroll Bartley came from his office. The chief closed the door and we all sat down.

The chief's desk was cleared off except for stapled copies of fresh, cleanly typed papers. I looked down to see my name at the top of them.

The chief spoke very softly. I leaned forward and let my eyes probe his. He looked away. "Bill, the city feels like since you are under a felony indictment, that there is only one avenue they can take, and that is to suspend you indefinitely without pay."

Candy-coated words. Bitter translation: "You're fired."

By using "the city" and "they," Bridgers was distancing himself from it all and depersonalizing this whole ordeal. He rarely looked me in the eye and spoke mostly to Denette as he explained the forms and formalities.

I yearned for some show of support from the administration of the police department. I fantasized that the brass at L.P.D. would go over to Ware's office, get in his face and say, *No way. We stand with Hubbard. We have already investigated this stuff inside and out, and Bill Hubbard has not committed any crimes.* That's what it was, though— just a fantasy.

There was no doubt in my mind that this administration was afraid of Ware and would never stand up to him about anything. The misguided philosophy was that since Ware was the only district attorney we had, if you stood up to him and made him angry, he would take it out on the police department by being as difficult as possible on every case we sent over. The only problem with that was, by not standing up to him, Ware got the idea that he could do whatever he pleased and the police department would lie down and take it. Case in point: the reaming out Ware had given Ronnie Goolsby. Ware obviously felt that he ran the police department and could do whatever he wanted to the police individually and collectively, with no resistance from "the corner office" which Bridgers occupied.

Chief Bridgers picked up the papers on the desk before us. "These are the terms of your suspension," he said to me as he handed a copy to Denette. She leafed through, looking unimpressed.

"You know, Don," Denette began, "what really concerns me here is Bill's insurance situation. He's not on any other plan, and here you are today, in effect, terminating him, and he's out there with no health insurance protection." She was forever looking out for my interests when I had no clue as to what I should be doing.

This was something Chief Bridgers had not anticipated, and I wondered if Denette had brought it up mostly to throw him off course and let him know that she was looking at the total picture of what was going on and all of the ramifications. She and I had not even brought up the insurance question prior to being there.

Bridgers was indeed caught off guard. "That's a question I can't answer for you, Denette," he shook his head, "but I'll find out and get back to you about it this afternoon."

Appearing nonplussed, Denette continued to leaf through the papers. I had seen this before. She looked like she was being quite distant and was not really paying attention to the paperwork, when just the opposite was true. She doesn't miss a thing.

Bridgers handed the rest of the papers to me. Mostly, they explained the terms of my suspension. With as many copies of it as I had to sign, you would have thought I was buying a house. One for me, one for the police administration, one for City Hall, and on and on.

As I repeatedly signed my name, the chief said, "Now, we'll check to see how much vacation time Bill still has coming this year, and we'll pay him for that. And you'll need to call the academy and make arrangements to turn in all of your city equipment."

"Okay," Denette said before I had a chance to answer.

"Then I guess we're through," said the chief, "except for what you have to turn in to me here today."

This was the part that I had dreaded the most. I handed over my gold shield, number 13, my commission card, and my city-issued .357 Smith and Wesson model 65#2111. I was no longer Sergeant Bill Hubbard. Like Erdmann, but for exactly the opposite reason, my professional title had been stripped. I was Mr. Bill Hubbard. It was the lowest day of my life.

I knew in my heart that I had never done anything to tarnish that badge. I had chosen Lubbock, which was not my hometown, and had sworn an oath of office to give my life to protect her citizens if the need arose. When I took that oath on September 3, 1979, I didn't even know more than ten people in the entire city. But in thirteen years Lubbock had become my home. I had led a life that I was pleased with, one in which I could stand before the Lord and say, "This is me." Not sinless, not perfect, but trying hard and taking my vow seriously.

For instance, when I moved to Lubbock and put that badge on, I was a teetotaler. My reasons for being a nondrinker expanded as I explored myself and the vows I had sworn to uphold. I decided I would never be in the position where I could not or should not respond to the call of duty because I had consumed alcohol. Whether I was on or off duty, for thirteen years I had not taken even a cocktail and was always fit for duty. I responded willingly to the needs of my chosen city and its citizens.

Lubbock had responded by being very kind to me. My pay was not extravagant but was adequate. I hadn't become a cop to make a lot of money anyway. Lubbock had given me a wonderful wife, friends beyond my greatest imagination, and an economy that allowed my pay to go quite a long way. When it came time to buy a house, we could afford a very nice one in which we lived not luxuriously but well.

Leaving that badge on Chief Bridgers's desk hurt beyond anything I could conceive. I tried not to show what I was feeling.

"I guess that about does it," Don said.

Denette and I got up to leave the meeting. As we walked out and met other officers, I tried to keep my head high but I could feel my heart contracting against my chest. No handshakes. No well wishes. No encouragement. No condolences. Those we saw appeared non-committal in every way, and that really tortured me. These men *knew* that I was innocent of the accusations. For Pete's sake, one of them was also my neighbor, but they did not for a second depart from their roles that morning. Fear of reprisal, fear for their own futures was written on their faces and in their eyes which did not meet mine.

Even worse, as I walked into the lobby of the chief's complex, gripping an empty gun case in my hands, every journalist in the area was there.

Facing the newspeople outside the jail yesterday had been easy compared to this. When I had been released from jail, I had seen the indictments and knew just how bogus they were, and was aware of the huge amount of evidence already in existence that would clear me. I will admit that, at the time, I naively thought it would be a simple matter of getting the grand jury back together and letting them hear me tell *all* of my story. I didn't know that an indictment by the grand jury was irrevocable, and I would have to face a trial.

As I walked on, the lights from television cameras blinded me. A whole gamut of emotions from indignation to anger to hurt filled me, so, at first, I left most of the talking to Denette. She let them know in no uncertain terms that these new charges covered the same old ground that the police department had dealt with and which I had been cleared of the year before.

"This is a joke," she said indignantly. "Not a very funny joke, but it's a joke."

I tried to remain calm and exhibit my best air of confidence, but blurted out angrily, "I will be back wearing a badge in this community." However long it might take, I would fight to proclaim my innocence.

The newspeople then asked, "What's next?"

I told them, "The first order of business is to get a job."

Denette went on to allege that some kind of behind-the-scenes dealing had gone on to make these indictments come about without the knowledge of the police department. She swore she intended to find out what it was and how it had been done.

We knew nothing of Travis Ware and Rebecca Atchley's secret meetings with malcontents from the Street Crimes Unit, nor what, if any, involvement Shane Phelps and Frank Briscoe had. Such deeds were possibly dirty and deeply buried, but Denette Vaughn announced to the world that day that she intended to get a shovel and start digging.

My next stop was my homicide office down the hall. I got some boxes and sorrowfully, I began to gather up my personal stuff. Then, feeling each act as a blow, I stripped my nameplate off the door. I claimed my Nolan Ryan memorabilia from the wall, as well as my Police Officer of the Year plaque. I moved slowly each time as the impact struck me anew. I hoped that the news crews would get tired of waiting and find another story to exploit.

When I was sure they had gone, I went to the office next door to see my officers in the identification unit. Closing the door, I addressed them, unable to keep emotion from my voice. "Thank you for accepting me among you even though you were initially opposed to having me for your new sergeant. You gave me a chance. We've worked very well together and become friends, and I am grateful."

As I began shaking hands, I lost it and started crying. Cops don't cry, especially in front of other cops. But they understood.

Detective Shields volunteered to take me and my boxes of stuff home, so I let Denette go about her business. My next stop was to see Captain Wiley.

I thanked him for the turnaround he had made toward me since my first day under his command and the "Teflon overcoat" speech. He said he had found me to be a good and hard worker who had caught on quickly to the areas of expertise needed in that division. I called him "Frank" for the first time in my life and said good-bye.

Before leaving the building with Shields waiting in the hall, I made one last stop by my office. I took out a plain white sheet of paper and a marker pen. On the paper I wrote, "I WILL BE BACK!" and signed my name. With tape, I posted it on the wall, closed my office door, and slowly walked out.

I don't remember much about the ride home or my conversation with Detective Shields. Things were happening so fast that I was rapidly approaching emotional overload. When we pulled into my driveway, I was glad to see that Richard Jackson, one of the out-of-town Texas Tech students to whom we had opened our home, had stopped by and was waiting there. Debbie was at work, and I had dreaded coming home to an empty house. Richard helped me carry in my boxes. Shields shook my hand, wished me well, and went back to work. I closed the front door and collapsed in uncontrollable sobs. Richard's compassion was immediate. He stayed right there, giving me comfort and words of encouragement. I don't know how I would have made it through those first few minutes at home without him.

* * *

On Sunday I fought the temptation to escape by sleeping in and avoiding the world outside. However, Debbie and my standard practice was to go to the early service at Trinity Church, which had been our congregation for about ten years. She encouraged me, and I knew I needed sustenance to reach out to the faith on which I depended.

As I walked into the huge sanctuary of this church of more than seven thousand members, I remembered how I initially had not liked the fact that the church was so large. However, senior pastor Randal Ross had a gift for the ministry the likes of which I had never seen before. Ross could really reach out and grab you. Part of this was because, I felt, he had not grown up as a "goody-goody" but had lived a rough existence out in the world before turning to Christ.

Our usual set of friends was as warm to us as ever, and I began to feel a little better. When the service was over, Debbie and I headed down the aisle to go home. Suddenly, I felt a tap on the shoulder from behind. I turned to see a familiar face, Detective Mike Beckham from the forgery unit at the police department. He also was the drummer for the church services. "Pastor Ross would like to see both of you in his study," he said and led the way.

When we got there, we found Ross changing his shirt. He works so hard preaching that he sweats through a shirt per service and has to change before starting the second service. With him was his wife, Andrea.

I started to apologize for interrupting.

"Come on in." He motioned and got right to the point. "Bill, the pastors and elders of the church are aware of your situation." With all the news about it on television, I wondered if anyone was *not* aware of my situation.

He went on, "Now, we don't know the ins and outs of all this and what led up to it, but we do know that what we are hearing about these charges is not consistent with the man we know." He smiled. "Trinity and I and Andrea are standing with you all the way. You and Debbie won't go in need. Whatever comes along that you guys need, just say so, and it's yours."

How good it felt to have someone like Randal say openly, *I believe in you!* Without asking a lot of questions, he just let us know that he cared. Randal and Andrea prayed for us and we left, but our step was a little lighter and our heads a little higher.

We also came away with a new verse to post on the refrigerator, along with Psalm Ninety-one: Isaiah 42:16. "I will lead the blind by ways they have not known. Along familiar paths I will guide them. I will turn the darkness into light before them and make the rough places smooth. These are the things I do. I will not forsake them."

Soon, Debbie had copied another verse and placed it beside the other two on the refrigerator. The one she chose was Matthew 5:10-12: "Blessed are those who are persecuted because of righteousness, for theirs is the kingdom of heaven. Blessed are you when people insult you, persecute you, and falsely say all kinds of evil against you because of Me. Rejoice and be glad, because great is your reward in heaven, for in the same way they persecuted the prophets who were before you." Those three passages would continue to be our inspiration in the difficult months to come.

Despite this, on each day that followed, my criminal charge was the first thing that came to my mind in the morning and the last thing I had to drive out at night so I could sleep.

When I told the reporters right after I was fired that my first task was going to be finding a job, I felt confident on that score. I had a college degree and was qualified to do many things. Now I was finding that this was easier said than done. Felony indictments close many doors. So does being high-profile, and my mug shot had been on television and in the newspapers. I was turned down for all kinds of security jobs, counseling jobs, and teaching jobs, because I bore the label *indicted felon*. I was also turned down to referee or umpire high school and college athletics because of the indictments. Not only my spirit, but my ability to earn a living was impacted.

After pounding the pavement and having doors continually shut in my face—sympathetically shut in some cases, but shut nevertheless—the next wave of depression set in. Now there was not only the feeling of helplessness as I longed for the legal battle to get over so that I could prove myself, but the feeling of frustration that I could not even manage to get hired at a minimum wage security job. Moreover, there was also a feeling of guilt that I had drawn my wife into a situation that threatened to ruin our financial security and possibly have adverse implications on the rest of our lives.

I could not help but think that this situation was the *real* goal of the people who had me indicted. They had to know that the charges could not stand up in a courtroom and that there was a good chance that the case could get dumped before it ever got that far. Their aim had to have been, at least partly, to smash my reputation, trash my police career, ruin me financially and "teach me a lesson" about standing up to their political power. Even when I beat the criminal charges, the losses could still be staggering. So, to me in this dark time, even the best case scenario looked pretty bad.

On the one hand, I had decided to tell the world the truth about Dr. Erdmann with my eyes wide open. I could have easily told the court in Canyon, "I don't know" or "I don't remember." That's an easy way out taken by some police officers. The cop gets off the hot seat, and it is almost impossible to charge perjury when you simply say that you don't know. It's called a "convenient memory." But to me, such self determined haziness meant a lack of integrity.

On the other hand, my whistle blowing had unfairly affected the person I loved most—my wife. Literally, overnight, our family income had been cut in half, and we were now facing not only the regular bills that come in every month, but legal bills that could run into tens of thousands of dollars.

"I'm sorry, Debbie," I tried to apologize one night. "I feel pretty guilty that I felt I had to open my mouth, and that got us into this. Everything we've worked for and all our dreams could come crashing in on us."

"Bill," she said, looking into my eyes, "one of the reasons I love you is your integrity. Your fighting for it is a necessity, not a problem. Anyway," she said with a wry smile, "I've put a calculator to it, and we ought to be able to make it on my income. It'll be tight, and we'll need to cut out some things we really like doing, but I think we'll be okay."

"But sometimes I feel so worthless now, like I'm not contributing to our existence," I said, looking away.

"Bill," she gently turned my face to hers, "you yourself said that this isn't about people and things. It's spiritual. We've never been let down when our faith was where it belongs, and this situation is no different. I'm making a good income, and we'll have the additional money coming in from my doing the Ad Club secretary stuff, so I really think we'll get by moneywise. And I'm working on getting your story out to those who can help us."

I knew my wife well enough to know that she had already "crunched the numbers," and was working on the rest. Her readiness to respond to this crisis was a great comfort to me.

"I love you, you know," I said.

"And that's what keeps *me* going," she replied.

Nevertheless, in the weeks to come, it was very hard for me to gather up the courage to ask Debbie for money. But there were times that I had absolutely none of my own, and even change to buy coffee had to come from her. Debbie handed me pocket money without the least bit of comment that could have made me feel even more worthless than I already felt. Even in small ways, she was always so positive.

Still, despite Debbie's upbeat spirit, sometimes late at night when things were still and I had stayed up by myself, a kind of guilt/depression came creeping upon me. Inside I felt a gnawing pain for getting Debbie into the middle of this mess. However, anytime I brought it up to her, she just passed over it lightly, saying that she could have left anytime she wanted, but chose to stay because she believed so much in me.

It was during one of these late night depressions when I was having my own personal pity party that the phone rang. It startled me at first because it was after 1:00 A.M., but I scampered quickly to answer before the second ring so it would not disturb Debbie. She was fast asleep in the bedroom and had to go to work early the next morning.

"Hi. It's me. Are you asleep yet?" Denette asked. She had more of a reputation of being a night owl than I did.

"Not yet," I said slowly.

"I just had a couple of things that I wanted to go over with you, and I thought we might talk about them now while the phones aren't ringing. Things get pretty crazy around here during the day, and somehow I knew you'd be up." She paused.

"Yeah, I can't sleep."

"Neither can I. Not with all this hanging over you."

Here it was, the wee hours of the morning, and my lawyer was calling me to discuss my case. Lawyers have notorious reputations for being "out of the office" and for not returning phone calls. But my lawyer was calling me—at 1:00 A.M., no less.

"What have you got now?" I asked drearily.

"Good grief, Bill. You have to have the same belief in yourself the rest of us have," Denette said, hearing the despair in my voice.

That was all it took. Emotions swept over me. Tears ran down my face and I could hardly talk. "It's just so unfair to Debbie," I said in almost a whisper.

"What? What's unfair?"

"Debbie suffering this way."

"Debbie? What about Debbie?" Denette demanded, not knowing what turn of events had put me in this state of mind and thinking that something awful had happened to Debbie.

"It just seems," I began, "that it's so unfair for Debbie to get dragged into all of this, having our income cut, having to squeeze the pennies, answering questions about this wherever she goes, seeing me on public display every single day in the paper and on television—it's just not fair to her."

"So *that's* what this is about," Denette sighed, her voice softening noticeably.

"Isn't that enough?" I asked.

"Bill, you have to stop," Denette said calmly. "Knowing Debbie the way I do, I'm sure that she would want no other course in life than to be where she is right now. What else could Debbie ask for than a guy who loves her with all his heart? A guy whose integrity doesn't stop just because the road gets a little rough? A guy who is willing to speak the truth no matter the circumstances? Gee, Bill, there are women out there who would give a king's ransom to be exactly in Debbie's situation, just to have a guy who loves her and has a backbone. Believe me, 'cause I know!"

Denette waited silently while I took several minutes to

regain my composure. She had said the words that I so desperately needed to hear. They could not have affected me more deeply, even if they had been spoken by Debbie herself. My tears that night were in humble realization of how blessed I was, not only for the wife I had, but also for my attorney who knew when to set lawyering aside and speak as a friend.

A few minutes later, we were able to get down to business and discuss the reason Denette had called. "Bill, this case is bigger than I think I can handle alone, since I'm a one-person law practice."

I started to protest. "I don't want any other lawyer but you on my case."

"Look," she went on. "There's a meeting at nine tomorrow morning at one of the biggest banks in town. Don't ask questions now, I just want you to attend the meeting and let me know what you think."

I didn't know what she was talking about, but I promised her I would go.

14

For the Defense

At nine o'clock the next morning, I slowly walked into the bank, mumbling, "What on earth is this all about?" Pushing the door of the meeting room open, I was stunned at what I saw. Assembled there were some of the biggest defense attorneys in the area. It soon became apparent they were there to talk about my situation, and they told me of others who wanted to be there but could not attend because of schedule conflicts.

It was a humbling experience, because, in the past, I had been guilty of treating some of these attorneys with my own brand of snobbish contempt. I had not been able to separate them from the clients they often represented. But I was to come to understand that those clients had just as much right to their full constitutional protection and competent counsel as I needed now.

These lawyers told me they knew and respected my work. I had faced them many, many times in court. Now they were here to help me.

"Travis Ware has gone too far this time," one of them

said. "If he can do this to you and get away with it, who's going to be next? Whatever you want from any of us, our firms or our clerks are yours for the asking. Just name it."

I began a long road of humble apologies to those lawyers that day, and as time went on, gained a new appreciation of the role a defense attorney plays in our society.

This is an appreciation that is not popular in law enforcement, because a lot of the mentality is, *That suspect is a scumbag and those lawyers got him off!* Let me tell you, enmeshed in my own legal disaster, I found out that if those "scumbags" don't have rights, soon none of us will have rights. If I could be indicted in retaliation for telling the truth, anyone who refuses to look the other way, who stands up to be counted, may find themselves attacked. And when you are unjustly accused, you'll need someone to help you fully exercise your rights.

After the meeting and a lengthy discussion with Denette, we decided to ask attorney Dan Hurley to be our co-counsel.

Mr. Hurley had a good reputation in the legal community as being very intelligent and committed to his profession. Having Denette and Dan Hurley both in my corner, along with the promise of help from other lawyers in nine different firms if needed, brought Debbie and me a new feeling of confidence and determination.

"Bill," Mr. Hurley told me when Denette and I went to his office for our first meeting, "you are the reason I went to law school. To have a client who is truly innocent and has been dumped on by the system is the ultimate call to battle for a lawyer. It's my honor and privilege to represent you, and we'll beat this thing!"

I had shed plenty of tears in these last days, but none more humble than those in Hurley's office.

* * *

At almost the same time, facing other realities, Debbie and I decided that my finding a job was not to be the primary concern for the time being, so we tightened up our belts and prepared to live on her income alone. Debbie continued to tithe and we saw that the Lord was faithful to His word. We went farther on 90 percent of her salary than we had thought possible.

That is not to say that we didn't have a great deal of help. Letters, cards, and cash had begun to come in. Prayer groups from all over the city sent us notes saying they were praying for us. Individuals and attorneys sent money or gave it to Denette. Soon, we were at the point of having to open an account for the Bill Hubbard Support Fund at the bank. That money was reserved for expenses that had directly to do with our legal costs.

Although the modern image of the legal profession is tarnished by depictions of greedy lawyers, neither Denette nor Dan Hurley was the least bit concerned about my paying them. There were no contracts, no discussion of charges, no talk of if or when I might pay them. The primary focus of everyone's effort was to wage one heck of a legal battle. Dan and Denette were committed to a cause and not to a dollar.

Despite my depression at times, I made the conscious effort to get myself out of bed every morning, shower, shave and walk across the hall to my home office. There, I would telephone potential witnesses, organize notes, write reflections on possible strategies, and generally stay busy doing things that would possibly help me or assist my lawyers.

In fact, my office was a really comfortable place, with a big roll-top desk Debbie had given me, a 1963 jukebox I had restored myself, and all my baseball stuff. At least in there I felt I was "working" and earning my keep.

And other developments also lifted my spirits. Not long afterward, a young patrol officer I barely knew,

Larry Manale, wrote an open letter to Travis Ware which was sent to him by certified mail. It said:

> *"Dear Mr. Ware: It has come to our attention at the Lubbock Police Department, through your quotes in the media, that you are under the impression that Sergeant Bill Hubbard is not well respected by his fellow officers. This letter is to inform you that this is far from the truth. There is no officer in this department who feels that he or she is above the law, as you implied in the October 25th issue of the Avalanche-Journal. As with all the officers in our department, Bill Hubbard joined the police department not for personal gain, but to help make his community a happier and safer place in which to live. This is why Sergeant Hubbard has been one of the more respected officers in the Lubbock Police Department. In the future, we would appreciate it if you could refrain from communicating your personal feelings relating to how we feel about one of our officers."*

Following the letter were the signatures of 151 really gutsy cops. This gave me a huge boost! I called Manale and told him how I admired his courage. "This is the kind of action that would get a man indicted in this county," I said. The rank and file in the police department had done what the administration did not have the backbone to do.

Within days, I began seeing bumper stickers and people sporting badges saying, "I BELIEVE BILL HUBBARD" in big blue letters. Chief Bridgers had to make sure that the officers understood that these were not to be put on city police cars. Instead, officers placed them on briefcases, clipboards and their personal cars.

A college student went so far as to have buttons made up urging people to "IMPEACH TRAVIS WARE." After they were seen at a Texas Tech football game, they caught on like wildfire. People from all walks of life began placing orders for the buttons, wearing them and handing them out to friends.

All of this attracted the attention of the local media, and they wanted to question me. I told them all the support was very gratifying, but it didn't get me cleared of the criminal charges, or get me back to work to pay the bills. "But it sure doesn't hurt!" I smiled.

On the darker side, reports came in that buddies of the Street Crimes officers who had helped make my original indictments come about were intimidating those who signed the open letter to Ware. Despite the great support from so many, there still seemed to be a sickness within the police department. The sickest part of all was that some of those officers who I heard were doing some of the intimidating would come by my house to visit and tell me, "hang in there, everything will turn out all right."

Nevertheless, Debbie and I were confiding to each other that good was finally beginning to do battle with evil. The Ware office should have begun to see the turning of the tide when the *Avalanche-Journal* published the results of their latest phone-in poll on November 3rd. The question was, "Is the Criminal District Attorney's office operating effectively and ethically under Travis Ware?" The results were: Yes, 31%; No, 69%.

Apparently, Ware and his associates could not believe this was true. One administrator called the paper and alleged that they had mistakenly reversed the poll results. When he was told that the results were printed correctly, the stunned man criticized the poll as being "unscientific."

15

Interference/Intimidation and Other Revelations

In the days immediately following my indictment, a flurry of other matters related to Ralph Erdmann came to public attention. On October 22nd, to many people's dismay, Lubbock's new forensic pathologist, Dr. Jody Nielsen, resigned.

Nielsen had come to Lubbock in July for all the right reasons and at personal sacrifice. Her husband, Jim, was still in his residency in thoracic surgery in San Antonio. For Jody to stay in the Lubbock job would necessitate having a weekend marriage.

When she moved to town, Jim helped her move a few pieces of furniture, along with one of the family cats, into a small apartment. Behind their car they pulled a horse trailer and boarded one of their horses at a stable outside of town, so Jody would be able to ride in her free time.

When I met her, I was struck by her professional demeanor and captivating personality. Excited by the fact that Lubbock would finally have a credible pathologist as well as a good citizen, I introduced her to Debbie. We helped Jody get acquainted with Lubbock and make some new friends. We had good times together, and it was even more enjoyable when Jim could come to town and share a weekend. All of the people we introduced them to found them to be entertaining and unassuming regular folks who immediately became good neighbors.

I have to admit that, in addition to her medical skills, the female Dr. Nielsen could be somewhat credulous, but in a fun sort of way. She was never bent out of shape when others laughed at her expense. She proved she could take it and dish it out as well. The amazing part was that, when she walked into the morgue to do an autopsy, she was a completely different person. Then we saw a competent professional who really knew her stuff. She had spent some time as a physician in the Air Force and then at Dr. DiMaio's medical examiner's office in San Antonio. She was practiced and professional, and Dr. Hoblit did a terrific recruiting job getting her to come to Lubbock.

And that was even more difficult in the aftermath of Ralph Erdmann. Professionals and public alike were already suspicious of forensic pathology. So, not only were the new pathologist's techniques and procedures doubly scrutinized, but she was asked to give many second opinions on Erdmann autopsy reports and possibly do second autopsies on exhumations. Nielsen accepted this as a challenge and a great career opportunity. She wanted to build a strong practice in the area and clean up the tarnished name of forensic pathology. For three months, she toiled, reorganizing and getting the office on a firm basis. But in the end, Nielsen felt she wasn't given a free hand in correcting the multitude of problems that so badly needed solving.

And there was another negative component. Among

the reasons she gave in leaving was that she resented "a certain public official" trying to interfere in her personal life. Some said that Ware contended he did not know to whom she was referring. However, the conversations Ware had with Dr. Hoblit, who in turn passed them on to Dr. Nielsen, and the recorded telephone conversation between Nielsen and Ware, would be revealed later in an effort to help Ware refresh his memory.

One day after Nielsen's resignation, Investigator Carrie McClain of the C.D.A.'s office also submitted her resignation. I advised her against doing that, since she had no other job lined up and was a new home owner with a mortgage payment to make each month. "I'm willing to flip hamburgers to get away from Travis Ware and his office," she said.

To the media, McClain said, "I'm leaving because of the lack of honesty and integrity in the criminal district attorney's office and because it's beginning to reflect on me. People question me about why things are going on in the D.A.'s office," she told the local media.

Ware countered that McClain had been a source of trouble since shortly after she was hired. "No investigator trusted her," he said.

"I never had any complaints from other investigators," she firmly replied.

Going one step further, Ware accused McClain of stealing county property as she left. McClain told the press exactly where she had left the items Ware said were missing. In fact, later rumors flew that Ware found them where Carrie said she had left them. McClain then demanded a retraction of the accusation of theft. Ware refused. McClain hired an attorney.

For a rookie in the public arena doing battle with the C.D.A.'s office, Desert Storm veteran First Lieutenant McClain waged an impressive fight. However, she would make cappuccino and sell lingerie for nine long months at minimum wage until another suitable law enforcement job came along. But, as she said, "I'm free."

Ware, meanwhile, continued his assault on me in the news media. On several occasions he stated that he had been complaining about Bill Hubbard to the police department "since 1987." He did not cite specifics, just "since 1987," and made it sound as if I had been a bad character for a long time and that I had finally gotten what was coming to me.

Though my despair over these events grew day by day, I could not help getting a laugh out of the "since 1987" business. The first day of January 1987, I had been promoted to sergeant and had been assigned to the front desk. I stayed there for thirteen of the most miserable months in my police career. When my desk assignment ended, I directed the police recruiting drive for another two months or so. So, from January 1987 until late April of 1988, I did no real police work at all! During that time, I did not work on any criminal cases or present any charges to the district attorney's office.

A further and even more startling irony was the file of letters of commendation I had in my possession, signed by Ware himself. They bore dates in May 1988, December 1988 and January 1989. In them, he used terms such as "superior police officer," "some of the best police work our office has ever seen," "professionalism and dedication to duty," and "a direct indication that police work has truly emerged into a profession."

Nevertheless, Ware now was trying to convince the public that I was a long time bad cop who had finally been caught.

Meanwhile, Denette Vaughn, Dan Hurley and I continued to meet and plan our legal strategy. One of the things we considered was that Blair Cherry would probably be the judge who would preside over my trial. Because of his past relationship with Travis Ware, we discussed filing a motion to recuse Judge Cherry from the case.

Judge Cherry beat us to the punch. Without our even asking him or filing a motion, he voluntarily stepped aside from the case and asked for a new judge to be appointed in his place. Rumors of an angry exchange between the judge and Travis Ware circulated around courthouse circles, and it was said that afterward the judge had decided to excuse himself. A visiting judge from Henrietta was appointed to preside.

Verifiable stories of some strange behavior on the part of Travis Ware started finding their way to us. We began to document them for possible later use. One news team told of Ware's coming to the conference room of their television station to pass out some documents. When he reached into his briefcase to retrieve the papers, he flashed the Uzi full-automatic machine gun he carried. The news crew said they felt rather intimidated having a district attorney in their newsroom brandishing a gun. When some reporters repeated the incident to me, I told them, "Investigator McClain has told me about Travis's shooting scores on the practice range, and you have nothing to worry about!"

Other print reporters and those who worked around television stations came forward with more stories of individual reporters being confronted by Ware, particularly if that reporter had participated in putting together a story that had put the D.A. in a bad light.

According to the reports, the confrontations did not always happen openly. We documented accounts of reporters who were leaving work only to have their cars hemmed in by two vehicles. From those cars would emerge Ware and usually one of his investigators who then wanted to talk to the reporters about the angles of their stories.

On more than one occasion, Ware showed up at the

Avalanche-Journal newspaper and got an audience with the editorial staff to try to drum up support for the "courageous officers" who "came forward" with information on Bill Hubbard, and who "deserved medals." When it became apparent to Ware that he would not get the editorial support he wanted—in fact, he continued to be the subject of editorials and polls that questioned his conduct—he would then launch into hour-long character assassinations of me.

Soon, it became obvious to those on my defense team that not only was I being attacked, but they were, too. Denette Vaughn's house was broken into five times. Dan Hurley's vehicle had the tires cut while it was parked on a county parking lot. A shotgun blast was fired under the bedroom window of Rod Hobson, another attorney and Ware critic. He told all of his family to get down on the floor, where they stayed until the police arrived. Then they went outside to investigate. Small dead animals were piled up under the window of the bedroom that his elementary-school-aged daughter occupied.

This sick behavior appeared to be more than coincidence. Newspapers evidently thought so, too. All of these "coincidences" became front page news.

Despite our uneasiness, Debbie and I decided that we needed to remain high profile and out in the public eye so that people would see we had nothing to be ashamed of. We tried not to let the indictments and our inner sadness change our habits. That did not mean we were not suffering. I saw the pain, despite her usual optimism, mirrored in my wife's eyes each time I gazed at her. Mine never went away.

About three weeks after my indictment, we attended a social function at the Lubbock Civic Center. Mingling with people there, we were approached by an older couple plus an attractive woman who seemed to know us. At first I did not remember them, but in the course of conversation I discovered that we had met years before. The younger woman was Travis Ware's former wife, and she was accompanied by her family.

"I'm so glad we ran into you," Mrs. Ware said. "Ever since I heard what happened to you, I have wanted to let you know some things. You have got to understand that you are in very grave physical danger. Travis Ware has surrounded himself with people who know people who will do *anything* for him. I mean *anything*!"

Startled, I snapped to attention. I was being told, by someone who was in a position to know, that I could be in severe danger. Though our conversation with them lasted only a few minutes, the content occupied our minds the rest of the night.

"This is getting out of hand," I told Debbie as we sat in the kitchen brewing some late night coffee when we got home. We'd always loved getting back home and sharing our evening's impressions with each other. Tonight was different. "You'd think I crossed the Mafia rather than a West Texas D.A."

"What are we going to do?" Debbie asked. "Should we let the police know?"

"Let the police know what?" I said nervously. "We don't have anything specific to tell them, just a reported hunch by some people who should know. We can't run to the police with something like that." It felt strange that I was referring to "the police" as "that group over there." Always before, "the police" meant "one of us." Guilt, remorse, and anger churned inside me.

"We can't just sit around and wait for something bad to happen and then hope we're still alive to deal with it. I feel we should do something," Debbie said.

"I wish we could," I said, shaking my head in frustration. Trying to put the thoughts of possible danger away, I tended the pot of coffee. But Debbie came and stood next to me, not willing to let me turn my back on the conversation.

"I'm so afraid. I never dreamed that anything like this was even possible here in our town. First, you make the wrong people mad, and you go to jail. Then, the lawyers who are trying to help you start having things happen to them. Now, we find out that you may end up in a ditch somewhere out in the country."

"Don't get weird on me here." I tried to smile and joke with her. "It's not like we're going to become hermits, scared to go out for fear something bad will happen. We're not going to be stupid, but we're not going to back off either. That's exactly what Travis and his buddies would want."

"And you plan to do just what? We need protection," Debbie demanded.

It was all too easy in our frustration to let my temper go and at the person I loved most. "I'll tell you what I'm *not* going to do. I'm *not* going to get all paranoid and start looking for the bogeyman behind every tree. And I'm not going to start carrying a gun. That would be the ammunition Travis needs. If I got caught packing heat now, he would have a righteous charge on me. Up to now, the charges are total garbage, and I can't afford to play into his hands and give him what he wants."

Debbie, too, felt the despair and lashed out, her eyes swimming with tears. "What about me? You're not always around when I'm coming and going from work or from late meetings downtown, or when I'm here at home alone."

"Here it's a whole other ball game," I explained. "When you're inside your own home, you have the right to defend yourself. You know how to use a weapon, plus we have a very good alarm system. If you are home alone, keep the alarm on and call nine-one-one if anything happens." I tried to be matter-of-fact but I could see that Debbie, who gazed at me with widening eyes, was becoming more frightened. I reached out, taking her hand in mine.

"As for when you are out and about," I said softly, "I think you should just carry on with business as usual. I don't think that even these guys are low enough to go after a man's wife when the beef is with the man himself. Just do the things which will ensure your safety, and you'll be okay. Park in lighted areas, don't walk to your car alone if it's late—you know, the usual precautions we've talked about and that you've used for years. Besides that, always keep your cell phone with you so you can use it if you need it."

"This is all so strange and intimidating. My stomach is churning," she said, her face harried.

"Darling, we can't let it run our lives. That's exactly what they want." I pulled cups out of the cabinet and poured us both some coffee. "Another thing, our social schedule should stay exactly as it is. We will be at all of the Ad Club functions, all of the holiday events. We will go out when we want to, and be where we want to be." I handed Debbie her cup. "Playing this whole thing high profile and out in the public eye is the one thing that will not only bug Ware and his buddies the most, but it will also keep us safe. It's a whole lot harder to do something to someone who is always out there with a group of people."

"I agree," Debbie said, taking a sip, "but tonight's warning really made me realize just how high the stakes are in all of this."

"It's okay to be afraid," I said, pulling her into my arms, "but what we can't do is freeze because we're afraid. You've heard me say, 'Stay afraid, stay safe.' It's kind of like when a cop has to go into a building to arrest a burglar. Any cop who says he's not afraid needs to have his head examined. Yeah, you're afraid, but you make that fear work for you, to make you more alert, more careful and stronger. You use the fear, rather than letting it paralyze you."

"Even without a badge, you're still the cop," Debbie quipped, finally smiling.

Some Ware supporters decided they had heard enough bad things about their district attorney. A petition drive was started to give him a vote of confidence, and a "public rally" was scheduled. The announcement for the rally was even carried as a public service announcement on some radio stations.

The rally organizer was a woman who worked for the same car dealership where Ware bought his vehicles and where the lightly-sentenced dope dealer also worked. I remembered her, too, because a few years earlier Pat Kelly and I had caught a burglar who had broken into her home. She was grateful then. She must have had a short memory.

The time of the rally arrived. But only twelve supporters stood on the courthouse steps and told the defense attorneys to leave their man alone.

Rod Hobson deadpanned for the *Avalanche-Journal,* "It was a Yogi Berra sort of day for Ware's supporters: They stayed away in droves. I've seen bigger crowds at real estate foreclosures. It's indicative of the general public's questions about what's going on at the D.A.'s office, and we join in with the editorial request for an investigation of what's happened and why, and who was involved."

Ware didn't take this lying down. He told a local television news crew that his office, in light of the recent indictments against me, was looking at more than five hundred cases in which I had been involved for other possible criminal violations. Some sixty-seven of the cases were said still to be active.

Five hundred cases! I had not realized I had been *that* busy.

Pat Kelly had proved to be an accurate prophet. Just as Kelly had predicted, an investigation of Kelly was initiated the day after his Canyon testimony, and now it was drawing to a close. D.A. investigators charged that Kelly had lied on the stand when he testified in Canyon.

Pat had retained counsel in anticipation of this threat. "There's an old expression, 'A district attorney can get a grand jury to return an indictment on a ham sandwich,'" Brian Murray, Kelly's lawyer, told the *Avalanche-Journal.* "Well, Pat Kelly was their ham sandwich."

Ironically, Kelly had received a letter of commendation from Randall County D.A. Randy Sherrod for his testimony at the trial of another murder defendant back in January. "I guess they believed Kelly then but can't believe him now," Murray said.

Soon, Kelly was indicted on a multicount charge of aggravated perjury. Attorney Steve Losch was furious. Two police officers had taken the stand in the pretrial hearings in which he was involved. Two police officers had been indicted. What kind of message was being sent to others who were under subpoena to testify? According to Losch, it was "lose your memory or lose your job."

"It's absolutely clear to me that the indictment of Pat Kelly, like the indictment of Millard Farmer, like the indictment of Bill Hubbard, is a vindictive act meant to intimidate people who testified about Erdmann," Losch angrily told the press. "If I were a betting man, I would believe that, when this is all over, if anyone goes to jail it will be Travis Ware and Randy Sherrod, rather than the courageous people who've been indicted."

Pat Kelly turned himself in the next day and was booked. When he put up the bond and went to the police station, he too was placed on the infamous "indefinite suspension without pay," and joined me in the ranks of the unemployed.

Four days later, the same grand jury issued subpoenas for attorneys Brian Murray and Rod Hobson, and of course, Millard Farmer had already been indicted. Now the lawyers were forced to hire lawyers! Murray and Hobson never found out what their required presence before the grand jury was all about, but they were not indicted for anything. The intimidation, however, had not gone unnoticed.

Lawyers literally from all over the country got wind of what was happening in West Texas and hurried to join the fight. When one of their own of the stature of Millard Farmer gets indicted, other lawyers stand up and take notice. "If you want to help me," Farmer told his high-powered lawyer buddies, "first help Bill and Pat."

I had no idea any of this was going on until I read about it in the *Dallas Morning News*. Suddenly, in addition to those at the bank meeting who had offered to assist me, we had the assistance of about fifty of the most prominent lawyers and national attorneys' associations. One of the most highly regarded attorneys, Richard "Racehorse" Haynes of Houston, volunteered to join the defense counsel for Pat and me. Even the National Association of Criminal Defense Lawyers, the Texas Association of Criminal Defense Lawyers, and the NAACP Legal Defense and Education Fund got involved. This changed the whole tincture of the fight as unlimited resources literally came looking for us. I didn't know any of these people, but never had I been so grateful.

"If the United States Justice Department were investigating these indictments, they would look at the racketeering statute to stop them," said Jonathan Gradess, executive director of the New York State Defenders Association. "It's an awful precedent and an outrageous abuse of state power. The idea that a prosecutor has the hunting license to pick off witnesses because he doesn't like their testimony is an outrage."

"I don't believe the indictments are coincidental," Gerald Goldstein, a rather prominent attorney, told the newspapers. "It's a shame that standing up and blowing the whistle gets police officers retaliation." The paper said Goldstein was very sympathetic to my cause. I was eager to meet him.

"It's absolutely criminal what's taking place in Texas," Gradess told the *Dallas Morning News*. "There's not a defense lawyer I've talked to who's not prepared to come to Texas and square off with those prosecutors and teach them a lesson they will not forget. If I had wanted to do the exact wrong thing as a prosecutor in Texas, I would've indicted Millard Farmer. Dumber than this it doesn't get." His words crackled with righteous indignation.

Gradess's last sentence would become our unofficial battle cry in the weeks to come.

Meanwhile, Travis Ware was having new problems. On November 14th, the double homicide of an elderly couple occurred. A young man named Chris Buss III became the prime suspect. Ware and Buss already knew each other.

Not long before, Buss had testified as a "jailhouse snitch" in another high-profile murder case in which Ware badly wanted a conviction. Coincidentally, Buss had not wanted to get sent away for a long time on the charges he was facing, so he had "volunteered" to be put in a cell next to the murder suspect. And, just as coincidentally, at the trial Buss gave exactly the right testimony to assure the killer's conviction. Buss received a light sentence for his crime and soon was back on the streets of Lubbock.

Now, Buss was himself a murder suspect. No matter how much evidence the homicide detectives piled on

Ware's doorstep, however, they could not get him to file capital murder charges on Buss. Speculation was rampant that some sort of deal had been cut for Buss in return for his testimony, or that he had made up his testimony and might now tell all about it in order to avoid the death penalty for murdering the elderly couple.

Evidence came out in the press that, at the time Buss had been sentenced for his own crime after his testimony against the killer, his prior conviction record had, at best, been "misplaced" by staff members in the district attorney's office. Some said the sentencing judge at the time had been misled so Buss would receive a light sentence.

It was also brought out that, when Buss had been sentenced in the first crime, had his real criminal record been taken into consideration, he would not have been out of prison and in a position to be a suspect in the current murders.

Ware and his administrators were tiptoeing around the question of why full disclosure of Buss's criminal history had not been made. It looked as if Buss was willing to tell all, but was he trying to avoid the consequences for his latest actions, or was he squealing because it was the truth?

Whatever it was, Ware was caught in the middle between Chris Buss and his credibility on one side, versus angry police officers with evidence incriminating Buss on the other side.

The *Dallas Morning News* did not help the Ware camp when it ran a lengthy article on November 22nd. The story recapped the whole sorry history of the Erdmann scandal, from the accident when a drunken assistant district attorney killed a young woman and her disputed autopsy, to the court of inquiry, and up to the indictments of Millard, Pat, and myself.

In addition to laying before the public the breadth of the scandal, the story contained two enlightening bits of information. It repeated the words Randy Atchley spoke to his wife, Rebecca, about why they didn't get me "when they had their shot." I was shocked to read these words I had never heard before.

But the most startling revelation came from Steve Holmes, chief administrator for Ware as he shared a meal with Ware, Atchley and *Dallas Morning News* reporter Lee Hancock. According to Hancock's story, Holmes acknowledged that the investigation that started with the Atchleys might never have begun if I had not "chosen to draw attention" to myself! In other words, I was being punished for my testimony in Canyon.

The article concluded with a quote from Ware: "This is not a game. We're playing for keeps." I saw the statement as threatening. Others confided that they did, too.

The *Lubbock Avalanche-Journal* fueled the fire with a December 9th editorial which referred to the "pall of public suspicion, mistrust and, in many cases, sharp hostility" that had fallen over the operation of the Ware office. It said that somewhere along the way of being relentless in the prosecution of criminals, Ware had taken on "the appearance of an excess in relentless, period."

The editorial concluded, "the air must be cleared," and called for a federal investigation.

On December 15th, the *Avalanche-Journal* ran the results of its own phone-in poll of Lubbock citizens on the question, "Is a federal investigation of the criminal district attorney's office necessary?" Results were 58% yes and 42% no.

The rest of the American public had its chance to respond to the bizarre scandal in West Texas when, on December 13th, Ed Bradley of *60 Minutes* aired the segment telling the nation of Dr. Erdmann's atrocities. Erdmann was interviewed in his kitchen/laboratory, as was an obviously nervous Travis Ware, who appeared to be struggling to answer Bradley's pointed questions. At the same time,

Ware maintained complete surprise at all that had been revealed about Erdmann and appeared shocked, saying that he had only come to know of it recently.

Appearance, of course, could sway public perception. But the polls and the news stories seemed to indicate that the public wasn't buying the images projected by Erdmann and Ware. They now wanted the truth.

16

Extra Mileage

Gerald Goldstein, the prominent San Antonio lawyer, who had spoken in my defense, called and volunteered to join our legal team at no cost. When I relayed his offer, Dan Hurley and Denette Vaughn seemed genuinely pleased. Their egos were not involved; they only wanted what was best for me. In fact, Hurley knew Goldstein from boards and committees on which they had served together, and Denette knew Goldstein from seminars she had attended. Both believed we were extremely fortunate to have his help. So did I.

However, we needed to go to San Antonio to meet with our new team member and to begin filling him in on the case. The problem was money. It was my responsibility to foot the bill for the three air fares. Unfortunately, though Debbie and I were making ends meet, there wasn't anything extra to pay a bill like this.

I knew it was not fair to expect Goldstein to come to Lubbock to meet with us. After all, he had been gracious enough to volunteer to join our team free of charge, and he was an extremely busy man. The normal retainer one would pay to hire him was in the neighborhood of $150,000. The least I could do was bring the others to him, but how could I get the money to fly us all there? For days, Debbie and I racked our brains. Then, one night at a holiday social gathering, I felt someone tugging at my sports jacket and turned to see who was there. Standing next to me was the wife of one of Lubbock's more prominent men, and a successful business owner in her own right. Astonished, I realized she had her hand in my jacket pocket!

Nothing was in the pocket except my car keys, but I was startled just the same. I'd been a cop too long not to jump when I thought I was about to get rolled!

The woman smiled and said, "This will help you and Debbie with the bills." She quietly turned and walked away.

I really wanted to look in my pocket then and there, but I didn't want to draw undue attention to what had just occurred. On the other hand, I couldn't wait to get back to my table, tell Debbie what had happened, and take a look. When I did, I could hardly believe what I found. A handful of hundred dollar bills! This was a truly wonderful, but totally humbling experience. I committed myself to being a very good steward of the funds and to seeing that the most mileage possible was gained from them.

In fact, literal miles were gained, because it made the initial meeting with Gerald Goldstein possible. Denette graciously bowed out of the trip claiming a virus, but I still believe that she put her ego in the backseat so that I had to pay for only two plane tickets.

Dan Hurley and I went to San Antonio in early December. We got to town in time to have a wonderful meal with Dan's wife's parents before meeting Goldstein. Hurley teased that he didn't want me to think he made a practice out of socializing with his clients and introducing them to his family.

Goldstein's office occupied the entire twenty-ninth floor of the Tower Life Building in the heart of downtown San Antonio. We walked into the office, and the staff treated me as if I were the wealthiest, most important client their firm had ever served. Not for one second was I ever made to feel like a charity case or that they were reluctantly doing me a favor.

Goldstein himself was short, slender and charismatic, with curly salt-and-pepper hair worn medium length. He called in one of his top assistant attorneys, Cynthia Orr, who sparkled as she took care of the plans her boss outlined for her. She was quick with a legal pad and an excellent lawyer in her own right. She knew exactly the way Goldstein wanted things done, and I would come to appreciate her guidance and compassion.

After we had been discussing the case for a while, Mr. Goldstein asked, "Would you like something to drink?" When I accepted his offer, he didn't reach for the intercom, but got up himself and left the room. Over and over, I would watch this man demonstrate servanthood both in small and large matters. I was in awe.

That awe carried over from the man to his environment. His office looked as if he had been honored by most of the civic and legal groups in existence. Along the baseboards, plaques were lined up edge to edge, five deep. I am sure each of them had a special meaning and was given with heartfelt appreciation, but I made a mental note right then never to give him a plaque.

While he was out of the room, I just couldn't help myself. Like a kid in a new environment filled with exotic toys, I jumped out of my chair and wandered around, taking it all in. His office was so cool! The view was unbelievable—I could see the Riverwalk, the Alamo, and the World's Fair complex. Then Goldstein popped back into the room carrying our drinks on a tray. I tried to regain my professional demeanor as I sat down.

Goldstein followed a lead that had been mentioned earlier by Jonathan Gradess, an attorney from New York. He believed that just waiting for my court date to come around was the wrong tactic. Goldstein opined, "I believe the charges were brought in bad faith, for the purpose of retaliation against you. I'm convinced that this is a civil rights issue and that we should pull out the stops and go on the offensive. I want to invoke RICO." Into my mind jumped images of the Mafia and gangsters. I stared at the dynamic man before me, trying to call up knowledge of the RICO statutes.

Prior to this, I'd had only a fleeting acquaintance with the term. I knew it meant Racketeer Influenced and Corrupt Organizations Act. I knew it was a federal statute, but I thought it had more to do with what I thought of as "traditional" organized crime. But, according to Goldstein, two public officials such as Ware and Sherrod, who were elected to similar offices, who were individually and/or collectively trying to silence opposition, certainly could be considered organized.

"I want to do some more research and talk it over with the other national firms who are helping out," Gerry said. "I know it's daring, but I'd like to pursue this tactic. I want to sue Ware and his office. We'd file a federal civil lawsuit against Travis Ware, Ralph Erdmann and others, alleging racketeering, conspiracy and violations of your constitutional rights."

Dan nodded, "I'll pass the information on to Denette, so we can start legal research to look at the matter on our own and be able to better advise Bill on a personal level."

The lawyers went to work, and the holiday season approached. Despite the turmoil, I was determined to make it a happy season, especially for Debbie, who was making tremendous sacrifices so that we could survive on her salary. To make a little money for the Hubbard Christmas, I took a job at the local mall driving a shuttle bus from the outer edges of the parking lot to the mall entrances. This was a free service for mall shoppers, and I was paid seven dollars an hour. I was also able to pick up some hours working in an enclosed plywood box at the remote controls of a giant stuffed bear that could physically respond and "talk" to children who came to see it. This also paid seven dollars an hour.

It was disheartening to be there every day, busting my butt for seven bucks. Especially when I saw mall security— most of whom were off-duty city cops whom I had outranked—making as much as twelve dollars an hour, often for simply providing a "presence." When I felt really low, I reminded myself of the humble lesson of the Lord whose birth we would soon be celebrating.

On the brighter side, some of the kids who came to visit the bear were very cute, and I figured out a good shuttle bus route that allowed me to get around the lot while avoiding many of the traffic jams.

Somehow, it got back to Steve Losch in New York that I was "running around in a shopping mall wearing a bear suit." He was outraged that a man of my education and law enforcement expertise was forced to do that to make a few dollars. He was somewhat appeased when it was pointed out to him that I was at the remote controls of a mechanical bear. "That's better," he said, "but not much."

On the night of December 17th, as closing time approached, I was taking a few minutes break from "being the bear." Taking a break meant putting the bear on animated autopilot with a tape recording of some Christmas songs. This gave me, the operator, a chance to get out of the five-by-five-foot control box for some air. Grabbing a cup of metallic coffee from the machine, I sat down on a bench near the bear. To my surprise, Larry Cunningham, whom

I knew from various civic functions, sat down beside me. I was aware that he had recently been relieved of his position as Lubbock's city manager.

"I probably shouldn't be telling you this, but . . ." Larry hesitated and then began a recital of facts that amazed me. They were about the exchanges Travis Ware had initiated in late August.

As he spoke, I shook my head vehemently. "Neither I nor my legal team knew about that," I said, shocked.

Cunningham said that Ware had wanted him to take action to get me out of my job, and if Cunningham didn't do so, Ware and Rebecca Atchley were prepared to dredge up accusations from the old internal investigation and get me indicted. Needless to say, Cunningham's revelations blew me away.

"In all my years of public service," Cunningham concluded, "Travis Ware is the meanest, most vindictive man I have ever met."

The next day, Denette called Larry Cunningham and he repeated everything he had told me. We got word to Hurley and Goldstein. We all felt that our ability to prove Ware's retaliation motive had been clinched. "Christmas has come early," I told Debbie, hugging her when I got home.

"I have doubts as to whether Cunningham sought me out to reveal what he told me tonight. I tend to think he just saw me there, walked up, and blurted it all out on the spur of the moment," I told her. I added, "The Lord does work in mysterious ways."

I have often wondered what would have happened if I had not taken that seven-dollar-an-hour job, had not been working that particular night, and had not been taking a break at that particular moment when Cunningham appeared.

* * *

Every day when we went to the mailbox, another blessing in some form was there. At this point, cards and letters were really rolling in. Some contained checks, and all contained encouragement. Prayer groups from many churches in different parts of the city sent notes that they were praying for us. What was surprising was that most of the names on these cards and letters were unknown to me.

To my further amazement, some letters came from people I had arrested at one time or another. One or two had even gotten a trip to the state pen, thanks to me. But not a single one of these letters said, *I'm glad you're taking a beating.* Each letter was kind and compassionate. Many of the senders said they were praying for me. And all told different stories of how their encounters with me had changed their lives. The arrests and the jail time were not resented. On the contrary, the writers cited their incarceration as being what finally got their attention and made them realize they needed to make positive changes in their lives.

Parolees offered to go anywhere at any time to be character witnesses for me. Many said I had been real tough on them and had really thrown the book at them. But they acknowledged that it was never more than they had coming and that I had always treated them fairly and with the least amount of force necessary to get the job done. Those letters made me proud of my record as a cop.

One other piece of mail, which had a profound effect on me, came to our house shortly before Christmas Day. It was a very generous check from our church. There was a note from an associate pastor that said they just wanted to make sure that Debbie and I were not in need of anything at Christmas.

I cannot describe the feeling that swept over us when we received this gift. We knew that our church collected a special offering on the fifth Sunday of any month that had five Sundays, and the money was used to help our own church families who were in need. We saw the check as much more than charity. It was love and concern in action. It said, *We are with you.*

Our financial need had not yet gotten critical. With the seven bucks an hour I was making and the belt-tightening we had done, we were holding our own. I knew the check was given to help us over the hump of the holidays, but I just could not cash it. With Debbie's support, I taped it under the canopy of my roll-top desk so it would be the first thing I saw each morning when I went to my home office. It was my constant reminder that we were not alone in this battle, and we resolved that the check would be cashed only if our need got critical.

17

RICO

On January 4th, attorneys from all across the country trekked to San Antonio. They came from other parts of Texas. They came from Chicago, Atlanta, New York, and New Mexico. And they came at their own expense. They assembled with all their expertise to form a think tank. Their mission: to work out the logistics of filing a RICO suit.

Into the meeting, they decided to join all three indictees—Millard Farmer, Pat Kelly and me—into one large civil suit based on the RICO and civil rights statutes. Attorney J. Mark Lane, of one of the largest and wealthiest law firms in the world, would take the pivot position in assembling all information and drafting the document. Mr. Lane worked out of the New York office of Skadden, Arps, Slate, Meagher and Flom. Their letter-head showed offices in places such as Washington, New York, London, Paris, and Beijing. The base office in New York operated around the clock. At any time of the day or night, you could call and get a warm body on the phone who was at least aware of and knew something about your case.

Because Millard Farmer had an excellent reputation among attorneys, lawyers from all over the country wanted to help him. Their interest in this matter ended up benefiting Pat and me, too.

Mark Lane kept us jumping. He was the designated hitter, but he needed all of the information we could provide for him. Lane gave marching orders for everyone across the country who was to be a part of making the RICO suit happen.

Lane knew the highlights of my case, but he wanted a complete rundown of the entire matter, including some biographical information about me and how my lawyers and I believed the cases on me came about. I was told I could dictate it into a cassette recorder in order to expedite matters.

I talked into three tapes and gave them to Denette, who added information from Dan Hurley. She then put the comments together with her own research assignment, and sent everything by FedEx to New York. The next day, when Denette called Mr. Lane, not only had the package arrived, but my tapes had already been transcribed. "The transcription is on my desk," Lane announced. We were tremendously impressed by the efficiency of his office.

As each of the attorneys who had helped lay the foundation of the RICO suit returned to their respective firms, each approached their firm for advice on participation in the suit. Every firm involved, including the ones helping me locally, gave a resounding commitment to the task. It was a huge effort in time and money, since the trial looked long and difficult, and would involve intense work on the part of everyone involved.

As I understood the lawsuit, our burden of proof was

twofold. In each of the three cases—mine, Pat Kelly's and Millard Farmer's—it had to be demonstrated that the decisions to bring charges against each of us were motivated, at least in part, by bad faith. We would also need to show that it was more likely than not that the charges were brought to chill or retaliate against us for constitutionally protected activity. This is a simplification, for the predicate acts and foundation of racketeering would have to be spelled out.

The judge who would hear the case was the Honorable Mary Lou Robinson, a conservative Democrat who had been appointed to the federal bench during the Carter presidency. The first thing we needed to do was convince her that she had jurisdiction and venue. When we had accomplished that, we would ask for a temporary restraining order that would call "time out" to the prosecution of the three of us in state court until the federal court could have time to hear our case and issue a decision. The third step would be a hearing in which both sides could present testimony. We would argue for the issuance of a preliminary injunction that would place a federal roadblock in the way, preventing our prosecution on the indictments. The final step would be a trial before a federal jury where we would seek damages, and ask for a permanent injunction that would forever ban any attorney from proceeding with the prosecution of our individual cases.

The document that Lane wrote was a legal work of art. It was one hundred and forty-three pages long and spelled out why our case was an instance of RICO from start to finish. In it, Pat Kelly, Millard Farmer and I banded together as the plaintiffs bringing suit against twelve people. Foremost were Randy Sherrod, Travis Ware, and Ralph Erdmann. Among the others were Frank Briscoe, and some key personnel and investigators.

Lane's was a riveting indictment. It gave background on the atrocities Dr. Erdmann had committed and how each of our indictments came about. It told of how Pat, Millard and I each exposed the wrongdoing of Dr. Erdmann.

The lawsuit brief then listed thirteen causes of action:

1. Violation of our First and Fourteenth Amendment rights, asking for injunctive relief against our various prosecutions—the three of us against Sherrod, Ware, Sherrod's assistant John Davis, and Assistant Attorney General Frank Briscoe.

2. The violating of our constitutional rights—the three of us against all twelve defendants asking for damages to be awarded for actual damages, attorney fees and punitive damages due to the malicious and willful nature of the damage inflicted.

3. Injunctive relief and also a complaint that the grand jury that indicted Farmer was unconstitutionally composed—Farmer against the judge where his case was pending.

4. A declaratory judgment against our various prosecutions for which all three of us asked.

5. Violation of the federal racketeering statute—all three of us against Sherrod, Ware, Davis, Erdmann, Woodson Rowan and Sherrod's inves-tigator Kevin Rush. This section alleged the fraudulent scheme (Erdmann's false autopsies and the measures taken to keep them quiet), the "enterprises" (Erdmann's business and the counties involved), the predicate acts (alleged mail fraud against Erdmann, the damage inflicted by several of his bogus autopsies, violations of the Hobbs Act on selling body parts and tissues, plus violations of laws of Texas concerning bribery and extortion), and

an ongoing pattern of the racketeering activity, which resulted in injury to us as plaintiffs.

6. Alleged conspiracy to violate the federal racketeering statute—the three of us against all defendants.

7. Aiding and abetting a violation of the federal racketeering statute—the three of us against all the defendants.

8. Alleged common law conspiracy—all three plaintiffs against all defendants. This basically alleged that the defendants had acted in concert to accomplish unlawful acts by unlawful means for the purpose of harming others.

9. Defamation because of statements Sherrod had made to reporters to damage Farmer's professional reputation—Farmer against Sherrod.

10. Defamation because of the statements Ware had made to Investigator Carrie McClain about my character and the statements he had made to Dr. Jody Nielsen that damaged my professional and personal reputation—me against Ware.

11. Defamation for statements in general about Kelly, Farmer and I, which accused us of criminal acts, thereby being slander—all three of us against Sherrod.

12. For intentional infliction of emotional distress—all three of us against Sherrod, Ware, Davis, Erdmann, Rowan and Rush.

13. Negligence—Millard Farmer against Ralph Erdmann. This alleged Erdmann owed to Farmer and to the public at large a duty to perform his office honestly and with due care. Erdmann's breach of duty had caused Farmer to incur considerable financial expense and other damages.

If our contentions were upheld, we would gain:

1. Preliminary and permanent injunctions prohibiting the defendants from prosecuting the three of us.

2. A declaratory judgment that the indictments of the three of us were obtained in bad faith and for the purposes of harassment and interference of our constitutional rights.

3. Orders directing the Lubbock Police Department to reinstate Pat Kelly and me, give us our pay, and back pay.

4. Actual damages to be determined at the trial.

5. Triple damages for damages occurring as a result of racketeering statute violations.

6. Punitive damages to be determined at trial.

7. Injunctions against Randall County as well as its current grand juries and a declaratory judgment that the current method of selecting grand juries in the county is unconstitutional.

8. Attorney fees.

9. "Such other and further relief as justice may require."

The brief concluded by asking for the final trial to be before a jury.

On an auspicious and, we prayed, lucky date, the eighth anniversary of the day Debbie and I married, Lane flew to Amarillo and filed our suit in United States District Court for the Northern District of Texas, Amarillo division.

Judge Robinson set a meeting to be held two days later, on February 4th, in her chambers. At that time, she would want to see and hear briefly from the parties involved. Then we would find out if she believed that she had jurisdiction and would hear our case.

We did not know what to make of the fact that she had, only two days after the suit was filed, set up this meeting. Had she made a snap decision against us? Was she just very sure of the direction in which she would go? And, if so, which side did she believe?

Those who knew the judge and who had been in her courtroom told us that the Honorable Mary Lou Robinson was not one to make quick decisions. In view of the early date she'd set, we agonized, was this a good sign or a bad one?

18

Accelerating the Pace

The two days between the filing of our RICO suit and the hearing in Amarillo seemed more like two weeks. The tension became combustible because of Judge Robinson's decision to hold a meeting. The purpose of the meeting was to enable the judge to identify everyone involved, to see that all parties understood the nature of the suit, and to tell us if she had decided whether she had jurisdiction to hear the suit.

Three months earlier, shortly after I had been indicted, I had complained to Dan and Denette that I was impatient and wanted something—anything—to happen. They both constantly reminded me that the wheels of justice turn very slowly sometimes, but they do turn. It seemed to me that in getting me indicted, the wheels of justice turned pretty fast, while getting the indictment undone was excruciatingly slow. But now, as the process accelerated, so did my anxiety. As one after another motion and event struck, Hurley quipped, "Well, Bill, are things finally happening fast enough for you?"

"Plenty!" I replied, exhaling a deep breath.

The day of the meeting, Debbie and I arrived early. Prior to entering the judge's chambers, all of the plaintiffs and all of their lawyers, as well as all the defendants and all of their lawyers, began squeezing into the small outer office. No one spoke. Even the air was filled with electricity.

Richard "Racehorse" Haynes was present as part of our legal team. He is not a large man physically, but his size in the legal community is of gigantic proportions. In the waiting room, he just happened to end up next to Travis Ware, who was standing just behind me.

Haynes eased slowly in front of Ware, reached up and sort of flicked Ware in the middle of the chest with the back of his hand. He obviously had read the *Dallas Morning News* story that referred to Ware as the "bulletproof-vest-wearing, gun-toting D.A."

"Hey, Travis." Haynes grinned. "Got your bulletproof vest on?"

I was about to erupt into laughter when the bailiff opened the door and announced, "Judge Robinson will see you now."

Since only parties to the suit and their attorneys were allowed in the judge's chambers, Debbie had to wait outside. She pressed my hand as I started in with Denette. "Get 'em," she said, smiling.

Fortunately, the judge's chamber was roomy. With three plaintiffs and our eight or nine lawyers, plus eleven of the twelve defendants and their host of counsel, the number of people crowding in was formidable. The one missing defendant was Ralph Erdmann—the man who was responsible for all the rest of us being there. He had chosen to ignore the suit and had not even sent representation. The newspapers had reported that Erdmann left Texas after pleading no contest in September to seven felonies in botched or faked autopsies.

As Judge Mary Lou Robinson silently studied the participants, she reminded me of my very strict sixth grade teacher, Mrs. Warren. Her stern look was compounded by gray hair slicked back into a tight bun. Lines of wisdom crisscrossed her forehead. Robinson did not look like someone on whose wrong side you would want to be. As the judge straightened her back, there was no doubt she was in charge and meant business.

"First," she announced, "Everyone in the room should identify themselves for the record, including who is corresponding counsel for which defendant."

The sheer numbers made this a time-consuming job. As Judge Robinson more or less called roll, there was little talking. I tried to whisper a couple of questions to Denette so I would know what was happening, but my mouth was so dry from nervousness I could hardly phrase the words. I didn't want the judge looking up to see where the talking was coming from, so I decided to keep quiet.

Finally, Judge Robinson completed the identification process. "I'll hear briefly from a spokesperson from each side, but will not allow lengthy arguments from anyone, because that is not the purpose of this meeting." Then, looking around, she decreed, "Keep your talks informal and you need not stand to address me." Though the last words were designed to ease the mood, little was altered.

Serious-faced Gerald Goldstein led things off by giving a very brief summation of what our suit was and what we could prove in a courtroom, particularly about the origination of the criminal charges against Pat, Millard and me.

Travis Ware stood up and the judge allowed him to speak.

"Your Honor, I had nothing to do with the indictments on Bill Hubbard." This was his standard speech, the claim he had been making to the press for months.

He insisted that the attorney general's office gathered the information that he had merely passed along.

Goldstein politely responded concerning what we intended to prove about the involvement of Ware and others long before the attorney general's office got that information. Ware remained standing throughout Goldstein's response.

"Sit down, Mr. Ware," the judge said sternly. He complied.

After the judge had heard short statements from some of the others present, she announced, "I believe my jurisdiction and venue are proper for the case, and I intend to entertain it in my courtroom."

"Yes!" Denette whispered.

With a few added words of explanation and some strokes of her pen, the Honorable Mary Lou Robinson issued a temporary restraining order that blocked the moving ahead of any prosecutions of Millard, Pat or me until such time as she could hear testimony for the possible issuing of a preliminary injunction.

Our first goal had been accomplished. We were absolutely ecstatic but tried to contain our emotions until we got out of the courthouse. However, to Debbie, who knew me so well, the expression on my face must have told the story. As I sauntered out of the judge's chambers, I couldn't wait to tell her all that had transpired, but first we had to get to a place where we could talk freely. Hand in hand, we went down in the elevator with our team of lawyers and headed out of the building to take the two-block walk back to the downtown office of attorney V. G. (Bill) Kolius, which was our temporary base.

Our lawyers had advised us not to talk to the press. As we walked, television cameras moved in on us. Reporters pushed microphones into our smiling faces. It must have been obvious to them that whatever had transpired inside had gone in our favor. As the persistent questions kept coming, "Racehorse" just couldn't stand it any more and broke the silence.

"Let's just say that it's a cold day when I'm smiling, and I'm smiling today!" he said.

The next morning, newspaper headlines around the country read, "Judge halts cases against Erdmann critics." The story began, "In a rare federal intervention in state criminal courts, a U.S. district judge Thursday halted prosecutions of an Atlanta lawyer and two Lubbock police officers indicted after they criticized discredited pathologist Ralph Erdmann."

Our next court appearance was scheduled for February 16th, a mere twelve days away. At that time, Judge Robinson would hear testimony in support of our suit as well as rebuttals from the defendants. That hearing was expected to last two days or so. After that hearing, the judge would study the situation and give a decision as to whether she would issue a preliminary injunction to bar our prosecutions until the permanent injunction trial, or if she would side with the defendants and refuse to grant the injunction. That move would invalidate the temporary restraining order and give the state the right to try us on our respective charges.

The defendants' feet were now to the fire. They had less than two weeks to prove to a federal judge that the charges were clean, brought in good faith and not for retaliatory purposes.

Back at our downtown base of operations, our jubilant team began putting our belongings together, preparing to go our separate ways for a few days until the showdown arrived. Though we felt satisfied, we were weary. Many of us had driven up from Lubbock. Gerald Goldstein had flown in from clear across the country and now would be heading back, so he could take care of other issues in the interim.

"I can't believe Travis told the judge that he had nothing to do with my indictments," I told Goldstein.

"He's gonna eat those words when we show the judge just how involved he was," Goldstein replied.

"I don't know how to thank you for your continued efforts on my behalf," I said, my voice cracking.

"Piece of cake!" He smiled and patted me on the back.

As the Goldstein group left, I saw Jed Stone, one of Millard Farmer's lawyers, gathering his files and other things to return to his Chicago home. I walked over to him.

Stone is a big bear of a man with a full salt-and-pepper beard and a definitive Chicago touch to his speech. He's not a loud, wild-eyed liberal or a soapbox type, but an intelligent, introspective gentleman. After I'd thanked him, we talked about the murder case, which was the crux of the Canyon hearing, and he started to talk about his belief on the subject of the death penalty.

Earlier in the day, before we went to meet with Judge Robinson, there had been opportunities to converse about a variety of subjects, and I had gotten to know Stone a little better. We even had the chance to extol the virtues of our favorite baseball teams—his Chicago White Sox and my Texas Rangers.

But now, as Stone adamantly began to voice his views, I knew almost immediately ours were very different. "You'll never know what it's all about until you watch a man, whom you believe to the depth of your soul has been wrongly charged, die by judicial order." When Stone said "watch," he meant literally, physically see it.

I leaned toward him, "Mr. Stone, you will never know what it is really all about until you are only twenty feet from a friend who has been gunned down only because he was a police officer, and you are pinned down by gunfire and can't get to him."

As we continued to explore the reasons behind each of our opinions, each was filled with compassion for the other. I really understood and felt sympathy for him as he had watched the execution of a client for whom he had fought clear to the Supreme Court. He seemed to truly understand and empathize with me as I described how I had watched Sergeant K. D. Fowler, my friend and compatriot, die because of the uniform he wore. Each of us could see tears welling in the other's eyes as we felt a shared pain.

"If just one person is wrongly executed, it just isn't worth it," he said.

"But, Jed," I said, my voice breaking, "the man who killed K. D. cannot die soon enough to suit me."

"Oh, Bill," whispered this huge man full of emotion, "even if he does die, it doesn't change a thing. Your friend is still dead."

We just stood there and looked at each other, our emotions too deep for words. We parted company, he still a foe of the death penalty and I still a believer in it. But we both left different from what we had been before.

Meanwhile, we all waited in nervous anticipation for the next and most telling move of the defense. Two major organizations, the Texas Criminal Defense Lawyers Association and the National Association of Criminal Defense Lawyers, reviewed our case. Together, they filed an "Amicus" or "Friend of the Court" brief in support of our motion for a preliminary injunction. They had done their own homework and also filed a fourteen-page review of the results of their research into the issues at hand. They cited fifteen cases that supported our position. Stories exploded in the newspapers that we were on the brink of making new legal history. Legal scholars were saying that asking a federal judge to intervene in a state criminal action was rare for any court, and probably unprecedented in our state.

"To my knowledge, it has never happened in Texas," Charles Bubany told the *Dallas Morning News.* Bubany had been a law professor at Texas Tech Law School for more than twenty years.

"It was more common back in the civil rights era when you had federal courts stepping in to block state prosecutions in southern states," Bubany went on. "It's very significant."

The fact that what we were trying to accomplish had never been done in Texas and had happened only about a dozen other times in the history of the United States neither intimidated me nor made me uneasy. I was no legal scholar, but I understood my situation very well, and the case law I had reviewed during the building of our suit emphatically supported our position.

However, though I had confidence we were in the right, I was still somewhat apprehensive. I had never been a party to anything this big before. On the other hand, I had never been indicted before either. Lots of "firsts" were happening in my life. Since most of them were not good, I was thankful for the prayers and all the expert legal assistance that Debbie and I received.

Now, the media's grip on the momentum tightened. My attorneys did not want to blow them off. But, more important, they did not want to have Judge Robinson turn on the television and see any of us spouting off about the case, the situation, or what we felt the judge could, would, or should do.

Gerald Goldstein simply announced, "We believe the judge will enter the appropriate order."

Although we were not saying much to the newspeople, the local media were making quite a noise of their own. The day that Judge Robinson entered the temporary restraining order and set the hearing date, Lubbock's leading Hispanic newspaper, *El Editor*, called for Travis Ware's resignation. An inside editorial explained that, though the allegations in the RICO suit had not yet been proven, "it remains that not only (Ware's) integrity but also his moral character and capability to represent people in our county must also be questioned.

"Travis Ware's lying and instigating of lying by witnesses is documented by many newspaper articles printed not only in this newspaper, but also in the *Dallas Morning News* and the *New York Times*."

A third point was then made that *El Editor* called the most serious. It cited "Racehorse" Haynes's statement that his main reason for intervening in this case was because of an "abuse of power." The paper said that Ware's abuses of power were "evident," "countless," and "documented."

After weighing integrity, moral character and credibility, the article concluded that Ware had lost the ability to represent the citizens of Lubbock and therefore must resign.

Ware scoffed at the notion.

Twelve days inched by. Judge Robinson circulated word to both sides concerning the number of hours she expected to allow for the next phase of the hearing, which she firmly stated was expected to last only two days. Our team spent the interim hard at work, trying to get our voluminous material compacted into what we felt could be introduced into court in such a short session.

Day and night, I worked to prepare summaries for my legal team that got straight to the heart of what each witness we expected to call could testify to. Though anticipated testimony was cut to the bare minimum, it still looked like a lot for two days. And I knew Kelly and Farmer would each have at least as much testimony from their witnesses as I anticipated from mine. We condensed our expected line of questioning and then condensed the condensation. It was like taking a work of classical literature and making it into a short story and then making "Cliff's Notes" of the short story.

One major problem I had not anticipated was the cost involved in producing our witnesses. For each witness there would be an initial witness fee, mileage, food and lodging allowances, and an additional reimbursement for each extra day they remained to testify. As I added them up, it was a sizeable sum. Fortunately, my parents, despite their health problems, stepped in at that point and sent us the three thousand dollars it would take to get the witnesses to the courtroom. I have to admit, the thought of paying for the likes of Randy and Rebecca Atchley really got my goat.

Those last few days before the hearing in Amarillo were really intense. None of us had a minute to spare. The matter was complicated by the fact that our legal team was separated by many miles, and the attorneys who knew the players best had to communicate everything they knew to our heavy hitters, who were in New York, Chicago, San Antonio, and Houston. Early in the afternoon of February 14th, Denette Vaughn and I went to Dan Hurley's office, and there we remained as the light of day turned to darkness.

In Hurley's office complex, we spread our legal papers, reference books and clippings all over the library, break room and secretary's area, not to mention every desk, table and inch of floor space. More research was being conducted in the library. I sorted papers in the break room. The copy machine and fax ran constantly. At Hurley's desk, Dan and Denette asked question after question for clarification and wanted the documentation to back each one up. Phone calls were either placed or received to update members of the team, and the appropriate documents were faxed or set aside to be hand delivered when we met in Amarillo for the hearing.

Intense? Yes. Exhausting? Yes! It was probably a good thing we were so busy that we did not have time to really stop and agonize about the immensity of what we were doing. We would soon be appearing before a federal judge, charging serious civil rights and racketeering infractions by some of the most connected and influential political figures in Texas. Then we would ask the judge to make a ruling the likes of which had probably never been made before. If we had really reflected on that, it might have caused us to pack up our boxes of paperwork and head on home!

The three of us worked late into the night. "We'd better get to Amarillo well prepared," Denette and Dan joked, "because if we don't win big up there, our law practices here in Lubbock will be finished." When we finally pronounced the job complete and got the brief all boxed up for the drive to Amarillo, it was after midnight.

"I'll pick you up about one o'clock tomorrow, pard," Hurley said. "Get some sleep."

Exhausted, I got into my old Jeep and headed for home. When I drove into the driveway, I was surprised to see lights still on in the living room. Quietly opening the door and going in, I found Debbie awake and the television on, but I could tell she hadn't been paying attention to it.

"Still up?" I asked, concerned. Debbie was not the night owl that I was.

"Yes. I just didn't feel like sleeping. How'd things go?" she said, anxiously.

"I guess we're as ready as we're ever going to be. Dan and Denette are really putting in the hours for me."

"For us," Debbie corrected.

"Yeah," I said. "That goes without saying. I'm completely worn out and really pumped up about this, all at the same time. Maybe I'll be able to sleep—from sheer exhaustion, if nothing else."

"You go on to bed. I think I'll stay up a little while longer," Debbie said, sighing heavily. "Bill, I'm afraid for you, for us, if it doesn't come out right.

I paused. "Debbie, don't worry." I tried to smile. She looked haggard but, as I bent over to kiss her, I did not question her. I was preoccupied and weary. I walked slowly down the hall to the bedroom.

As I got undressed and fell into bed, Debbie stayed in the living room with the unwatched television still on. I knew that she too was exhausted, not so much from work, but from watching someone she loved under the most intense pressure of his life.

Don't worry! How could she not worry? She must feel completely excluded from all the preparations and plans the legal team and I were making. She couldn't tell for sure how we all felt the evidence was stacking up. And she had to feel torn.

In addition, the pressure of her work had been heavy. She was introducing one of the mall's biggest promotions at a press conference tomorrow, just when the hearing would be beginning. Her boss and her friends at the mall had been wonderful, supporting her in every way possible, and she couldn't let them down. Not that there was any chance of Debbie letting anyone down. So she would hold the press conference, then drive to Amarillo with Denette, who also had morning commitments.

I knew the sorrow that was weighing on her tonight was not merely because she felt left out. I could tell from her words and mood that only in these hours had she faced the reality of what might happen if Judge Robinson ruled against me. If I lost and Travis Ware was to continue prosecuting me on the bogus charges, even going to trial, the consequences for me were too dire to consider. In her heart, Debbie knew I would never allow myself to be sent to prison. Prisons are hazardous environments for former police officers, and if I was incarcerated, the chances of being tortured and killed were too strong. I would never permit that to happen. No one knew that better than Debbie.

Suddenly, it was all too much for her. Rarely did Debbie shed tears, but I heard her sobbing. "I'm not going to cry," she cried out. "I'm okay. Bill's okay. But are we going to be all right, Lord?"

There was no holding back her emotions. She buried her face in her hands so she wouldn't wake me. She thought I was already asleep. But lying still, eyes wide open in the darkness, I heard her. At that moment, recognizing my insensitivity, I jumped out of bed to go to Debbie and promised myself that from then on, instead of trying to shield her from the news, I'd involve Debbie in all the plans for the suit. When I reached the living room, I walked up to the sofa, bent down and gathered Debbie in my arms. We didn't speak, but I led her to our room, where we could comfort each other.

On the afternoon of Monday, February 15th, a severe cold front swept into the area bringing driving winds, pounding rain and freezing temperatures. Steve Losch had come to Lubbock early to assist with the project, so he and I rode to Amarillo with Dan Hurley in his four-wheel-drive vehicle. Debbie and Denette would not be able to come up until the next morning.

Though we had to drive slowly, Losch, Hurley and I made it into Amarillo without any problems. Our team was staying at an "all suites" hotel, and Millard Farmer, Mark Lane and Jed Stone were already there when we arrived. Gerald Goldstein and Cynthia Orr were expected soon. Pat Kelly and his team were still working in Lubbock and would arrive the next morning in time for the start of the hearing.

Our first order of business: Eat. We really filled up at

a barbecue restaurant, locally famed for its ribs, chicken and the abundant portions.

Back at the hotel, I was amazed all over again at how organized and prepared our legal team was. One room had been rented and outfitted as a complete office and conference room. A computer, two telephone lines, a fax machine and a high-volume photocopier were already set up. This office would operate on a twenty-four-hour basis for as long as the hearing would be in session.

As the evening wore on, the finishing touches were added to strategies that would be put into motion the next day in the courtroom. Mark Lane was kept busy on another front. Negotiations were going full tilt with attorneys from the other side to settle the matter before the hearing.

From these meetings, Lane brought the question back to us: "What do you want to settle this right now?" The thought of money had not even occurred to me. Coursing through my mind was an image of my gold badge with #13 on it. And to be free of the criminal charges. Back pay would be nice. And assurance that I would get my old job back in homicide.

However, despite preliminary overtures, the meetings didn't go well. I was their key target and one they were intent on keeping, and of course they were mine. The rest of the deal apparently had been accepted, but the Lubbock Criminal District Attorney absolutely would not agree to any deal that would mean dismissing charges against me.

Fine, I thought. Why would I not want to go to this federal hearing and argue for an injunction? I wanted vindication. I was jobless and under indictment, with an unknown toll being taken on my professional reputation every time Ware spoke to the media. By going ahead with the hearing, I had little to lose and everything to gain.

19

Truth and Lies

The morning of February 16th we woke up shivering to a deep freeze. The high temperature for the day was not expected to get above ten degrees. Add some West Texas wind, and the result was a wind chill factor of minus zero. We had to rely on booster cables to start our cars for the slip-and-slide ride downtown to the courthouse.

When you add subfreezing temperatures outside to the lack of heat in most old courthouses and then add a frigid atmosphere of fear, you get an ideal situation for shivering in your shoes. I tried to keep my emotions in check, but the long hours and pressure were taking their toll. I badly needed the support of my lawyer and even more, that of my wife. So I felt very relieved when I saw Denette and Debbie drive up earlier than I expected, despite the slick roads.

"How'd it go this morning?" I asked as I hugged Debbie, referring to her press conference.

"It went great. All of the newspeople were there. They

were joking and complaining that they were going to have to make this drive to Amarillo today, too. One of them said that all she had planned for the day was to follow the Hubbards around. I asked her in my best southern belle voice, 'Press conference in the morning, court in the afternoon—what *do* I wear?'"

Debbie always knew how to make light of even the heaviest situation. We all laughed, but then Denette's face turned serious. "Okay, you two," Denette's voice of reason broke in. "Let's get going. There's business at hand."

We made our way up to the lobby outside the courtroom where the hearing would be held. The most intimidating time of all was upon us. Virtually all of the plaintiffs, defendants, some twenty lawyers, plus all of the witnesses and courtroom observers were scattered in the lobby, waiting for the courtroom doors to open so we could go in. It was quite obvious from their somber faces and tapping feet that many of the defendants really didn't want to be there, and resented that we had made them come.

Travis Ware had his own little entourage staying off by themselves in a corner of the lobby. Occasionally, their cutting glances and stares darted around the hall checking to see who was being friendly to whom. Some witnesses stood at a distance and spoke to no one at all, probably because of Ware's scrutiny, fearing that there might be a price tag to pay for being friendly to the wrong person when everyone returned to Lubbock.

I appreciated those who made small talk with us. It helped to cut the tension. There were a few handshakes and smiles. Some brave souls dared to come over and wish us good luck. Nevertheless, apprehension pulsed in the dimly lit old lobby, and the atmosphere was heavy with anticipation.

Suddenly, Debbie whispered to me, "I feel like I'm smothering. I have to get out of here." She hurried down a short hallway toward the water fountain. I followed, seeking comfort from her presence. She took only a sip of water, then leaned wearily against the wall.

"I just had to get out of the scene for a minute," she said. "I felt like I couldn't breathe."

"It's pretty tense."

"It's like before a prize fight, when everyone on both sides is glaring and sneering and trying to intimidate the opponent."

"But Debbie, we're here because this judge can stop this insanity."

"I know."

"And remember, I'm not on trial here. We are asking for relief. We have everything to gain by being here and absolutely nothing to lose. If we fail in this court and don't get the injunction we're seeking, we still have the criminal trial, and I'll be found not guilty."

"I know you will," Debbie answered, looking into my eyes. "I'm positive, but I wish it would never happen."

"That's the point of our being here." I tried to smile. "If we succeed now, that trial will never happen. It's Ware and Briscoe and Sherrod who've got their butts on the line in this courtroom."

"I understand what you're saying," Debbie conceded. She took a deep breath. "I just hate even being in the same room with these people."

Nevertheless, linking her arm with mine, she allowed me to shepherd her back to the lobby. She squared her shoulders as we continued to wait.

The session was late getting started. Like us, the crowd in the lobby continued to wait, some talking desultorily, some reading, others having quiet conversations with their lawyers in a corner, but all under the watchful eyes of Travis Ware and his associates.

The bailiff let us know the judge was busily embroiled sentencing some drug pushers. When the judge finally finished, she took a needed recess. As the doors opened, the dam broke and we flooded in. A major rearranging took place, as each defendant sought to find a place in front of the rail with his lawyer, and the lawyers jockeyed for the places of power. For a time, it was defendant lawyer versus defendant lawyer as they vied among themselves for the position in the coming battle they thought most advantageous for their clients.

Our group moved in front of the rail, but on the far side of the courtroom. There were only three plaintiffs— Millard Farmer, Pat Kelly and myself—but we had our own army of nine lawyers, their clerks and assistants. When all of the boxes of materials were stacked on our side of the room, it was cramped for space. Debbie and I were forced to sit in the front row of the area outside the railing designated for general seating of courtroom observers.

Finally, all of the setting up and shuffling for position was finished, and the loud voices in the room slowly became a low rumble.

When the Honorable Mary Lou Robinson reentered the courtroom, all activity ceased. Like it or not, ready or not, the time was at hand. Debbie moved closer to me so that our shoulders touched. Each side was allowed some time for an opening statement. Our attorneys explained what we intended to prove by the testimony that was forthcoming.

I had braced myself for the fact that the defendants were going to paint as bad a picture of me as possible, even resorting to rumors and hearsay. It did not take long for Ware's attorney, David Mullin of Amarillo, to go for my throat, telling the judge that I had a long history of abuse of my police authority and he intended to show it. Further, he said he would show that the bringing of indictments was the right thing to do. When he said there would be no evidence that Ware had any animosity toward me, I wanted to stand up and shout the truth: that this was all about Ware's animosity toward me.

After the opening statements, it was finally time for the plaintiffs to call witnesses. At the top of our list was Lubbock's former city manager, Larry Cunningham. He was called to the stand.

Gerald Goldstein had not been comfortable about calling Cunningham. In the weeks that had followed after the former city manager made his revelations to me in the mall, he had repeated his story to my lawyers, but would not give a sworn statement or deposition. We could understand why he was hesitant. However, Goldstein had the hard and fast rule that an attorney doesn't put anyone on the stand if he doesn't know what the witness is going to say. There was grave concern that, for whatever reason, Cunningham would have a sudden lapse in memory.

Nevertheless, I believed Larry Cunningham would honor the oath he would take upon being sworn in. Many people had not liked him while he was city manager, but in my dealings with him, I had come to know Larry as an honorable man. I felt he would not lie.

As Cunningham approached the witness stand, I was struck all over again by the smallness of his stature. This day I hoped he would have a lion's heart.

Gerald Goldstein stood up and strode to the witness stand. He had on a pair of tortoise shell glasses which highlighted his dark eyes in a way that was mesmerizing. He put them on whenever he looked at something up close and then took them off to address the court. The ear pieces were loose, and he had an interesting flick of the wrist which opened them so he could put them on one-handed. They made a little sound whenever he did this: snick snick. In a two-minute address, he would put those glasses on and off five or six times, snick snick snick.

Now, he took the glasses off and twirled them shut. Snick. Very quickly, Goldstein established Cunningham's identity: that he had formerly been Lubbock's city manager, that he had worked for the City of Lubbock since 1966, and that he had been city manager during 1992.

"Did there come a time when you had a conversation with either Travis Ware or Rebecca Atchley, his first assistant, with regard to my client, Bill Hubbard?" Goldstein asked, his face intent. The fire was there but subdued. He studied the witness.

Cunningham was outwardly nervous but composed in his answers. "Yes, sir. I did."

"Could you describe to the court, first, on how many occasions you had conversations with Travis Ware regarding Bill Hubbard?"

"There were several occasions."

Goldstein moved in quickly but cautiously. He asked tentatively, "Mr. Cunningham, were they by telephone or in person?"

Cunningham lifted his chin. "Two of them were by telephone and one was in person."

Goldstein caught the look and became more deliberate. "Did all of these come after my client had testified with respect to a cover-up of the Erdmann affair in April of nineteen ninety-two?"

Cunningham nodded. "Yes. They were in approximately August of ninety-two."

"Could you state for the court what Mr. Ware said with respect to my client?"

After Cunningham did so, Goldstein asked, "Why was he coming to you telling you that you needed—or 'we needed'—to do something about my client, the police officer, Bill Hubbard?"

"He had indicated that he had previously talked with the (police) chief, and that he felt that perhaps he needed to go ahead and bring this to my attention, and to see if I could help in dealing with some of the problems with regard to Mr. Hubbard."

A short interchange, then Cunningham went on, "He had indicated to me that Mr. Hubbard was not performing well and he was not respected by other police officers, and that he felt like we needed to do something with him. And when I told him that was a matter for the chief of police, he indicated to me that perhaps we could reassign him to a less sensitive area of the police department."

"Would that have taken him out of the homicide identification unit where he would be in contact with the medical examiner?"

Cunningham nodded. "That was my understanding of what he was requesting."

Rumbles in the courtroom. A few more questions, then: snick. The sound of Goldstein's glasses closing resounded in the courtroom. "Did there come an occasion when Travis Ware actually came to you in person?"

"Yes, sir." Cunningham looked Goldstein in the eyes.

"Who was with him, if anyone?"

I sensed Goldstein was reaching a precipice. In his eyes for a fleeting second, I could read doubts about a witness he couldn't control. Then he plunged forward and said again, "Who was with him?"

"No one. He was by himself. The first occasion, which I just described, he had asked me about some of these problems, complaints, and I told him I would talk to the chief of police—and I apologize for sharing this, but I need to tell you in order to explain his coming—but then I called him back a few days later after I talked with the chief and reported to him that the chief had looked into those allegations and reported to him (Ware) what the findings were.

"A few days after that, Mr. Ware came by my office. He dropped in, saying he wanted to visit with me a few minutes. He shared with me that he had just had lunch with Rebecca Atchley, I believe is her name, one of his attorneys, and that they had discussed what could be done with regard to Bill Hubbard. And that they felt probably the best approach and plan was to take the administrative findings of the police department to the grand jury in hopes of getting some kind of indictment. I asked him why he was telling me this, and he said as a courtesy so I wouldn't be surprised when something came out."

Quick, impressive and stylish, Goldstein flicked his glasses closed and leaned closer to Cunningham. "In essence, he told you that he and Rebecca Atchley intended to dig up this year-and-a-half old investigation and present the charges in that investigation to a grand jury to seek an indictment against Bill Hubbard?"

Cunningham nodded. "Well, he told me that they had discussed that and come up with this plan and that was what he said that they were going to do."

Goldstein's voice sounded through the pin-drop quiet of the courtroom. "That was their plan?"

Cunningham echoed, "That was their plan. I don't know what he was going to do. And he indicated that he did not want me to share this information with anyone."

"Did he warn you what would happen to you or what the effect of sharing that with someone would be?"

Cunningham shook his head. "He didn't say anything about what would happen. He just said that if there was a leak that he would know where it came from, because only Rebecca and he and I knew it. And I assured him that I would not say anything to anyone, because I didn't have any reason to. That was his business."

I sighed heavily.

"Question after question pitched by Gerald Goldstein, and Cunningham slugged them all over the center field fence," Debbie whispered. There was no doubt in our minds that Cunningham's testimony negated both Ware's words in the judge's chambers on the fourth of February and Mullin's insistence in his opening statement that Ware bore me no animosity. I watched Judge Robinson listening intently to Cunningham's every word.

When he stepped down from the witness stand after a very brief cross-examination, Debbie squeezed my hand. We felt our side had made a strong beginning toward proving the two things we needed to get the injunction. At least part of the motivation to seek charges against me was bad faith, and the charges were more likely initiated in retaliation for constitutionally protected activity.

The next morning's headline in the *Avalanche-Journal* read, "Doubts cast on Ware's claims." The story said, "Former Lubbock City Manager Larry Cunningham on Tuesday disputed Criminal District Attorney Travis Ware's denials that Ware sought the October 1992 indictment of police sergeant Bill Hubbard. Cunningham's testimony in federal court also implicated First Assistant Criminal District Attorney Rebecca Atchley in a plot with Ware to have Hubbard convicted."

Still, there was much work yet to do and much headway that needed to be made for Pat and Millard. There were still defense witnesses to come.

Later that day, Goldstein called to the stand Frank Briscoe, who had been the special prosecutor who got the indictments against me. As we prepared for my criminal trial date, it had seemed most peculiar that we had not been able to get Briscoe to respond to our motions for discovery. We had filed all the necessary requests to see the file that was used to indict me. Briscoe would not cough it up.

When we had subpoenaed him for this hearing, in spite of his being a defendant, we specifically requested that he bring with him this file. Now Goldstein called him to the witness stand to testify. He said he "forgot" the file. It was still in his office in Houston, but he promised to mail a copy as soon as he got back.

By that time, however, the hearing would be long over. There was one pressing question on all our minds at the moment. What was it about that file that they were trying to keep away from us?

Under Goldstein's pointed questioning, Briscoe admitted that he had done very little investigation into the case prior to taking it to the grand jury. He would not be specific, but he gave the impression that his total investigation had consisted of reading the material that had been sent to him.

Now, Goldstein looked at Briscoe and whipped open his glasses. Snick.

"Is this the type of investigation that normally is done in the attorney general's office?" Snick.

"Is this the way you did things while you were district attorney in Harris County?" Snick. Goldstein did not let up.

When court ended that day, Debbie and I were elated. We felt as if we had gained a great deal of ground and had kicked some major butt. My attorneys, on the other hand, were more reserved. They warned me that this was far from over and that I would "take some licks" before the other side was through. However, they promised we were not going to lie down and surrender. "We're going to wage one hell of a battle and we're going to win."

That night, I learned what being part of Gerald Goldstein's legal team was not about. It was not about sleep. It was about work. Hard work. Unceasing work.

After each break, or whenever a new witness came from a witness room into the courtroom for the first time, Goldstein reintroduced himself to the court. Every time he would say, "Gerald Goldstein, Your Honor, for plaintiff William Hubbard." I was proud that this guy, the captain of our team, was for me! With the organization skills of Cynthia Orr, who provided the oil, Goldstein was an absolute legal machine.

Goldstein approached the court battle with an attitude that can be explained only as obsessive mania. No point eluded him. He went over and over our case so there would be no loopholes. "Sleep is a luxury, not a necessity," he told me. "Three hours a night should be sufficient. And they don't have to be consecutive hours." After a night of trying to keep up with him, I decided it was amazing that the man had not dropped dead long ago because of this work methodology. Probably the only thing that saved him, I came to the conclusion, was the regimen of an athlete that Goldstein maintained. I noticed that he ate right and exercised every day.

Goldstein had given us our marching orders. Orr saw that we carried them out precisely. At one point, I was given the task of arranging and putting reference tabs on a pile of paperwork. Being the organizer that I am, I decided to help out beyond what Cynthia had asked, and I reordered the documents in what I believed would be an easier way to access. I found out real fast that Goldstein is accustomed to working in a particular manner, and Orr keeps things exactly the way he likes them. I got to do the entire project over again, and this time I did it as specified!

While each team member finished their project, Goldstein catnapped. We were told to wake him up so he could review what we had done. I made the mistake of allowing him to sleep longer than it took for me to complete my assignment. I did it solely out of concern for his well-being, but I got set straight on that as well. When my work was pronounced okay, I could go to bed. Then Goldstein got up and worked through the night on the material we had given to him. About 5:00 A.M. or so, he got another hour of sleep. After that, he got up again and started making wake-up calls to whomever he needed. We got in a couple hours of more work, showered, shaved, and began to dress. That night, a snowstorm had hit.

Early that second morning, the first order of the day was to get cars dug out of the heavy snow and jump-started so all of us could get to the courthouse, with the piles of "stuff" we lugged.

The musty smelling courthouse, built in the days before metal detectors and courthouse security, was badly in need of modernization. The entry lobby outside the elevators was small, and into it had been crowded a conveyer belt and metal detector, like the ones in airports. We caused quite a logjam when twenty lawyers plus helpers, many with boxes of legal documents on hand trucks or dollies, tried to get through the checkpoint. Goldstein, Farmer, Lane, Stone, Debbie and Denette remained friendly and talkative, while the defense lawyers were tight-jawed and taciturn. Some elected to use the stairs—boxes and all—rather than ride on the elevator with us to the fifth floor where the courtroom was.

When we got off, the acoustics of the tall ceiling came alive with sound. "It makes you feel you have to be careful even whispering," Debbie murmured. "The sound amplifies for blocks."

I nodded.

When court was in session, we opted for passing notes. We didn't want to be corrected by Judge Robinson, who missed nothing as she looked down from the bench.

The second day of testimony, Wednesday, February 17th, Lubbock Police Detective Sergeant Randy McGuire spent a lengthy time on the witness stand.

McGuire had not only been the point man on Pat Kelly's investigation of the young woman killed by the intoxicated district attorney, but after the D.A.'s people brought over the initial statement, he had also been one of the investigators assigned to the court of inquiry.

There was no doubt that he was extremely knowledge-
able about the entire situation concerning Erdmann's
autopsy.

McGuire is an intelligent officer and has spent
enough time in police work and on witness stands that
he does not get rattled under intense questioning. "It
must be difficult for you to sit still and watch Pat Kelly's
lawyers try to wear McGuire down," Debbie whispered. I
nodded. I counted Randy as a friend and a respected supervisor. He had been my sergeant when I was involved
in the only shooting incident of my career, back in 1983.
It was largely McGuire's compassion and professionalism
that night that had helped me survive the situation from
an emotional standpoint. Nevertheless, though I liked
him personally, I strongly disagreed with his present position, one that he obviously believed in.

He handled each question directed toward him
thoughtfully, and he projected an air of willing disclosure.
He testified about the investigation he had made, along
with Detective Doug Davenport, into Kelly's Canyon testimony. These statements made Kelly look bad.

Before he got off the stand, however, Kelly's counsel
was able to introduce documents that solidified for the
court the time frame as to when each development had
occurred on the day of the autopsy. That time frame
seemed to cast doubt on some of the statements
McGuire and Davenport had made.

"That seems to give a lot of credence to Kelly's statements," Debbie said quietly when we met during a break.

"Thank goodness the truth's coming out," I replied.

The headway gained in Pat's behalf while McGuire
testified had been small, but our hope was that the judge
had caught it. Once again, Mary Lou Robinson seemed
to be listening intently.

Later that day, Justice of the Peace Jim Hansen of Lubbock took the stand and testified as to the problems he

had in working with Dr. Erdmann. He told of the "lost head" case and how that had come about. He also told of two detectives coming to his office shortly after he had assumed his position and those two officers telling him about "problems" with Dr. Erdmann. One of those detectives, Hansen told the court, was Randy McGuire. The other was my predecessor, Thomas Esparza.

The justice told of Erdmann's becoming obstinate in providing autopsy reports to the justices of the peace who ordered the autopsies in the first place. Hansen testified that, as he confronted Erdmann about providing autopsy reports, Erdmann referred to Ware as his "boss," and Erdmann believed he needed to answer only to Ware. It was an established fact that Ware's signature was on Erdmann's county contract, but it was still not known why.

During our third day in court, we called Captain Bill Knox to the stand. Knox had been my captain while I was assigned to the Street Crimes Unit, had been the primary investigator into the allegations made against me during the internal investigation in the summer of 1991, and was also the captain over the Street Crimes officers when some of them testified before the grand jury in October that led to my indictment. Knox had brought his file from the internal investigation to court, and it was introduced into testimony.

As evidence was entered, if it had to do with Millard Farmer it was preceded by an "F." If it had to do with Pat Kelly it had a "K." Evidence that was mostly to do with me was labeled "H." The file from Knox was entered into evidence as H-13.

Captain Knox testified about how the internal investigation had been done and about the statements he had taken from various witnesses after allegations had been made. His investigation led him to conclude that I had not committed any crimes, and, if any departmental procedures had been violated, they were minor. Knox's investigative file was fat with notes and documents that were very much in support of my position and disproved the serious allegations that were made against me in the internal investigation.

Knox was also questioned about the day after I was indicted, when he attended a meeting with Colonel George Ewing and Sergeant John Gomez, who was the new supervisor of the Street Crimes Unit. Knox testified that Randy Atchley had asked for the meeting because he felt he owed his supervisors an explanation as to how these indictments had come about.

Knox said Randy Atchley had told the assembled supervisors that he and his wife, Rebecca, were watching me on television after my testimony in Canyon, and he asked her, "Why didn't y'all do something about that (expletive) when you had the chance?"

Bill Knox's testimony went a long way toward validating the testimony of Larry Cunningham. The idea of a dark plan to have me indicted which had started with the Atchleys and grew to include Travis Ware loomed in the air. The next morning, headlines screamed, "Witness impugns Atchley's motives" and detailed that police captain Bill Knox's testimony "gave weight to Tuesday's testimony by former City Manager Larry Cunningham that Lubbock Criminal District Attorney Travis Ware and his first assistant conspired to have police sergeant Bill Hubbard indicted."

Kelly's lawyers then put Detective Doug Davenport on the stand briefly to demonstrate that there were inconsistencies in the statements of that detective and McGuire. The two officers were in conflict when it came to determining exactly when Kelly had divulged certain information to them concerning problems with the pedestrian death

autopsy and what they did with that information during
the court of inquiry.

Next, Pat Kelly took the witness stand, after his team
decided that the judge would need to hear from Pat
himself to clarify the key issues that had come to the
forefront during previous testimony.

Pat handled questioning from both sides very well and
in a professional manner. He testified that he had been
afraid to speak out about the Erdmann problems until
he was put under oath in Canyon out of a fear of retaliation "for opening up a can of worms."

It appeared Kelly had been indicted on one count for
testifying that a meeting had taken place with Ware, Erdmann, the accident witness, and the justice of the peace,
at the end of which the reported intoxication level of the
victim had seemed to change. Kelly clarified that his testimony had been that the J.P.'s secretary said that the
meeting had taken place, and Kelly had believed her. It
was important for Judge Robinson to understand the
subtle yet distinct and important differences between
the two accounts.

Millard Farmer also took the stand and was questioned under direct examination by Goldstein. In his
charismatic way, Farmer told about his background in
the legal profession and how he came to be involved in
the Canyon case. He made it plain that he had received
little payment in return for his services.

The day of Millard's fateful visit with Woodson Rowan
was recounted.

"To me it clearly indicates," I said, leaning toward
Debbie, "that Millard was on a quest for truth and not on
a mission to try to get a witness—Erdmann—to lie or
change his testimony."

Most of us had brought only enough clothes for two
days in court. By Friday morning, the fourth day of testimony, we were recycling our shirts with cologne, airing

them out, and then wearing them again with a different tie. Still, the end didn't seem in sight. We all hoped fervently that this would be the last day, but had begun to think we might be back next week.

Though it wasn't the last, Friday was a telling day. When Rebecca Atchley was called to the stand, it was not the Rebecca Atchley I knew. Instead of the hard-looking, business-suit-and-briefcase prosecuting attorney, the woman who came to court was attired in a flowered dress with a peasant collar, and she spoke in a soft, little-girl voice and wore a wide-eyed, innocent look. The Rebecca up there on the stand did not look like the kind of person who could prosecute a felon in the courtroom.

During the early part of her testimony, the story Rebecca Atchley told painted a picture of a benign relationship between her husband, herself and me.

With a flick of his glasses Goldstein asked, "And what is the relationship between Randy and you on the one hand, and Mr. Hubbard, prior to 1992?"

"In August of '90, before Randy and I were married, he was assigned to the Street Crimes Division after being transferred to the Homicide Division. And so Bill Hubbard would have been his immediate supervisor. I have known Bill Hubbard since I started working in Lubbock in 1987."

"Had you had a friendly relationship with him?"

Rebecca looked thoughtful for a moment, as if trying to remember, and then responded, "Fairly so."

"And was there any animosity between you and Mr. Hubbard prior to 1992?"

"I wouldn't describe it as animosity. Distrust by myself of Mr. Hubbard would be what I call it," she said looking at the judge.

"Did you still like Mr. Hubbard?"

"Yes."

"Do you still like him?" Goldstein asked pointedly.

She drew a breath. "Yes."

After some more questions about her feelings toward me, Goldstein brought Travis Ware into the picture, and Rebecca's testimony became very interesting. Atchley became almost chatty for a few moments as she and Goldstein went back and forth.

She told him, "He (Bill Hubbard) talked about how Travis Ware had sat across the table at Carrie McClain's graduation dinner. She is one of our—was one of our investigators in our office that Travis hired." She went on, "He said something about that Travis had sat across the table from Bill Hubbard's wife and bragged about how he had gotten Bill Hubbard in this internal affairs investigation, and that he was bragging about giving Carrie McClain a job and how many favors he had done Carrie McClain."

As she spoke she flashed a disdainful look. "At that time, I was very uncomfortable because my husband had made a complaint against Bill Hubbard. And so basically, my answer to all of that was, it was just a bad thing for everybody all the way around."

Rebecca Atchley continued testifying that I had a vendetta against Travis Ware and that I constantly attacked his character. Despite her demure appearance, looking at her sent chills up my spine.

Soon the questions turned to the matter of Ralph Erdmann. Atchley painted a very different picture of Erdmann than I or the media had come to know.

"Okay," Goldstein began, "Now, are you familiar with Dr. Erdmann; is that right?"

"Yes, I am," she said matter-of-factly.

"Now, up until January 1992, had you put on Dr. Erdmann as a witness in any cases?"

"A few."

"And you had dealt with him in connection with some cases?"

"Yes, I had."

Goldstein continued with a steady stream of questions, the only other sound being the snick, snick of his glasses. "And you also knew that he was involved in cases that other attorneys in your office were handling and had been involved in cases when you were up in Potter County?"

"Yes, sir."

"With respect to Dr. Erdmann, at that time, had you been made aware of any complaints—first of all, complaints of Dr. Erdmann?"

She bit her lip. "I can't recall anything that anyone ever complained about other than he never showed up on time and he never brought his Autopsy Protocol with him, and he was real hard to get to answer the question on the stand. He would ramble and start talking about other things and it was—he was difficult to handle on the witness stand for anybody."

"Was he the kind of witness that would give you a few hours to woodshed him before you got to put him on?"

A ripple of laughter passed through the courtroom.

She reddened. "I—not me. I have never spent more than maybe a minute with him prior to putting him on the stand."

"And why was that?" Goldstein asked.

"You were lucky to get him there to testify."

"And did you—in any of the cases that you had handled, had you ever seen him destroyed on the cross-examination?"

She replied confidently, "I never saw the cause of death in any case I tried with Dr. Erdmann ever challenged in any way."

Atchley continued to answer questions about Erdmann for a few more minutes until Goldstein turned toward the subject of my indictment. In response to his questions about her role in the matter, Atchley denied that the idea to put together enough select documents to get an indictment against me had been hatched in her living room. With an innocent, almost shy look on her face, she told the judge that it could not have been as a result of a television broadcast because she did not watch television news.

A first assistant district attorney in a county the size of Lubbock who doesn't watch television news? Incredible! Then she said she didn't read newspapers. If this were true, she had to be one of the least informed public officials in the business. *Surely, the judge won't buy this testimony,* I prayed.

One of Pat Kelly's attorneys, Charlie Dunn of Lubbock, then directed some questions at Atchley concerning the knowledge she and the Ware office had about Erdmann's incompetence. Dunn had defended Zane Lee Ham when Erdmann had made the incredible "fifty-five-hour" testimony that had put the dead child in Ham's care when the injuries were allegedly inflicted. That was the case the court of appeals had thrown out and had chastised the prosecution for its incompetence.

Dunn asked Atchley if she was aware of that case having been overturned. "Based on your education, training, and experience, and knowing that this happened, shouldn't you have launched an investigation?"

"I don't know. I think I'd be concerned about him," Atchley answered.

"Yet, Ralph Erdmann was used by the D.A. for five more years!" Dunn retorted. And Atchley admitted that Erdmann's testimony was used to help obtain more convictions even after the overturning of the Ham case.

Even after acknowledging that she knew of the overturning of the Ham case, that she thought she would be "concerned" about Erdmann, and in earlier testimony, stating that Erdmann was an unreliable and unpredictable witness, minutes later she contradicted herself

by telling the court that she never questioned Erdmann's knowledge of pathology.

"I had no reason to question him," she said.

At the end of the day on Friday, Rebecca Atchley was
still on the witness stand. Gerald Goldstein was convinced that Atchley had crossed herself up several times.
"But I want to be sure," he said as we gathered up our
boxes, "so my next line of questioning can be precise."
Before we left the courthouse, he went to the office of
the court reporter and asked what it would cost to have
a copy of Atchley's testimony up to this point in his
hands by Sunday afternoon. The court reporter named
his price. Goldstein wrote him a check. I almost had to
be picked off the floor. It was about a week's pay for a
police sergeant.

Thank God for the weekend. It was good to get some
time off, if only to get some sleep. Five days straight of
working for Gerald Goldstein had about killed me.
Debbie and I went home to Lubbock. Goldstein and his
entourage flew to Colorado both to work and to ski a
little. Farmer and his people took off for New Mexico for
a dose of culture in Santa Fe and Taos. Mark Lane and
Jed Stone were too far away from home to go back for
just two days, and they were too tired to visit even the
best sights of New Mexico. They opted for some rest in
Amarillo.

Saturday night, Debbie and I had a commitment to go
to the Lubbock Advertising Federation's annual awards
banquet. We felt we needed to honor the commitment,
even though we were too exhausted to want to be there.

The news media had saturated the public with the
events in Amarillo. This made us apprehensive but,
when Debbie and I stepped onto the stage Saturday
night, we were greeted by a standing ovation. It made us
feel so good to be respected by Debbie's colleagues and

business associates. It helped ease our fatigue and made us glad to be among friends.

Our weekend was over way too soon, and Sunday evening we began the trip back to Amarillo.

Rebecca Atchley resumed her testimony on the stand on Monday morning. Goldstein had the transcript of her testimony from Friday. He asked several pointed questions that seemed to leave her groping for explanations to explain her previous statements. She continued to insist that she and her husband played no role in my indictment.

Goldstein was about to slash the proper portrait of a credible Ralph Erdmann. He took off his glasses with a small flourish and dug in. Snick.

"You indicated, I believe, that one of the forensic pathologists who did a review of Dr. Erdmann's autopsy reports was a David Hoblit, I believe?"

"That is correct."

"Is it your—"

Atchley broke in. "I didn't call him a forensic pathologist."

"All right. Perhaps I misheard. He is not a forensic pathologist; is that a fair statement?"

"That is correct."

"And the reviews that he and Dr. Bux did were not, in fact, of a determination, a reautopsy, were they?"

"No, they were not."

"In fact, they did not review the quality of Dr. Erdmann's autopsy reports or the accuracy of Dr. Erdmann's testimony, rather, they only focused on, in fact, what had killed the victims; is that a fair statement?"

"I am not sure if they looked at the accuracy of his testimony or not. I don't know about that."

Putting his glasses on, Goldstein inclined his head. He

was about to close that loophole. "Your Honor, if I may tender to the Court Plaintiff's Exhibit H-33. And if I may display it to the witness."

Judge Robinson nodded her approval and gestured to him to continue.

"Were you aware of the fact that it was reported in the newspaper that Hoblit had told the attorney that his review of these reports was focused on what had killed the victims?"

"I am reading from the third column, last paragraph, Your Honor, of Plaintiff's Exhibit H-33," Goldstein explained, turning to the judge. Turning back to the witness stand, he continued.

"What had killed the victims, not the quality of Erdmann's autopsy reports or the accuracy of Erdmann's testimony. Were you aware of that statement by Dr. Hoblit?"

"No, I was not."

"You had indicated, I believe, and there was—if I may use Counsel's chart—that sometime prior—and I understand your testimony was that Dr. Ralph Erdmann was indicted in Hockley County on February 24th, is that correct, of '92?"

"I believe that is when he was indicted."

"All right. And is it safe to say, and I am correct in assuming that, in fact, you first had an opportunity to speak with the criminal district attorney of Hockley County, a Gary Goff, sometime prior to the February 24, 1992, date; is that correct?"

"Yes."

"Do you recall, if you can, when prior to that date you first had an opportunity to speak with Mr. Goff about the—I believe it was the autopsy of a Craig Newman; is that correct?"

"Yes."

"That was the deceased?"

"Yes."

"And am I correct that, in fact, this Craig Newman case had come up because a relative—"

Atchley bristled, "I have no personal knowledge of that, why it came up."

"Well, were you aware of the fact that what triggered the indictment was the fact that Dr. Erdmann had filed an autopsy report—"

"Yes." She sighed.

"—weighing a spleen"

"Yes."

"And this would have been the deceased Craig Newman's spleen?"

"Yes."

"And that, in fact, a brother of Mr. Newman had come forward when he saw the report to the newspaper. The concern was that the deceased had been pronounced dead of a drug overdose of some sort?"

Atchley shook her head.

"I don't know."

"But what you did know was that Dr. Erdmann had indicated that during the autopsy, he had, in fact, extracted or removed the body organs, including the spleen, and had weighed it and gave a weight to the spleen?"

"That is correct."

His eyes brightened. The glasses came off. Snick.

"And that, in fact, the brother came forward and indicated to—publicly that he was aware of the fact that his brother had previously had his spleen and gallbladder removed, and that caused a concern?"

"I don't know how any of it came to be. I only know what the allegation was."

"Well, and the allegation clearly was that Dr. Erdmann had not, in fact, removed a nonexistent spleen and weighed it?"

A long silent moment. Then she answered.

"Yes."

Goldstein's lips twitched in a slight smile.

"All right. And this would have been prior to—"

"If I may, Your Honor."

"Yes."

"—prior to February 24th; is that a fair statement?"

"What would be prior to?"

"When you learned that, in fact, there was an indictable offense against Dr. Erdmann, that the—"

"Yes."

"And, in fact, how did you come to speak with the criminal district attorney of Hockley County about this matter? Did he call you or did you call him?"

"The best I can remember, it seems that he came back to our office. He had been in to visit with Travis, and I guess told him about the fact that he was planning to present this to a grand jury. Shortly after he left—and he may not even have left our office. I am not sure whether he left and came back or whether he was still there. Travis sat me down and he said, you know, 'You are not going to believe this,' and told me what Gary Goff had told him."

"So suffice it to say, prior to February 24, 1992, your boss, Travis Ware, had been apprised of the fact that Dr. Erdmann had apparently claimed to have performed an autopsy and removed a spleen, when, in fact, he had not?"

Once again Goldstein forced an admission.

"Yes, he did."

"And I believe you even assisted in preparing the indictment at the request of your own boss?"

"No. What I did at the request of my boss was to help Gary however he needed it."

"And was that one of the ways?"

"What?"

"I'm sorry. Was that one of the ways?"

"He told me to get him a copy of any—the orders to exhume a body, which I did."

"And you forwarded those to Gary Goff?"

"I handed them to him."

"All right. The district attorney—"

"Yes."

"—of Hockley County? Did you hand them to him at that point or was that on another day?"

"I don't remember."

"Suffice it to say, you did meet with him on several occasions, either by telephone or in person, discussing with him the preparation of an indictment—"

"Yes."

"—to present to the grand jury in Hockley County?"

"I believe once or twice we had a phone conversation about that."

"And in addition to assisting him with determining what charges would be applicable to such a crime and perhaps the parameters of the indictment, you also helped him with the preparation of the paperwork necessary to exhume the body of Craig Newman?"

"I gave him a copy of an exhumation motion and order."

A few minutes later he forced another.

"And, in fact, did you later learn that the body of Craig Newman was, in fact, exhumed and, in fact, it was determined that he had not had a spleen and that Dr. Erdmann had not, in fact, conducted an autopsy to weigh that organ?"

"That is what I heard."

"Did you have any further discussions with your boss, Travis Ware, about these startling revelations that you and your boss learned sometime prior to February 4, 1992? When I say 'startling,' I assume they were startling to you."

"They were startling to both of us."

"You had relied upon Dr. Erdmann's testimony and his autopsies in numerous cases?"

"Yes."

Goldstein could not resist a jest.

"Sort of like the clock that strikes thirteen, the concern you had was that called into question almost everything that had come before?"

Atchley didn't smile.

"Yes, in my mind it did."

"And you discussed that with your boss, Mr. Ware?"

"I don't know that we sat down and specifically discussed that. We certainly thought that and took steps to see if that were, in fact, true."

"There was no question in both of your minds that these revelations caused you concern about Dr. Erdmann both in terms of his autopsies and his prospective testimony? Any lawyer would feel that way?"

"Sure, it did."

"Calling your attention to April 2, 1992, and that, to refresh your recollection, would have been the date that my client, Bill Hubbard, testified in Canyon City, which you have related to, it would have been April 2, 1992."

"Something to that effect, that everybody was saying what he was saying was that it was a cover-up, and he didn't think that is what Bill Hubbard had said."

"Let me call you attention to—"

"If I may, Your Honor."

"Yes," the judge nodded.

With an almost undetectable movement, Goldstein's glasses were back on. He glanced down at some papers before continuing.

"Plaintiff's exhibit H-30, which is a transcript of those proceedings, and ask you—in particular, calling your attention to Page 186, Lines 13 and 14, and ask you if the statement, 'He, Travis Ware, enjoined all of us there to keep that meeting quiet,' a reference to the February 5, 1992, meeting.

"Would that be something you would interpret to be a cover-up; that is, keep it quiet?"

"No," she said firmly.

"The next line, continuing at Line 15 on Page 186 of Plaintiff's Exhibit H-30. QUESTION: 'Not to mention the contents of that meeting?' 'Yes, sir.' Would that indicate to you that someone was testifying as to at least a cover-up?"

Atchley hesitated then replied. "Not necessarily."

Goldstein was not about to let go.

"Calling your attention—continuing on that same page, Page 186 of Plaintiff's Exhibit H-30, beginning at Line 22, it is again, 'Did he tell you why to keep it quiet?' ANSWER: 'Yes, sir.' QUESTION: 'Why did he tell you?' ANSWER: 'He said, "because if it gets out, the defense attorneys will have a field day with it."'"

Snick! Off came the glasses. Goldstein's eyes blazed but his voice was cold, sober.

"Was that a concern that either you or Travis Ware shared?"

"I don't even know what it is talking about. What is the 'it'?"

"'It' refers to a February 5th meeting at which Mr. Ware discussed matters relating to Dr. Erdmann with several members of the Lubbock City Police force."

"If the meeting gets out?"

"If the subject of what he had discussed got out."

"Well, that depends on what the subject was, I guess."

As I sat there listening to this exchange, it appeared to me that Rebecca Atchley was feigning ignorance or confusion to avoid answering the question.

"Did you ever," Goldstein paused then went on, "just out of curiosity, were you in Lubbock, Texas, during the month of February 1992?"

"Yes, sir."

"And in that regard, I believe you had indicated that prior to August of 1992, you were positive that your boss, Travis Ware, didn't have any information with regard to the internal investigation regarding Bill Hubbard, was that—did I understand you correct?"

"Yes, that is correct."

"All right. Now, that—"

Atchley interrupted, "When you say 'didn't have any information,' he didn't know what the allegations were or what was contained in the statements. I think he knew there was an investigation."

"Now, that date would have been during August of 1992; is that correct?"

"Yes."

"And that is when you indicated that you and your husband had that conversation; is that correct?"

"Yes."

"A conversation in which your husband had suggested, 'Why didn't we get Bill Hubbard when we had a chance?'; is that correct?"

"That is not what he said," Atchley snapped.

Goldstein wasn't put off.

"Is that what you said?"

"That is not what I said either."

Goldstein stared at her.

"Let me ask you in that regard—" He paused then and looked at the judge. Snick.

Goldstein looked down at his notes. "Your Honor, calling the Court's attention, if I may, to Plaintiff's Exhibit H-5, a copy of which has been tendered to both counsel and the Court."

Snick. He looked back at Atchley, his face betraying for a moment disgust, then he said coolly, "Were you familiar with a newspaper report of a statement made by your boss, Travis Ware, to the effect that, 'The prosecutor, Mr. Ware, said his office knew little about the case until late August when his chief assistant's husband—I presume that is referring to your husband, Randy Atchley?"

"I assume so."

"—when his chief assistant's husband, a police officer, began talking about problems with Sergeant Hubbard and asked, 'Why didn't y'all get Hubbard when you had your shot?', close quote."

Mullin stepped in. "Your Honor, I am going to object to him using documents that are fourth level hearsay and they know they are fourth level hearsay and putting them up on the screen and using them as exhibits when there is no way that is admissible."

Goldstein wouldn't desist. "Your Honor, I believe even at trial, under Rule 801(b)(2)(d), these are admissions of a party opponent. They are nonhearsay. This is a statement attributable to a party—"

Judge Robinson nodded at Goldstein and spoke. "You can cross-examine using these documents."

"Thank you."

Goldstein went on with his attack. "Is the quote, attributable to your boss, not accurate as far as your recollection goes?"

Atchley admitted. "It is probably pretty close to part of what he said."

Goldstein's voice took on a razor edge. "In that regard, was your boss also correct, and is it correct when he is quoted as suggesting that it was a coincidence that two Lubbock police officers and a noted capital defense lawyer who helped to reveal Dr. Ralph Erdmann's wrongdoing both face criminal indictment?"

Atchley appeared rattled. "I don't know what your question was. I'm sorry."

"My question is," he hammered her, "Did you ever hear your boss suggest that the fact that two Lubbock police officers and a noted capital defense lawyer who have helped bring about the revelations about Dr. Ralph Erdmann now face criminal charges?"

Atchley denied that Ware was involved with anything but Hubbard's indictment.

A few minutes later Goldstein picked up on this.

"You had indicated that your boss, Travis Ware, did not—and you were certain, or positive that he had only fleeting familiarity with the investigation of my client, Bill Hubbard, some year and a half before; is that correct?"

She appeared to nod and he went on.

"And did you—or were you made aware of the fact that on the very day after my client's testimony, your boss was quoted in the newspaper as bringing up my client's, Bill Hubbard's, investigation from some year and a half before in the same article that reported in headlines in your city that this officer had testified that Mr. Ware had been involved in a cover-up?"

She drew a deep breath.

"What is the question?"

"Were you aware of that fact?"

"No. No, I was not."

"You had indicated, I believe, if I am correct, that your husband had been concerned for some time about activities by my client, Bill Hubbard, is that correct?"

"I think what I testified to was that he had been concerned about what happened on the investigation. He had not been under Bill Hubbard but for a little—I am trying to think—a little less than a year when this happened."

"So nothing happened between the investigation and my client's indictment of any consequence or you would have turned that over to the attorney general's office, as well, I presume?"

"If I knew about it, I would have."

"And if your husband had been complaining about it, you would have known about it?"

"If he knew about it, he would have."

"All right. And you didn't, and he didn't?"

"That is correct."

"Were you aware of the fact that in the file which has now been marked Plaintiff's Exhibit H-13 was an affidavit from your husband?"

"Yes."

Goldstein turned to the judge and asked permission to show Atchley an affidavit. Upon her approval, he gave the affidavit to Rebecca and let her look it over.

After a moment she looked up at him and said, "It is my understanding that is what happened."

He glared at her.

"Were you aware of the fact that your husband had sworn at the time of the investigation that whatever problems that they were having with Bill Hubbard, 'These times occur when members were'—that is, the complaints about his manner with them, 'when members were unable to perform to his expectations, which were many times out of our control'? Did you know that your husband had sworn to that?"

Atchley admitted she did.

And then Goldstein delivered the coup d'état.

"And then the following paragraph which is general, your husband swore, 'Even though I have disagreed with Sergeant Bill Hubbard's methods at times, I feel that he is a very intelligent, hardworking and dedicated individual and that his intentions were to produce what he felt was expected of him.'"

Goldstein watched closely as she answered.

Then he turned slightly from her for a moment, caught my eye with his and winked.

When questioned concerning why she and Ware recused themselves from prosecuting the case against me and opted to take it to the attorney general's office instead, Atchley said it was because she felt Ware's office would not be able to maintain objectivity. A short while later, under Goldstein's prodding, she stated that, in her opinion, she did not have a problem maintaining her objectivity when prosecuting cases where her police officer husband was a witness. She said she had never recused herself from any case where Randy was a witness or the arresting officer.

Randy Atchley was then briefly called to the stand. He denied that the idea to gather information and set the ball in motion to get me indicted was triggered by seeing news about my Canyon testimony on television. Just like his wife, Atchley testified that he didn't read newspapers or watch television news. His memory became cloudy, however, when Goldstein questioned him as to precisely when and what he told his sergeant, John Gomez, about how the indictments against me came about.

Atchley's foggy memory was nothing to be concerned about, however, because Sergeant Gomez was sitting outside in a witness room waiting to be called to testify, and we did not believe there would be anything at all wrong with his memory when it was his turn to get on the stand.

Meanwhile, there were other important battles to wage.

20

The Team Fights On

The sixth day of testimony turned out to be of huge significance. We could hardly believe that Judge Robinson had allowed the hearing, despite her stated time constraints, to continue this long. We had expected a two-day hearing, and now we were in the second week. At every possible opportunity, the judge reminded everyone to "keep it moving," but it also seemed that she was going to hear everyone out so there would be no crying at the end that any one individual did not get to have his say, call his witnesses, or cross-examine someone else's witnesses.

Now we awaited a major player. Tall, elegant in his expensive suit and heavily starched white shirt, his tan incongruous with the subfreezing temperatures outside, Travis Ware was called to the stand by his own attorney, David Mullin. As he took his seat, Ware exhibited an air of confidence. Mullin lobbed him the easy questions and got the same kind of answers. As he testified, however, the press later reported, Ware's confidence gave way to cockiness, an attitude many felt Judge Robinson would not like.

After learning in February of 1992 that Erdmann was to be indicted in Hockley County, Ware testified, he "was eager to find out if Lubbock County had been victimized by misconduct."

Ware answered questions concerning the February 5th meeting about Dr. Erdmann that had been held in his office, and his reflections on my testimony about it in April.

"Hubbard did not tell the truth in his testimony," Ware said under oath. "Hubbard didn't say there was a cover-up, but he also didn't say there wasn't a cover-up. I defended Hubbard and said he didn't say anything about a cover-up."

This testimony was definitely confusing to me. In three short sentences he had told the judge that I did not tell the truth and that he had defended me! Under questioning from Goldstein, Ware then acknowledged that, a couple of days after my Canyon testimony, he had told a reporter that I had not lied under oath. Ware knew we had that reporter waiting in a witness room just in case he wanted to deny having said it.

"I recall saying Hubbard did not lie," Ware told the court. "He did not tell the truth. He didn't lie, but he grossly distorted the truth."

To me, it appeared that Ware was trying to tiptoe all around by not confirming what he had said to reporters at the time, and also by not saying that my testimony was accurate. We had a full transcript of my Canyon testimony ready to introduce as evidence in case Judge Robinson wanted to see for herself that my testimony had been factual. In addition, witnesses still were available who could corroborate what I had said.

Ware acknowledged under questioning that he had gone so far as to contact Chief Don Bridgers even before a word of testimony had been offered by me in Canyon, because he was concerned about what I would say. He said it was because, after the February 5th meeting, he did not trust me.

When Ware left the stand, an assistant from the Ware office testified in very general terms about a case of mine he "remembered" from years ago. The prosecutor did not remember it well enough to present the actual file in court, but he gave sworn testimony to Judge Robinson about the case just the same. It had to do with my preventing an arrestee from swallowing drug evidence as the unhandcuffed suspect was trying to stab me with a used syringe.

This prosecutor evidently forgot the part about what the suspect was trying to do with the syringe and tried to make the judge believe I was some sort of a brutal cop.

"If there is a 'gift' Bill has in police work," Debbie often says, "it is the ability to remember names, incidents, license numbers of suspect vehicles and other such information for long periods of time." I smiled at her. While this prosecutor was testifying, I wrote in the margin of my notepad the name of the person who had been the arrestee in that incident and the address where the altercation had taken place, even though it had been about four years earlier.

Even though this prosecutor's testimony really had nothing to do with the questions before the court in this hearing and sought only to soil my reputation, at the next recess, I had the police report from that incident faxed to Amarillo. I was able to locate in my box of files the sheet the prosecutor had filled out when the case was originally submitted for filing of charges.

The report differed considerably from the vague generalities the prosecutor had testified to, and the prosecution sheet in his own handwriting had commended me for my restraint. The report clearly showed that a felony could have been filed on the offender, but the prosecutor had filed a simple resisting arrest charge.

We entered the report and prosecution sheet into evidence without a great deal of fanfare so that Judge Robinson could see once again the kinds of smear tactics that were going on here. They really had nothing to do with the questions before the court about the motivation behind the present charges against Kelly, Farmer, and me.

Next, Lubbock County morgue manager Woodson Rowan briefly took the stand. It was difficult for me to see Woodson as a defendant in the suit, because he and I had always gotten along and worked well together. But Woodson was a key element in the charges against Millard Farmer.

Rowan testified that, after Farmer and his investigator had visited with him, he called and left a message with Erdmann's wife about it. He also called Erdmann's attorney, who at the time was John Montford. It was Montford who then called Randy Sherrod's office. However, Sherrod took no action on the information until about six months later. Then he did so on the day before Farmer was to oppose Sherrod in the courtroom.

Rowan did not feel threatened or intimidated by Farmer's visit, he told the court, and he had nothing but respect for me. It had been others who had interpreted Rowan's notification of Farmer's visit as completely different from the way he intended it.

As the lunch recess was announced on Tuesday, our attorneys were finally provided with a copy of the file that had been used to indict me. These were the documents that had been selected and compiled by Rebecca Atchley and that had been hand delivered by she and Travis Ware to Assistant Attorney General Shane Phelps. The same file special

prosecutor Frank Briscoe had not, despite our lawful rights
to it, turned over to us for so long.

Though we were all curious to see it, Denette was chafing at the bit and grabbed it first. "Finally," she said exasperatedly.

"I'll second that." Debbie, who had walked up, shook
her head.

While the other members of the team ate the Goldstein health fare of fresh fruit and saltine crackers and discussed strategies together in the courthouse conference room, Denette Vaughn was busy poring over the files in front of her. Debbie and I walked over.

"Watching Denette work is entertaining in itself," I
whispered to Debbie.

"Prime time," she quipped.

Denette's "piling system" consisted of a pile of papers here and another pile there. In Lubbock, her whole office looked like a disaster zone. But at any given moment, she could dig into the exact pile and come out with the document she needed. "Always piled but never wild" was her motto.

This lunch break was no exception. Denette was absolutely driven to know why the opposition had tried so hard to keep these documents from getting into our hands. With testimony set to resume in less than an hour, she had precious little time to find her answer, but she wasn't about to fail.

The other thing I knew about Denette's work habits was that she works best under the greatest amount of pressure. I have often mused that she was probably the kid in school who waited until the night before a term paper was due to even start on it, stayed up all night doing it, and turned in an "A" paper the next morning. It was not how I would choose to do things, but it works for her. I have seen her repeatedly turn in the winning performance at the last possible minute. Needless to say,

it can also drive a client crazy, feeling he or she is hanging out on a limb until the very end.

Today was no different. The piles were growing in all directions while Denette gradually became submerged. I
pulled up a chair and watched. With a pen, a highlighter,
and a pad of sticky notes in front of her, she made notes.

"I want to know," she told me, "what is different about
the indictment file when compared to the police department file?"

To learn that, she compared one to the other, page by
page. It soon became obvious that the file that Travis
Ware and Rebecca Atchley handed Shane Phelps, the
one which ultimately landed on Frank Briscoe's desk
and in front of the grand jury, was quite a bit thinner
than the police department's internal investigation file.

Denette went on comparing the indictment file to the internal affairs file, explaining to us what she found as she went
along. "Okay, these pages are the same, and this one, too."
She picked up another. "But here's one that is in the police
file but not in the indictment file." She put a sticky note on
it and marked it with a "one." When she reached the end,
she found that the police file contained twenty-six documents that the hand-selected-and-delivered-to-Austin file
did not contain. Most of those missing documents weighed
heavily in my favor. They contained the results of the investigation that was conducted during my suspension. The indictment file, on the other hand, contained primarily
accusations without any responses.

"This really makes me mad," I said, stiff-jawed, catch-
ing Debbie's eye. "If the attorney general's office had
bothered to make an inquiry at the police department,
they'd have known there wasn't anything there to get an
indictment with."

"Heh heh." Denette laughed her patented throaty
laugh. "Don't you see? If they had done that, the police
department would have known that they were up to

something, and then that would have filtered back to
you. You would have told me, and I sure as heck would
have found out what was going on.

"Plus," she continued, "if they had the police file, they
would have had to intentionally ditch twenty-six documents to make this whole thing look bad enough to
obtain indictments. By not seeing it, they could at least
feign ignorance and say they didn't know the other documents existed, or if they existed, they would be able to
claim they didn't know the contents.

"See," Denette explained, "if they'd gone through the
right channels, they would have never been able to get
an indictment at all. To achieve what they wanted, there
had to be carefully selected people with carefully selected documents that would ensure secrecy."

Angry, I tried to keep myself busy gathering up the
remnants of lunch and tossing them in the garbage.

"We're not finished," Denette said. "Our next job is to
do the reverse of what we just did and find out if there
are documents in the indictment file that are not in the
police file. That's what could really prove interesting."

I had to admit that such a thought had never crossed
my mind. I could tell from the shocked look on Debbie's
face she hadn't thought of it either.

We continued to work behind the closed door of our
conference room, with team members occasionally stirring outside to seek a file or take a stretch. Debbie never
moved from our side. The look on her face was one of
complete dedication to the task.

A law clerk's wife, who was part of our team helping
out as a gofer, left our conference room to go to the restroom next door. Expecting to find it empty during the
lunch recess, she was startled to find Rebecca Atchley
with her ear pressed to the common wall between the
restroom and our conference room!

That discovery was immediately reported back to us.

"She could face discipline from the bar for that," one of our attorneys said, shaking his head. "Even though she's up here as a witness, she's still a lawyer."

"We'll let it go for now," Goldstein interjected. "They've done wrong, they're caught, and they know it. I guess they feel they have to try to do something to win, even if it's listening through bathroom walls."

Denette had continued working throughout this conversation, and it was now almost time to go back into the courtroom. She motioned for me to approach her desk.

"Look at this. Have you ever seen this?" she asked. I leaned down. In front of her was a photocopy of a page in David Hagler's handwriting. Hagler was a member of the Street Crimes Unit and the initiator of the original internal investigation against me.

"I thought I was familiar with all of the documents from the internal investigation, but I've never seen this before," I said slowly, feeling a shiver creep up my spine. And I knew immediately that it was the reason everyone from Atchley on up the chain had tried so hard to keep the file from us. It was also the reason David Hagler had been released from his subpoena and did not testify before the grand jury that indicted me.

The document was a handwritten, two-page account giving a detailed description of the incident where we had arrested a drug offender as he and his brother left their apartment. I had eventually gone back into the place to lock it up and found some dope out in plain sight. Hagler's account corroborated, in almost exact detail, the arrest report I had written the day the incident occurred. I shook my head. "I don't understand it," I said to Denette. "Hagler's own notes agree with me and dispute almost every detail of the indictment that was handed up concerning that incident!"

Denette grimaced. "It's unclear exactly when this document was written," she said. "If it was written early in the internal investigation, it was never turned in and never became part of that investigation." I felt a surge of anger rise in me. "If it was an early document," she went on, "Hagler would have to answer in federal court under oath why this document was not turned in as part of the original internal investigation." Denette bit her lip.

"Let me see it." Debbie reached over to get a better look. As she read the first few sentences, color rose in her face.

My own anger spilled over. "Was it because it cleared me, whom he loathed? Was it because, after he had written it, he discovered that it conflicted with the account being formulated by the other officers who made allegations against me? If so, did he just toss this first try into a file and write another account?"

"You have a right to be incensed, Bill, but we need to think clearly now." Denette looked at me.

"His 'other' account of the situation, which was part of the police file, was considerably less detailed and simply said the incident had not occurred the way you reported it, but gave no specifics." Denette rubbed her chin. "Had they intended to leave this document out when the selective collection was put together to deliver to the assistant attorney general?"

The other possibility was almost as damning. If this document was written late, possibly as Mrs. Atchley and Mr. Ware were putting together documents against me, the creation of a new document would tend to show that they weren't just collecting papers as they had claimed, but were actively seeking additional information—selective information.

Was this why Frank Briscoe "forgot" the file when responding to federal court? Was this why David Hagler was released from his subpoena before he testified to the grand jury? I believe the answer to both of these questions is yes. It is clear that this document was the weak

link in the chain and could have made the whole thing
fall apart before indictments on me were gained.

When, shortly after lunch, David Hagler took the
stand and was questioned by Mr. Mullin, Denette passed
the ammunition to Gerald Goldstein. When it came
time for cross-examination, Goldstein was loaded and set
for the hunt. "I'm ready for big game," he whispered.

My indictment was projected on an eight-foot square
screen so everyone in the courtroom could see it. After
asking a few preliminary questions, Goldstein went to
work. With a flick of his glasses, he handed Hagler the
document in Hagler's own handwriting that Denette
had finally received less than an hour earlier.

"Calling your attention to Exhibit One of the defendants' exhibits. Is this the handwritten report you
prepared?"

If I live to be a hundred, I will never lose the picture
of Hagler's face absolutely freezing as he began reading
those sheets of paper.

Snick! The sound of Goldstein's glasses broke the silence and seemed to wake Hagler from a state of shock.

"It's a copy of the report," Hagler managed.

Goldstein didn't let up. "Do you recall writing out
what is titled, 'Summary of Events' entitled document
one of plaintiffs' exhibit H-Thirteen?" Snick.

"Yes, I do," Hagler responded in a shaky voice.

"And, in fact, with respect to the entry into the Baylor
Street residence, you recounted, did you not, that the
arrest in fact was occasioned by you and Corporal
Rendleman, did you not?"

"Yes, I did." His voice was barely audible.

In five swift minutes, Goldstein not only put the finishing touches to denouncing the dark plan that had indicted me, but he also demonstrated for the judge that
I was not guilty of the original charge! Our purpose had

been to answer the "bad faith" question, but Goldstein had done that and much, much more.

Even after this startling testimony, the case did not end that day. Tiredly, we headed into day seven of testimony. That meant yet another night for Debbie and me in the Goldstein late-night work chamber. "Back to the inner sanctum," Debbie said, half in jest, half in weariness. We spent most of it finalizing the questions to be asked of our rebuttal witnesses while Goldstein organized his final argument.

It looked as if Wednesday, February 24th, would finally be the day of testimony when John Gomez would rebut Randy Atchley's foggy memory and take the stand. We'd enter some sworn affidavits, and then we would be ready for closing arguments.

"Sergeant John Gomez," the bailiff called.

Gomez had become sergeant of the Street Crimes Unit when I was assigned to homicide. Some of his staff was good, but he'd also inherited some officers who were quick to complain and slow to work. Inspiring them and inculcating new work ethics wasn't easy. When I was indicted, his job became even more difficult. He knew that at least part of the action that had culminated in my indictment had come from men under his command, and that they had kept it secret from him. Gomez explained to the court how he came to know about my indictments, saying the explanation had come from Randy Atchley.

Gomez testified, "Bill Hubbard's indictment was a shock, and Lt. Joe Stone told me to go down to Street Crimes and see what I could find out about it. I asked Atchley what he knew and he said he knew nothing about it and refused to comment on it.

"But that evening, he called me at home and asked to come over and talk to me about it. He said he wanted to let me know about the indictment before I read about it in the papers."

There was a long pause, the kind that catches everyone's attention. As I sat there, I felt my stomach churning.

Gomez went on. "Randy said he and Rebecca had started the indictment."

The day after the indictment, Gomez said, Atchley had requested an opportunity to meet with his chain of command to explain it all to them. He met with Gomez, Captain Knox, and Colonel Ewing. Gomez said Atchley told the same story to all three men as he had told Gomez the night before.

Captain Knox had testified about this meeting earlier in the hearing. Atchley had taken the stand and denied it under oath. Now, Gomez confirmed Knox's story, and Ewing was still available to further corroborate the Knox/Gomez version.

After Gomez testified, it appeared to our team, to reporters, and to many others that David Hagler and Randy Atchley would have some explaining to do when they got back to the police department, not the least of which was withholding information which would have cleared me of the bogus charges brought against me. Not to mention other questions internal affairs might want answered about withholding of evidence during their internal inquiry.

However, even though an assistant chief of police sat through the entire proceeding and heard all of the testimony, Hagler and Atchley would never be made to answer to the police administration any questions concerning subversive conduct within the department. Though an investigation into Pat Kelly's testimony had been vigorously launched after he testified in Canyon, these two officers would never have to answer a single question concerning whether or what had been their participation in the dark plans that put me through the internal investigation, and then, a year later, brought on false charges.

Some speculated that the lack of action on the part of the police administration was because of their "ignore it and maybe it will go away" management philosophy, and others believed it had to do with the fact that Hagler and Atchley were both part of the apparently untouchable SWAT team. A current joke circulating in L.P.D. circles was that SWAT stands for "Six Wackos Armed to the Teeth." They appeared close knit and untouchable. Whatever the reason, a glaring double standard was revealed that has left many officers wondering why some must adhere to standards from which others are exempt.

Our final witness was Detective Ronnie Goolsby. He told about the investigation that had led to his being called by Ware's chief investigator, Jeff Creager, to come to a meeting with Ware and Atchley.

Goolsby, in his quiet, unassuming way, testified to what had transpired during their three-hour meeting that day, the rage Ware exhibited toward me, and what he perceived as Ware's attempts to intimidate him. "I remember on one occasion, Travis brought up that Hubbard was about to be indicted," Goolsby testified. "Ware told me that if I had anything to do with Hubbard, I would follow in his footsteps."

Goldstein went on to ask if Goolsby took it as a threat.

"I believe it was more to intimidate me," Goolsby replied.

"With regard to that statement, can you remember the precise words, leaving out epithets, the precise words that he used in telling you what was about to happen to my client?"

"Well, ultimately he would be indicted."

"What was he saying about you?"

"That if I had anything to do with Mr. Hubbard that I would basically follow in his footsteps."

When Goolsby was allowed to step down, Ware's team called Jeff Creager to the stand. Creager not only gave a different version of the events to which Goolsby had testified, he said most of it didn't happen at all.

One of these men lied in federal court. To me, it was clear who had been truthful.

Then we submitted into evidence sworn statements by Dr. Jody Nielsen, along with a transcript of her by now infamous telephone conversation with Ware, plus a statement by Investigator Carrie McClain, which told of the situations concerning me that she had witnessed while she was part of the Ware staff.

I was all set to testify, and Goldstein originally had told me that I more than likely would do so. He was also sure that if he didn't call me, our opponents most definitely would. But it didn't happen. Goldstein was satisfied. "We've made our case without your having to take the stand. They would just want to distort it and humiliate you. That's a no-win situation," he insisted.

Instead, closing arguments began. However, Judge Robinson still wasn't through. She ordered summaries from each plaintiff and each defendant, and she wanted them on her desk at nine the next morning. There would be yet one more night in the Goldstein salt mines.

At least Goldstein allowed us a nice leisurely dinner, our first. We went to an Italian restaurant before he put us back to work. In the ten days we had been together, we had all become very close. The three teams of lawyers and their clients had thought together, worked together, planned strategy together, taken meals together, and had a few precious laughs together.

Though our team was diverse in backgrounds and in political viewpoints, we worked like a law firm that had been together for years. And, although we had our moral and political differences, there was a tolerance and understanding of each other, while being committed to a common goal. "It's this lesson," I said, "that makes these days in Amarillo a valuable experience for my life regardless of how the judge will eventually rule."

The serious times, however, had far outweighed the funny ones. Each of us was always quite aware that the stakes were high. If this went against us, Millard Farmer stood to lose his law license and Kelly and I our peace officer credentials.

After dinner, "Captain" Goldstein rallied the troops one last time, and we headed downtown to our temporary office quarters. We spread out in the conference room and three offices as we sifted through everything we had presented in the hearing. We tried to get down to the absolute heart of the evidence that proved our case and then condense it into a concise, organized format.

At times, the testimony had to have seemed to the judge somewhat disjointed as our team offered some beneficial to Millard, then some for me, another witness for Millard, then two for Pat, and so forth. This ping pong approach was sometimes necessary to accommodate the schedules of the witnesses. But now it was time to give the case a final organization to guide the judge through what we had presented.

It took three drafts and an all-nighter, but at 6:00 A.M., we believed we had a summary that highlighted the very heart of the case. After turning it in, Debbie and I took Goldstein and Cynthia Orr to the airport so they could go home to San Antonio.

"What do you think?" Debbie asked our strategist.

"I believe we've proven our case, but I am not going to jinx us with a prediction."

Before Goldstein got on the plane, I tried to find the words to express my thanks. "The way you labored night and day for me, I hope you haven't cut a few years off your life."

"This *is* my life." He winked. "Piece of cake."

On the way back to Lubbock, Debbie, who was totally worn out, curled up in the seat next to me. Like her, I was exhausted, but my mind wouldn't wind down. As I drove, I relived not only the testimony given by various witnesses, but also the poignant moments as our teams had talked and worked together, inside the courtroom and outside. Emotion overwhelmed me, and tears of gratitude ran down my face. On the two-hour drive home, I had to stop three times and step out into the cold Texas air to stay awake and to regain my composure. When we got home, Debbie showered and put on fresh clothes and makeup. She kissed me good-bye. "Bill, we've met the test," she said, tears glistening in her eyes. Then she hurried out the door to work. I fell into bed to rest, reflect, and wait.

Judge Robinson did not return an immediate decision. The longer we waited, the more we nervously speculated as to what ruling she might make. She could grant the injunction for all three of us, for only two, for one or for none of us. I played "What if?" with Dan Hurley and Denette Vaughn, trying to be ready for whatever came. They tried to get me to understand that we had several more legal options if the ruling went against us.

But I wanted the nightmare to end. We *had* proven our case. I *knew* we had. All I asked was that the judge have the courage to make the ruling that she had the legal authority to make and that we had supported with the evidence. But I was also mature enough to know that difficult decisions were not always popular ones and that politics could always play a role in the outcome. On the other hand, after watching Judge Robinson's strength during those days, I felt she would be influenced by nothing except the law and the evidence. At least, that is what I prayed.

So Debbie and I waited.

The first of March came and went, with no word from Amarillo. *What is she doing up there?* I asked myself.

On the second of March, the Lubbock *Avalanche-Journal* ran the results of its latest poll question: "Do you believe there was a conspiracy in the Lubbock Criminal District Attorney's office to seek indictments on police and others who testified against forensic pathologist Ralph Erdmann?"

The results: Yes 65%. No 35%.

21

Decision Time

Two more days went by. There was still no ruling.

It was disheartening going into my home office and trying to work on my defense for a trial that would be inevitable if Judge Robinson ruled against us. I felt frustrated and wondered what in the world could be taking so long. Since we had gotten back from Amarillo the morning of February 26th, it had become increasingly harder to get up and face each new day.

On the morning of Wednesday, March 4th, at eight o'clock, the phone rang. I was still lying in bed pondering the trial and my fate. When Debbie said it was for me, I wasn't thrilled about talking to anyone, but getting on the phone, I grunted what must have sounded like a greeting.

"Hey, bud, there's news." I recognized Pat Kelly's voice.

"News?" I still felt sluggish and now a little irritated because Pat just loved knowing something I didn't.

"We won! All three of us! The judge's ruling is just now coming over the fax machines, and we won!"

Shocked, I didn't even take time to hear whatever else Pat had to say. "I've got to go see Denette and Dan," I said hanging up. I called to Debbie, "The ruling's coming in and it looks good. Real good!"

Then I dressed hurriedly and ran out the door on my way to Dan Hurley's office, promising Debbie I'd call her at work. Dan, Denette, and I waited around the machine as the ruling came in one slow page at a time.

When I saw the words "Preliminary Injunction" at the top of the first page, I realized that Judge Robinson was, in fact, blocking the prosecution of all of our cases in state courts. That was good. But it was the wording of the document that was *very* good. We didn't have to read past the second paragraph to see that it was an extremely emphatic decision. That paragraph began:

> After hearing evidence and the argument of counsel, the Court is of the opinion that Plaintiffs have shown a substantial probability that they will prevail on the merits in their application for permanent injunction in that the Plaintiffs have offered *substantial evidence* that the prosecutions were brought in bad faith and for the purposes of retaliation against the Plaintiffs for the exercise of their constitutional rights. The Court also finds that *substantial evidence* shows that it is more likely than not that the prosecutions would not have been brought in the absence of such retaliation. Accordingly, the Court finds:
>
> 1. A substantial likelihood that Plaintiffs will prevail on the merits;
>
> 2. A substantial threat that Plaintiffs will suffer irreparable injury if the injunction is not granted;
>
> 3. That the threatened injury to Plaintiffs outweighs the threatened harm the injunction may do to the Defendants; and

4. That granting the preliminary injunction will not disserve the public interest.

The short, three-page document ordered a halt to any prosecutions of the indictments of Millard Farmer, Pat Kelly and Bill Hubbard.

I knew that all this did was put a blockade in the way of Ware's prosecution of my case until a final trial could be held in federal court. There we could ask a jury for a permanent injunction and to award us damages. But I also knew that Judge Robinson's ruling was so decisive, that there was a glimmer of possibility that the City of Lubbock would give me my job back until such time as the federal case was finally finished.

Dan Hurley said, "The judge's ruling is so emphatic that Travis and the others won't want to face us again in Robinson's courtroom only to watch us carry away their assets." The shoe definitely was on the other foot.

Following the three-page injunction was an equally impressive document. It was a twenty-four-page opinion containing the points on which Robinson had made her ruling. The first four pages dealt with the background of the case and how all the Erdmann stuff had resulted in charges against the three of us. She then explained her understanding of the law on which she should base a ruling. She explained that the law precludes federal courts from enjoining state criminal prosecutions unless the prosecutions are brought in bad faith. She also cited the "strong federal policy against federal court interference with pending state judicial proceedings absent extraordinary circumstances."

And so she wrote: "The Plaintiffs must show 1) that the conduct allegedly retaliated against or sought to be deterred was constitutionally protected, and 2) that the state's bringing of the criminal prosecution was motivated at least in part by a purpose to retaliate for or to deter that conduct." If plaintiffs meet their burden of proof on these two issues, the state must show "by a preponderance of the evidence that it would have reached the same decision as to whether to prosecute even had the impermissible purpose not been considered."

Obviously, Judge Robinson believed we had met our burden of proof and the defendants had not.

The opinion document then set the legal standard for the issuance of an injunction, which was the same four-part paragraph cited in her three-page injunction. Beginning at page eight of her opinion, Robinson expressed her belief concerning how Millard Farmer's indictment had come about, based on the testimony she had heard. The visit to Woodson Rowan and the way that information got to Sherrod's office was included, as well as the timing that was involved in the return of the indictments against Farmer.

Beginning on page thirteen of the opinion, Robinson vigorously expressed her understanding of how the indictments against me had come about.

The Hubbard Indictment

There were bad feelings between Lubbock police officers Bill Hubbard and Pat Kelly, on the one hand, and Lubbock District Attorney Ware, on the other, long before the Erdmann controversy developed. Hubbard and Kelly made no secret of their intense dislike of Ware, and Ware disliked and mistrusted Hubbard and Kelly.

Hubbard and Kelly were both subpoenaed by Millard Farmer to testify in hearings in the case concerning Erdmann. Both testified. Both were indicted.

Hubbard was indicted in Lubbock County on October 21, 1992 on five counts: two counts of aggravated perjury, two counts of tampering with a

governmental record, and one count of securing execution of a document by deception. The
charges against Hubbard relate to an internal
police investigation more than a year before the
Hubbard indictment.

The Lubbock Police Department investigation of
Hubbard grew out of complaints by five of the six
officers in the Street Crimes Unit. Hubbard was the
sergeant in charge of this unit. Complaints included
Hubbard's failure to authorize overtime pay for
unit members and allegations that he falsified and
ordered his officers to falsify police reports dealing
with searches conducted by the Street Crimes Unit.
An investigation was undertaken by Hubbard's
chain of command. It lasted from May to July 1991.
No overtime was paid. No criminal charges resulted, although Hubbard was reprimanded for violating departmental policies. On August 27, 1991,
Hubbard was transferred to command of the homicide victim I.D. section. The matter was considered
closed.

Esparza, the outgoing section commander of the
victim I.D. section, turned a private file dealing with
Lubbock County autopsies performed by Erdmann
over to Hubbard as incoming commander. Hubbard was instructed to continue to maintain this
file.

In mid-October of 1991, Hubbard's supervisors
directed him to undertake an investigation into
improper autopsy procedures by Erdmann. In the
course of this investigation, Hubbard studied
accepted autopsy practices and compared those
standards with the actual practices of Dr. Erdmann.
He began to develop an autopsy protocol. In January of 1992, Hubbard and other Lubbock police officers complained to Travis Ware about Erdmann's

improper procedures. Ware, meanwhile, had been developing an autopsy protocol also.

On February 5, 1992, Ware met with Hubbard and other officers to discuss Erdmann and to adopt autopsy protocols to be presented to Erdmann. At this meeting, they discussed Erdmann's failure to follow generally accepted autopsy procedures. They discussed, among other problems, that Erdmann generally refused to do cranial examinations, and that he was estimating, but not actually weighing, body organs. At this meeting, Ware praised Dr. Erdmann as a witness. Ware asked those present to keep quiet about the meeting because if the information got out, "the defense attorneys will have a field day with it."

Back in Randall County, at least fifty witnesses were subpoenaed to testify at the Merriman (Canyon) exhumation hearing scheduled for April 2, 1992. Among those persons subpoenaed were Lubbock police officers. Ware had had a bad relationship with the former Lubbock police chief, but he had a good relationship with the new chief, Don Bridgers. On the day before the hearing, Ware called Police Chief Don Bridgers and expressed concern about police officers' potential testimony. Specifically, Ware expressed concern that Hubbard might misconstrue Ware's remarks at the February 5th meeting concerning Erdmann.

Hubbard testified at the exhumation hearing about Erdmann's autopsies. As Ware feared, Hubbard also testified about the February 5th meeting with Ware and Ware's statement that the matter should be kept quiet. Hubbard's attorney expressed concern that Hubbard might be retaliated against because of his testimony.

Shortly after the Hubbard testimony, Rebecca

Atchley, Ware's first Assistant D.A., was watching a television news report concerning Hubbard's testimony at the Canyon hearing with her husband, Randy Atchley, who is a Lubbock police officer and Street Crimes Unit member. Assistant D.A. Atchley stated to her husband that she "couldn't believe that Bill was doing this." Officer Randy Atchley responded by asking why Ware's office didn't get Hubbard when they had the chance at him. In the ensuing conversation, Officer Atchley discussed the allegations of false reports by Hubbard that were a subject of the 1991 police department investigation of Hubbard. Rebecca Atchley reported the conversation to Ware, who instructed her to get more facts and evidence.

On April 15, 1992, twelve days after Hubbard testified, Ware summoned Carrie McClain, an investigator in his office, to his office. She stated by affidavit:

> Travis Ware threw in my lap a bunch of pictures of homicide victims and in an extremely agitated state, Travis Ware told me that Bill Hubbard was going nuts, was trying to get killers off, has lied on the witness stand in several cases. Travis Ware then expressed his concern that Bill Hubbard would try to manipulate me for information going on in the district attorney's office. I got the impression that if I had associated with my good friend Bill Hubbard from that point forward, my job would have been in jeopardy. Later that summer, Travis Ware again warned me not to hang around Bill Hubbard.

McClain resigned as an investigator with the district attorney's office on October 24, 1992, purportedly for what she perceived as a lack of honesty and integrity in the office.

Sometime later, Ware called Lubbock City Manager Larry Cunningham and asked him to reassign Hubbard out of the homicide identification unit to a less sensitive area of the police department. Ware told Cunningham that the Chief had already refused to do so. A few days later, Ware went to Cunningham's office and told Cunningham that he and Atchley had discussed what should be done with Hubbard and that together Ware and Rebecca Atchley had decided to take the Hubbard problem to a grand jury in hopes of getting an indictment. Ware warned Cunningham not to share this information with anyone, and told him that if there was a leak Ware would know where it came from, since only Ware, Rebecca Atchley and Cunningham knew of the plan.

By August or September of 1992, Ware and Rebecca Atchley had decided to take the Hubbard matter to the Texas Attorney General's office for possible indictment. The decision to refer the matter to the attorney general was made in order to avoid an appearance of retaliation or bias.

On September 8, 1992, Dr. Jody Nielsen, the forensic pathologist brought in to replace Dr. Erdmann, called Ware saying that she understood that he wanted to talk to her. Without Ware's knowledge, Nielsen recorded their conversation in which Ware repeatedly warned Dr. Nielsen of Hubbard's hostility toward him. The transcript of this conversation is in evidence. Ware asked Nielsen not to publicly associate herself with Hubbard. He urged her to meet with himself and Rebecca Atchley in the district attorney's office to discuss Hubbard and suggested that it would be best if she talked to Rebecca Atchley woman to woman. Dr. Nielsen stated in an affidavit that she received the message from her conversations with Ware that anyone who crossed Ware could be subject to criminal indictment, and that there were problems in Lubbock County of which she wanted no part. Because of this, she resigned as Lubbock County pathologist in October of 1992.

The same day that Ware and Dr. Nielsen spoke about Hubbard, Ware called into his office a twenty-one-year veteran of the Lubbock Police Department, Ronnie Goolsby. Goolsby was at the time a detective in the crimes against persons division. Goolsby testified that during a three and one-half hour meeting, Ware expressed to Goolsby his unfavorable opinion of Hubbard, the officers in the Lubbock Police Department generally, and Goolsby himself. Goolsby testified that Ware told him that Hubbard was going to be indicted, that Goolsby might be next, and that other Lubbock police officers might follow.

The next day, on September 9, 1992, Ware and Rebecca Atchley traveled to Austin to personally hand-deliver a portion of the police file on Hubbard to Shane Phelps, an assistant attorney general. Ware told Phelps "to take a good look at the case." Phelps, who was involved in investigating allegations that Ware's office acted improperly concerning the John Young probation plea, decided not to handle the case himself. On October 5, 1992, the file was turned over to Assistant Attorney General Frank Briscoe. On October 21, 1992, Briscoe presented evidence to the Lubbock County grand jury and Hubbard was indicted. Although Briscoe had personally interviewed Lubbock police officers concerning Hubbard's alleged crimes, Briscoe did not present arguably exonerating testimony from certain live witnesses to the grand jury.

On October 22, 1992, the day after Hubbard's indictment, Officer Atchley told Sergeant Gomez, then his commanding officer in the Street Crimes Unit, that Atchley had reported information from the police department's investigation on Hubbard to his wife Rebecca. Atchley later repeated this information to superiors in his direct chain of command.

In every instance where Judge Robinson had a choice to make concerning whose testimony had been credible, she decided for the testimony from our team. Her opinion was the truth, the *whole* truth.

Robinson summarized the internal investigation of my conduct, and how, at the end of it, "The matter was considered closed."

The next part of the opinion had to do with how the judge believed Pat Kelly's indictment came about. This section was much briefer, but told of how the decision to investigate Kelly's Canyon testimony was made the day after he testified, and how Steve Holmes of the D.A.'s office had taken a second statement from the J.P.'s secretary that contradicted her previous testimony. Lubbock police investigators, as well as Steve Holmes, met with Randall County D.A. Randy Sherrod and then presented testimony to a grand jury, which indicted Kelly.

The judge also said it was her belief that the testimony and exhibits revealed serious questions concerning the autopsy of the pedestrian, Darlene Hall, who was killed by a car driven by the assistant district attorney. She enumerated a few of those serious questions.

It was obvious that the judge did not believe the motivation in the decision to investigate Kelly had been clean either.

In fact, the judge wrote, "The Plaintiffs have offered *substantial evidence* that each of the indictments was brought in bad faith and to retaliate against them for their exercise of constitutional rights. There is *substantial evidence* that it is not likely that the prosecutions would have been brought in the absence of a motive to retaliate. The defendants have not shown that it is more likely than not that the prosecutions would have been brought in any event. In reaching its conclusion, this Court recognizes that the indictments were returned by a grand jury, that the indictment of Kelly was secured by the Randall County District Attorney and not by Ware, and that the indictment of Hubbard was secured by a special prosecutor. Prosecution tainted by impermissible prosecutorial misconduct is not cured by turning it over to a new prosecutor, or even a grand jury." She cited the cases *United States v. P.H.E., Inc.* and *Smith v. Hightower* for "a prosecutor may not insulate himself from a finding of bad faith by having a special prosecutor take the case to a grand jury."

Bingo! went my heart.

The opinion concluded: "The Plaintiffs have shown a substantial probability that they will prevail on the merits of their application for an injunction enjoining the prosecutors from proceeding in the prosecutions of Millard Farmer, Bill Hubbard, and Patrick John Kelly. Accordingly, it is the opinion of this Court that a preliminary injunction should issue.

"It is so ordered." Signed, Mary Lou Robinson.

Clutching the papers, I read them and reread them. From the beginning, I believed that the three of us, Kelly, Farmer and I, would prevail in this hearing. Particularly after the testimony of former city manager Larry Cunningham. However, I had not ever imagined the judge's ruling to be so heavily and absolutely in our favor. The judge had even gone so far as to say that she expected that when we came back for the trial before the jury for the permanent injunction and damages, that we would win at that time, too. This was an emphatic, historical, and amazing ruling!

No sooner had the fax machines stopped buzzing than the news teams descended on us. They all wanted interviews, video, and photos. The banner headline of our hometown paper, the *Avalanche-Journal*, the next morning was my favorite of all: "Judge condemns Ware's tactics."

Typically, Ware was quick to place himself above even a federal judge. "I hate to argue with a federal judge, but I know there wasn't enough evidence," he said.

I think Ware was saying that he still had not grasped what was at stake and what needed to be proven in order to prevail. The entire matter had just blown right on by him.

However, Professor Charles Bubany of the Texas Tech Law School certainly seemed to grasp the importance of the ruling. "The significance of this decision has two aspects," he told the newspaper. "One, it's significant just how unusual this is because you don't have the federal courts step in very often to stop prosecutions. Two, it's significant that she found substantial evidence that the allegations against Hubbard, Kelly, and Farmer were brought in bad faith and were in retaliation for exercising their constitutional rights.

"I don't know what this means for Travis Ware," Bubany continued, "but this certainly is not good for the C.D.A.'s office. If I'm the D.A., I'm extremely troubled. I don't want a federal judge telling me I'm a crook when my job is to prosecute crooks."

His words echoed my thoughts.

22

Vindication

We had worked long and hard, and Judge Robinson's ruling proved that. We had acted with integrity. The truth had finally been heard and believed. I was ready to put the past where it belonged and get back to work.

We expected this to happen within days. However, it didn't. Weeks after this most emphatic ruling by a federal judge, I still had not been reinstated to the police force.

Fortunately, the media wasn't just standing by and taking it all in. When I picked up the March 7th *Avalanche-Journal*, the lead editorial called for Ware's resignation!

"Mr. Ware: Step Down," read the headline. Then the paper said, "For some time we have had reservations about Mr. Ware's willingness to target people who would differ with him. The court ruling in Amarillo Thursday contributed mightily to crystallizing our views—and quite likely the views of others." It concluded that Ware should resign also because "prosecutor vs. police politics" had begun to dominate the affairs of the Ware office, rather than the job of prosecuting criminals.

Ware scoffed at the idea. To the chagrin of many, he argued that much of Judge Robinson's ruling had vindicated him. Pat Kelly's lawyers counterargued that Ware obviously wasn't reading the same document the rest of us were. It looked as if Ware's "truth vs. appearance" tactic was untouched by the hearing and the verdict.

The following morning, the top rock radio station in Lubbock, KFMX, broadcast the "Five Top Things on Travis Ware's Mind Today:

"Number five. Call *60 Minutes*. Hang up.

"Number four. Put away that skull ashtray, Dr. Erdmann.

"Number three. Pick up another quart of hair tonic.

"Number two. Put the letters UMB and SS under the letters D.A. on his door.

"Number one. Call U-Haul."

By March 12th, picketers were out in front of the courthouse, demanding Ware's resignation. The Friday picketing would continue for months. By December 1993, they were still at it, and Ware still hadn't resigned.

On March 16th, Ware pushed for the outright dismissal of the RICO suit. He said that, to his knowledge, his lawyers were not involved in any out-of-court settlement negotiations. And he continued to defend the findings of his latest review into the work of Ralph Erdmann!

Though Ware denied it, by the twenty-sixth of March the papers were reporting that an out-of-court settlement was close at hand. The "talks" involved Ware and his codefendants agreeing to a permanent injunction against our criminal charges, and then paying us more than a quarter of a million dollars to let them out of our RICO suit. This did not sound like the kind of negotiation a D.A. would participate in when he claimed to have done no wrong!

Finally—F I N A L L Y—word came that the police department was willing to put Kelly and me back to work at our old positions, with full back pay. The date was April fifth.

On that day, gold sergeant's badge number 13 was mine again. I was restored to my full rank and seniority with orders to return to my former job in homicide. That job had remained vacant, as had my office, for the six months I had been gone. The men in my unit had worked shorthanded rather than have a replacement.

It was great to attain the prize. I definitely felt we had run the race with perseverance that was set before us. On the other hand, it was bittersweet. Members of the police administration reinstated me and returned my police credentials, but offered no congratulations, or even a simple, "It's great to see you back." To do that might be an admission that dismissing me had been wrong, or it might be interpreted as a statement of support of me and against the officers who had gone outside the confines of the police department to help gain my indictments. And, no one was about to put those officers under the microscope, for fear that they would cry that they were being retaliated against for what they did. So, the unspoken law to "do nothing and hope it all takes care of itself" was put into motion. It was a law the administration knew well. I have likened it to being thrown overboard by a bunch of mutinous shipmates, only to have the captain say, "Well, at least he's a strong swimmer!" rather than throw me a life jacket and squelch the mutiny. Nevertheless, I felt that people really were glad I was back and just were not allowed to say so.

The guys from my unit returned my office keys and my pager, as well as the keys to my unmarked police car. When I opened the door to my office, I found that everything was just the way I had left it. Still on the wall was the sign I had placed there on October 22nd: "I will be back!" My fellow officers had left it there, believing that I really would be back and get to take it down myself. This gesture touched my heart.

What was lacking in the reception by the administration was more than made up for by the rest of the police department. Greetings and congratulations beyond my wildest dreams met my return. For days, it was difficult to get any work done. A steady stream of officers came into my office. Some wanted to give me a handshake, others a high-five, or just talk about the ordeal. The majority of the rank and file of the Lubbock Police Department proved all over again that they are some of the best who wear badges anywhere.

With badge number 13 back in my pocket and my weapon on my hip, my next stop was the personnel office. There, I was presented with a check that amounted to six months' back pay.

That night, I experienced a further joy. When I got home, I led Debbie straight over to my roll-top desk. With Debbie's hand clasping mine, I took down the check that our church had sent us before Christmas. We were thrilled to send it back uncashed, along with our written testimony, "The Lord has been very good to us during this ordeal and has met our every financial need as it arose."

The next morning, I kept another promise. The previous Christmas, Debbie had willingly given her bonus check to the general household fund, to pay bills and to make ends meet. In years past, that bonus had always been hers to do with as she pleased. Now I withdrew the cash equivalent of her bonus in one hundred dollar bills and that night, I gave them to her. This was the best!

More affirmation of our position came when the rumblings about an out-of-court settlement proved not to be just rumblings. The defendants pooled resources to offer us $300,000 to drop the RICO suit. In addition, they would agree to a permanent injunction and forever be prevented from prosecuting the three of us. When Denette and Dan approached me about the settlement, I reminded them, "This was never about money. It was the defendants who brought it to this point. All I ever wanted was to be vindicated."

On the other hand, I also knew that similar whistle-blower suits were being awarded millions by the courts. However, I was aware that there was no guarantee I would be granted such a sum. Besides, considering the fact that all of my lawyers had, as yet, charged me absolutely nothing for their work, I felt it was only fair that they should get some compensation. So, I accepted the deal.

The settlement money was split evenly among the three plaintiffs, and my attorneys were allowed one-third of my cut to split among the three of them. True to the end, Vaughn, Hurley, and Goldstein did not sway from their commitment to me even though they were not able to recover their expenses, much less be fairly compensated for all the many hours of time they'd devoted to my defense. But all three were quick to point out that they had taken my case because it was the right thing to do and not because it had the potential to pay off.

Lubbock County and the City of Lubbock had to foot a hefty portion of the settlement bill. The county would also pay more than $50,000 for Ware's personal attorney and the city would pay somewhere around $35,000 for lawyers. Their price, both in negative publicity and actual costs, had indeed been steep.

The *Avalanche-Journal*'s editorial, "The Price of 'Retaliating,'" said it now knew the price tag of retaliation and didn't care for it.

In fact, as the article stated local taxpayers had to help pay Lubbock's $200,000-plus share of a $300,000 settlement to the parties.

"The settlement became necessary to end a suit in

which Mr. Ware and officials in Potter and Randall counties were accused, with discredited forensic pathologist Ralph Erdmann, of racketeering, conspiracy and violations of the rights of the officers and Mr. Farmer."

"Recall that officer Hubbard was accused, among other things, of aggravated perjury after testifying in 1992 that the district attorney had told policemen to keep questions about Mr. Erdmann's competence to themselves."

It went on to comment, "The cases against the three plaintiffs began to collapse, however, in March. U.S. District Judge Mary Lou Robinson ruled that the trio had 'offered substantial evidence that each of the indictments were brought in bad faith and to retaliate against them. . . .'"

The paper said, "It always has been revealing to us how Mr. Ware chose to go after officer Hubbard, toward whom he had expressed unfavorable opinions: He turned the prosecution over to the attorney general's office in Austin."

The article further quoted Judge Robinson: "The decision to refer the matter to the attorney general was made . . . to avoid an appearance of retaliation or bias."

Finally, the paper stated its own opinion. "We suggested last month, when the prosecutions of the policemen and the lawyer were temporarily barred by the judge, that it would be in Lubbock's best interests for Mr. Ware to resign.

The cost of this week's settlement which specifies that Mr. Ware and other prosecutors call off the dogs—only reinforces our view."

Meanwhile, Ware still scoffed at the notion of his resignation. He was still trying to persuade the public that his agreeing to the settlement was the prudent thing to do since taxpayers would have to foot the bill. Again and again, he reiterated that he would have won the lawsuit but it would have cost too much to do so. So it was in the taxpayers' best interest to settle.

If what Ware was saying were true, no major cases would ever be tried because of the immense expense involved. If his argument was valid, plea bargains would have to be accepted in every potentially "expensive to prosecute" case.

In addition, if Ware's argument could be believed, all a criminal had to do was get a high-powered lawyer to file a federal suit and the state would not only drop charges, but pay him lots of money, too! That's how it would be if the only criterion for justice was expense.

The people weren't buying his argument. Newspapers were filled with irate taxpayers' letters and quotes calling for Ware's resignation. However, Ware and the others weren't finished battling the tide which had now turned against them.

On October 13, 1993, a motion to dismiss the prosecution against me was heard in the Seventy-second District Court in Lubbock by the Honorable John P. Forbis, a senior judge of the One Hundredth District Court of Childress, Texas. Judge Forbis had presided over one of the earliest cases that involved a botched Erdmann autopsy. Tommy Turner, the prosecutor who obtained the original indictment against Ralph Erdmann, was the prosecutor pro tem representing the state.

I went to the hearing with Dan Hurley and, of course, Debbie at my side.

Judge Forbis called the court to order, and Mr. Turner proceeded. He explained that he was replacing Frank Briscoe as the lawyer for the state because, after the federal hearing in Amarillo, Briscoe's lawyer told Turner, "The attorney general doesn't have a dog in this fight."

Turner entered into evidence Judge Robinson's

preliminary injunction and opinion, quoting extensively from each. Turner stated that being the respected jurist that Judge Robinson was, her opinion was good enough for him. Turner also stated on the record that he had reviewed the police department files in regard to my criminal charges, and he had a good idea about the lack of any substantial evidence concerning my guilt on these charges. Even if there was evidence, he observed, it would be moot, because of the permanent injunction that had been part of the settlement agreement. And, even if he wished to risk the contempt of Judge Robinson and move ahead with the cases, his chance of getting a jury to give any credence to the cases was virtually nil.

Judge Forbis rendered his decision immediately. "I think it would be foolhardy, not just a mistake in judgment, but a foolish mistake, for me as the presiding judge of these two cases, to do anything other than to dismiss the prosecutions, and I will sign an order dismissing the prosecution in each of the two cases. This is the end of a long, hard experience, I am sure, for everybody, including Mr. Hubbard," he concluded.

I had never seen a judge reach over the bench and offer his hand to a defendant. But that day, Judge Forbis shook my hand and wished me well.

It was exactly one week short of a year since a Lubbock County grand jury had blindly followed what they *thought* was untainted testimony brought by a cleanly motivated investigation of my activities. Indicting me on charges of which I'd already been cleared had taken only a few minutes on that day. It had taken fifty-one weeks and much anguish and pain for Debbie and me to get it undone.

But, at long last, with a stroke of a judge's pen, it was truly and finally over. As I reached over to kiss my wife, I whispered, "We have our lives back."

Her eyes said it all.

Epilogue

In the months following the settlement of the RICO suit and the subsequent dismissal of the criminal charges against me, my life as a police officer was not without its ups and downs. Nevertheless, the work was challenging, and I derived great satisfaction from doing a good job. The average cop on the beat that I encountered always had kind words for me and rough ones for the district attorney and for the police administration. Hardly a day went by that someone didn't approach me and offer his or her congratulations for the fight we had waged and the winning back of my job. That part of my life was a joy.

On the other hand, a simple trip to court to testify even in a minor case became a media event and cause for me to consult my attorneys or even have them present in the courtroom. This was necessary because Travis Ware, Rebecca Atchley, her husband, Randy Atchley, and four other past or present members of the Street Crimes Unit began showing up at my cases to testify for the *defense*!

After I took the stand and explained how I made the case, affected the arrest, and seized the evidence, these seven people were there to testify that I had poor credibility and a reputation as a liar. "The only credibility problem I have ever had," I explained again and again, "is the one that these seven people created."

However, what Ware and Atchley did to damage my credibility came back to bite them. There were still some high profile "need to win" cases pending that had been filed before I was indicted. Now that I had my job back, I remained a key witness in many of those cases, including the killing of police sergeant K.D. Fowler.

Ware and Atchley were between a rock and a hard place. In an "insignificant" case, they were willing to take the stand and trash my credibility, but in the high profile "need to win" cases, they needed my testimony as a lead witness in order to get a conviction. Great lengths were gone to avoid putting me on the stand.

The criminal district attorney's office also cut some disgraceful plea bargains on old cases still pending in which Ralph Erdmann performed the autopsies. In one case, a murderer got a ten-year sentence with the possibility of parole in less than a year.

One of the most controversial cases to come to the public's eye was that of Chris Buss III. Buss was the prime—and only—suspect in the brutal slaying of an elderly couple. They were killed during the course of a burglary of their home. In this case, under Texas law, there were three ways to go for the death penalty: burglary with intent to murder the husband, burglary with intent to murder the wife, or committing a double murder. But you can't get a stiff penalty if you can't get the case into a courtroom.

Ware had no excuse not to fully prosecute this case. Erdmann was long gone when the murder occurred, and I was off the job under indictment. All Ware had was Chris Buss, who said he wanted to talk. It was what Buss wanted to speak about that became news. He wanted to talk about his earlier deal with Ware, where it was alleged that Ware intentionally kept a portion of Buss's conviction record out of the testimony during the plea agreement. Buss might also have wanted to talk about his work for Ware as a jailhouse snitch and whether the testimony he gave that helped send another inmate to death row was true, or if Buss made it up in order to ensure his own plea bargain.

The problem of the first plea bargain Buss made after snitching for Ware was about to come out. So Ware's office gave him another incredible deal in the current capital murder case. Buss eventually was allowed to plead to one count of simple murder in return for a life sentence from which he eventually hoped to be paroled. That was a far cry from facing a death penalty, and it would keep Buss quiet.

The outrage within the police department did not start and stop with me. Each time someone like Buss got a deal, the detectives who gave the case their sweat and tears in order to bring a murderer to justice shook their heads in disgust and pledged to vote in a new district attorney.

The Buss deal came to light the same week that Ware was on the television news blaming all of the problems in death penalty cases on the defense attorneys because they oppose the death penalty. Fortunately, the public seemed to be wising up to the fact that you can't blame defense lawyers if you don't take the case into a courtroom in the first place.

I still struggle with my own feelings about the death penalty. On one hand, I feel it is in the Bible that if you take someone's life, you should pay for it with your own. On the other hand, in today's society and legal atmosphere, I question whether the death penalty can be fairly and uniformly dispensed. The words of Jed Stone—the lawyer with whom I had an empassioned discussion during the RICO trial—ring in my ears: "If we put one innocent or wrongly charged person to death, it is too many!"

However, my cases were having problems long before they ever got to the courtroom. One morning, the midnight shift officers came in as I was getting to work. They had been at the scene of a brutal burglary and rape where a suspect had forced entry in the middle of the night into the home of a woman who lived alone. He got a knife from her kitchen and a pillow from a bed, then pounced on her as she slept. Putting the pillow over her face and the knife to her body, he savagely raped her.

When the officers came back from the scene, they had some fingerprints from the window the assailant had used to gain entry and from the headboard of the victim's bed. There were no witnesses, and even the victim had not gotten a look at the suspect, because of the pillow over her face. I worked all day on those prints, enlarging one to enhance clarity and then entering it into the statewide fingerprint database. The computer provided me with a list of possible matches to the print. From that list, I identified the correct suspect and matched prints not only from the point of entry but also the headboard. Within a day of the crime, an assistant district attorney had filed charges, and we had the suspect in jail. The daily newspaper announced the case was cracked and hailed my fingerprint analysis.

The following day, Travis Ware told the assistant district attorney and the press that the case would not go forward to a grand jury or be prosecuted unless someone else examined my print matches.

The police department had a problem. If they had someone reexamine my fingerprint work, it would cast doubt on my credentials as a court certified fingerprint expert, which would render my work useless in cases both past and future. There was also the added problem that I outranked all of the other print experts. The police department didn't want an officer supervising the work of their supervisor.

The police administration did nothing, apparently hoping the issue would go away. They did not order my work reexamined, nor did they stand up to Ware.

As a result, the rape victim had to hire a lawyer to ensure that her case didn't get trashed or fall through the cracks because of a vendetta the D.A. had for a cop.

Meanwhile, Travis Ware continued to fight for his political future, but the tide of public perception had completely turned against him. It surprised few that he composed yet another letter that "cleared" him of any wrongdoing. It extolled the virtues of Ware, told of the "errors" in Judge Robinson's ruling, and sought to "set the record straight." This one was from his own attorney, David Mullin, and was originally addressed to Jay Harris, the editorial page editor of the *Lubbock Avalanche-Journal* and Ware's personal friend. Not even Harris's influence or Ware's visit to the newspaper publisher could get this one printed, however.

After he was unsuccessful in getting the letter printed, Ware made dozens of copies of it and began distributing the letter on his own when he had public speaking engagements. The letter was critical of the *Avalanche-Journal* reporter who covered the Amarillo hearing, which could have been one of the reasons the *Avalanche-Journal* would not print it. Whatever the case, Ware's public distribution of the letter made the reporter believe that he was being publicly slandered by Ware, so he hired an attorney and filed a lawsuit. Ware won this one, however, as the court ruled "no slander."

Since Ware wouldn't resign, primary election day in Lubbock on March 4, 1994, was anticipated eagerly by many. Finally, voters would have the opportunity to express their views about Travis Ware, who was running for reelection in spite of everything that had happened during the previous year.

Shortly before the election, a "Pulse of America" poll in Lubbock, done in cooperation with the *Avalanche-Journal*, reported that 63% of those polled said they would not be voting for Ware in the upcoming election. About 18% were still uncommitted. Ware chose not to believe the poll was valid.

On election day, the ballot was clouded by the fact that there were four Republican candidates for the position of criminal district attorney. All four of them had at one time or another been card-carrying Democrats. Ware's campaign people confidently reported that their polls showed Ware was clearly the front runner. Independent polls continued to indicate otherwise. Most political observers were predicting a runoff between Ware and a local attorney, Bill Sowder, who had come to the head of the pack by basing his campaign on the shortcomings of the Ware office and promising to restore the integrity and trust of the C.D.A.'s office.

Ware ran a tough campaign. His small base of support came through with a massive amount of campaign funds, and he was able to spend freely. However, the public had not forgotten the events of prior years. That, coupled with the Lubbock Professional Police Association's very vocal endorsement of Sowder, set the stage.

I had firmly committed my support to the Sowder camp, walking blocks for him, contributing to his campaign, and talking to anyone who would listen to me. Within half an hour after the polls closed, the ballots were tabulated from the absentee voting. Sowder pulled ahead to a 53% lead, with the rest of the vote split between Ware and the other candidates. During the remainder of the evening, Sowder's announced lead never fluctuated more than two or three points. By 11:00 P.M., he was the outright winner with 55% of the vote. Had he received another seventy votes, he would have had twice the votes of Travis Ware. The public had spoken!

Travis Ware refused to call Bill Sowder to offer his congratulations, as is customary for a defeated incumbent.

However, there was no doubt that the eight years of Travis Ware's tenure as district attorney were coming to an end. Both the L.P.D. and the citizens of Lubbock were looking forward to a fresh start.

Shortly after being voted out of office, Travis Ware filed suit against the *Lubbock Avalanche-Journal* for what he believed to be an unfair, negative slant on him during the Erdmann controversy and later during his reelection campaign. Word around the courthouse was that Ware believed the suit would win him somewhere around $100 million. However, before the case ever saw the inside of a courtroom, a judge ruled that the $100 million suit actually had no merit, and he issued a summary judgment in favor of the newspaper. In addition, Ware was ordered to pay the costs the paper accrued in fighting the suit.

Ware is now in private practice.

The citizens of Randall County, where Randy Sherrod had been criminal district attorney for nineteen years, also spoke loudly at election time. In the primary election in the same month that Ware was defeated in Lubbock County, Sherrod's opponent was a former employee of the Lubbock Police Department, Jim Farren, who had gone on to law school. Farren pulled more than 70% of the vote.

Farren told Lee Hancock of the *Dallas Morning News* that the Erdmann scandal, plus the indictments of Pat Kelly and Millard Farmer, had hurt Sherrod at election time. "They could have run Daffy Duck against Sherrod and won," he said.

Lubbock Police Chief Don Bridgers retired on January 31, 1994. His tenure was summarized by many as, "What a great guy, but what an awful chief." He was a good and decent man who, in my opinion, just did not have the intestinal fortitude to do the job effectively.

In 1994, despite his lack of prosecution of Erdmann, Frank Briscoe was promoted to head the Attorney General's Prosecution Assistance Division, where he had been a staff attorney. The word is that he has his eye on a possible judgeship.

Shortly after receiving probation in his deal of the century, Ralph Erdmann moved to the state of Washington. Months later, police who responded to his home on an unrelated matter found more than one hundred firearms.

Even though he was on probation, Erdmann was still a convicted felon. By federal law, convicted felons cannot possess guns. To compound the problem, one of the weapons was a fully automatic machine gun! So Erdmann faced federal gun law charges, and his probation was revoked. Erdmann ended up doing serious time in a real penitentiary before being paroled in the spring of 1997, but most of his secrets remain buried on the plains of West Texas.

There has been a lighter side to some of this. I received several gifts, some from unknown admirers, such as the real-looking plastic eyeball "from Ralph" and the headless doll "from your buddy, Dr. Erdmann." A person in the media presented me with a briefcase. Inside was a fake plastic Uzi, remarkably similar to the Uzi that Travis Ware carried in *his* briefcase. Some quips about the case even got written up in *Texas Lawyer* magazine.

Hanging in my office is a professionally framed piece that includes the front page of the *Avalanche-Journal* reporting Judge Robinson's ruling: "Judge condemns Ware's tactics." On one wall of my office I hung other collected memorabilia, including an "I believe Bill Hubbard" bumper sticker, an "Impeach Travis Ware" button, and the business cards of my legal team. The wall is impressive, at least to me. Fortunately, the First Amendment and the L.P.D.'s management philosophy ensure that I can keep those things up there.

Ware continued to make statements to the public. He said that he participated in the settlement agreement because of his concern for the taxpayers' money and how expensive it would have been to proceed, even though he maintained that, eventually, he would have won.

I felt that the public had the right to know the truth. In my one and only press conference, I told how the RICO suit could have been settled the night before we went to federal court, *for no money*. If it had been settled that night, the taxpayers' bill for the city and county's legal fees would have been considerably less.

Among other things, I said:

> My issue has revolved around telling the truth when that truth might be very unpopular and could have a detrimental effect on me personally and professionally. I do not view basic truth to be open to compromise, regardless of the consequences.
>
> Beginning in August of 1991, when I became a supervisor in the homicide division of the Lubbock Police Department, and for the next several months, I became aware of and experienced firsthand not only the problems associated with the forensic pathologist who was practicing in West Texas, but also the unwillingness of certain prosecutors to own up to this problem and do something about it.
>
> When I was subsequently subpoenaed in April of '92 to a court in Canyon, Texas, the death penalty

certainly was not on my mind. Truth and fairness were my major concerns. Under oath that day, there was absolutely no denying my personal knowledge and documentation of the problems with this pathologist, but also the fact that some prosecutors and others were aware of the problem and could not get past their denial to deal with it. The pathologist himself had taken the stand the same day I did and pleaded the Fifth Amendment over two hundred and thirty times.

Afterwards, my testimony was described in the press as a bombshell. The logical conclusion was that it called into question literally thousands of autopsies in criminal and noncriminal cases where this pathologist had been used.

My testimony also had repercussions for prosecutors who had gained convictions behind the testimony of the pathologist, so it came as no real surprise to me when some six months later I was indicted for bogus things unrelated to my testimony but which nonetheless would call my fundamental truth and veracity into question. It was a lame attempt to discredit the one who had discredited them.

Two others—Detective Kelly and attorney Millard Farmer—were also indicted. Kelly, the only other officer to testify about his knowledge of the pathologist's practice, and Farmer, for working to expose the breadth of the problem. The message was clear: Tell the truth, go to jail.

Today, Kelly and I have our former positions back at the police department, largely due to the generous efforts of an army of attorneys who hold the Constitution dear enough to fight for the rights of those who dare to stand and tell the truth, even in the face of adversity.

* * *

The settlement money certainly hasn't made us wealthy. It has, however, allowed Debbie and me to recover some of the financial ground that we lost during the months I was off work. And although we were able to refinance the house to lower our monthly payments, things are pretty much the same. Mostly, Debbie and I have sought to be good stewards of the money, and it has allowed us the privilege of providing some assistance to friends of ours in the mission field.

No amount of money could begin to compensate us for what we went through. When I told this to Denette Vaughn, she was quick to point out, "Our society has no other way to make people right wrongs except to make the ones committing the wrong pay for their actions." When Ware claimed that the settlement was not an admission that he had done anything wrong, one of Pat Kelly's lawyers observed, "Losers pay. Winners cash checks."

Even though Debbie and I feel that we have passed through fire and been singed because of this ordeal, we feel more hurt than bitter. Our home and marriage were strong before this came along, but with it behind us, we feel that the Lord has given us added strength and prepared us to face whatever life brings in the future. Nonetheless, the scars cannot be denied.

Some of my police buddies couldn't believe that police work—especially in Lubbock—still could give me satisfaction. However, after my reinstatement, I still got up early every day and really looked forward to going to work. I still got excited when I cracked a big case or provided assistance to another detective.

In the fall of 1994, Debbie discovered a business opportunity in one of our favorite vacation spots in northern New Mexico. Early in our marriage, we each promised the other that if one of us got "the chance of a lifetime," that

person could feel free to take it, and the other partner
would go along. Beyond this, I felt privileged to give the
support to my wife which she so willingly and loyally gave
me in my time of need. Thus, Debbie began her new
career as the owner and broker of her own property management business.

However, finding law enforcement work in that part of
my home state proved to be quite difficult. The openings
were few, and the pay in most of the places left a lot to be
desired. So I stayed on at the Lubbock Police Department
until I sold our house and tied down other loose ends.
Then, at just the right time, the Red River Marshal's office,
a small but extremely professional department, had an
opening. The position was offered to me.

Debbie and I were ecstatic about being together again
after fifty-one weeks of "commuter marriage." Though
we were both happy we had made the change, we discovered that sometimes big dreams have big price tags.

Small town, mountain law enforcement has presented
new challenges, and we are constantly having to adapt to
the wide variety of tasks that are set before us. I still get
opportunities to use my skills as a homicide investigator,
as I also have taken a position as a deputy medical investigator for the State of New Mexico, covering the north
central part of the state.

In addition to my thankful feeling that I have walked
through fire and survived, my entire experience in Lubbock has had, I believe, a further positive impact on my
daily police work. Before all of this occurred, my zeal in
trying to bring a criminal to justice seemed so simple
and uncomplicated. Sure, there were times when the
case didn't proceed exactly the way I wanted it to go.
There were times when I felt evidence we should have
had was lacking. Prior to having been indicted, however,
if I had that gut feeling that the criminal had committed
the crime, I had absolutely no problem writing up what

I had—shortcomings and all—and sending it straight over to a prosecutor to see if they would file. If it was filed, I felt satisfied that the criminal would be tried in court and made to answer for his actions.

Things changed for me after I sat on the other side of the table. I've lived the nightmare of being wrongfully indicted and charged, of being wrongly dragged into "The System." That has changed my attitude toward others accused of crime.

Now, as I go about my law enforcement duties day in and day out, I am much more cautious in evaluating evidence before I ask that a criminal charge be brought against an individual. If an unknown "something" is lacking in a case, I keep the case in an investigative state so I will have an opportunity to find that "something" and be sure I have the right person.

Others have commented, and I feel within myself, that this added caution and going the extra mile in an investigation has made me a better police officer, a better investigator, and a better human being than I was before these traumatic events happened. Painful as they were, they have made me grow as a person and as a professional. I also believe I act more compassionately to those I charge or arrest, being careful to hate the crime, not the person. It's tough at times, but I'm getting better at it.

I have been asked many times what I would change if I had to do it all over again. The point is, the choices were not mine to make. I made a commitment to serve the people and seek justice. I followed orders, did my job, and testified under oath to the truth. The events that transpired as a consequence of my doing my job were beyond my control. So, if I had it all to do again, I would simply do it all over again. I wouldn't *like* it, but I *would* do it.

What others may not understand is that my ultimate goal as a human being and police officer has never changed, nor will it ever change, even in the face of adverse circumstances where I must risk my life or livelihood.

Joshua (24:15, NIV) said it best, as he addressed his people in Old Testament times. "But, as for me and my household, we will serve the Lord."

Afterword

Ralph Erdmann was paroled from the Texas Department of Corrections to Travis County on March 7, 1997. In paroling him by a two-to-one vote, the Board of Pardons and Parole put one new condition on Erdmann. The board prohibited him from seeking or holding a medical license or from practicing medicine. Erdmann settled into a quiet existence in the Austin area. His own family believed his punishment was excessive, while families on whose loved ones Erdmann had plied his trade would never believe his punishment had brought justice to the matter.

Meanwhile, the wars raged on concerning cases in which he had been involved. Old cases were constantly being revisited, new cases were being brought to trial, and prisoners on death row were seeking to appeal their convictions based on Erdmann's involvement in their cases. With the proliferation of the Internet, Ralph Erdmann even gained the distinction of having his own entry in *Wikipedia,* the free online encyclopedia. Memorialized there, he would forever be the forensic pathologist who, *60 Minutes* discovered, was keeping his laboratory specimens in his kitchen refrigerator, next to the condiments.

The June 16, 1998, edition of the *Lubbock Avalanche-Journal* announced, "Another botched autopsy in West Texas," as though botched autopsies had become the rule, rather than the exception. The object of this article concerned the 1989 death of infant Anthony Lynn Culifer. When the baby died, Ralph Erdmann had done the autopsy and ruled the cause of death as pneumonia. In late 1997 and early 1998, new witnesses and information came to light and the baby's body was exhumed. The results of the second autopsy caused Swisher County district attorney (DA) Terry McEachern to comment:

"Even almost a decade later, there were clear signs of physical injury and facial injury that are consistent with smothering. This was not pneumonia." Never mind that this statement was in stark contrast to that of forensic anthropologist Dr. Robert Paine, who stated in his written report that "no conclusion can be made from the skeletal remains in assessing a cause of death."

Nevertheless, David Earl Johnson Jr., the boyfriend of the baby's mother, was indicted for allegedly smothering the baby. Ralph Erdmann was contacted by reporters and declined comment. His wife told the Associated Press that her husband did not even remember this case, and that the police were using her husband to cover up their own "shoddy work."

Prosecutors, armed with the information from the second autopsy, plus new scrutiny of the original autopsy photos, along with witness testimony of a thirteen-year-old sister of Anthony—who was barely two years old at the time of Anthony's death—convicted David Earl Johnson, Jr. in 2000 for causing Anthony's death. He was convicted of involuntary manslaughter—not murder—and sentenced to ten years, the maximum for that crime.

Erdmann testified at Johnson's trial. An October 2002 article in the *Texas Observer* quoted Erdmann as saying to Johnson's mother as he left the courthouse, "You had better get some legal help, because they're railroading your son here."

All of this is very hard for me, who saw Ralph Erdmann's work and demeanor "up close and personal." Of the over one hundred bodies that needed to be exhumed and reexamined in the Lubbock area—and knowing that only nine or so actually got such reexamination—I can still only wonder. I wonder not only about which cases were convicted on allegedly contrived testimony, but mostly I wonder who it is that may be walking free, because homicides made it to the grave with an "official Erdmann ruling" of death by natural causes, accident or some medical reason.

The Ralph Erdmann debacle has become the battle cry of defense attorneys across the country when calling for more accountability and better science in the area of forensics and forensic pathology. A May 2001 resolution by the National Association of Criminal Defense Lawyers cited the Erdmann scandal as ammunition in calling for a fully funded, independent investigation of the Oklahoma City Police Department Forensic Laboratory. With bizarre situations like those caused by Ralph Erdmann and others, as well as the proliferation of television shows like *CSI*, public interest seems to be at an all-time high.

That brings us to death row, where Erdmann's name still echoes down the halls leading to the death chamber. On January 31, 2002, Randall Wayne Hafdahl, Sr. was executed for the 1985 murder of Amarillo police officer James D. Mitchell, Jr.

Ralph Erdmann had conducted the autopsy in that case. Not only that, but he testified at trial that—based upon his reconstruction of the crime scene, and on the distance and angle from which each shot was fired—only one shot, the one in Officer Mitchell's wrist, could have been fired when Officer Mitchell was standing. My own training and experience in crime scene reconstruction, as well as projectile trajectory, reveals this to be an intricate and exact science, with many variables that would need to be considered before an expert opinion could be rendered. I never knew that Ralph Erdmann possessed such expertise. I have my doubts.

Should that testimony at trial be the basis for an appeal? Should it be the basis for commuting a death sentence? Must all testimony in a death row case be pristine and held to a higher standard than in other cases? Does raising these issues minimize the heroic death of a valiant police officer, who died serving his community? The answers to these questions are mostly academic questions of justice at this point, for Hafdahl has been executed for killing Officer Mitchell.

Granville Riddle was executed in Texas on January 30, 2003, for the 1988 murder of Ronnie Hood Bennett. A jury convicted Riddle of beating Bennett to death with a tire tool. Ralph Erdmann had performed the autopsy on Ronnie Bennett and subsequently testified at trial. The cause of death was the head injury caused by the multiple blows of the tire tool to the head of Ronnie Bennett. An issue during Riddle's appeals was the fact that Erdmann actually testified to the *sequence* of the blows inflicted, stating that Bennett was struck first in the head and not the knee, as was Riddle's account in building a "self-defense" defense. Erdmann also testified that the first blow was not the fatal blow.

Was Ralph Erdmann qualified to render such an opinion? Is such an opinion even *possible* in this particular case? More importantly, though, is the question of whether or not the fact that Ralph Erdmann was thoroughly discredited should be the legal basis for virtually overturning any case in which he was involved. The bottom line is that the ripple effect of the Ralph Erdmann saga continues on.

After nearly five years as a Deputy Marshal for the town

of Red River, New Mexico, I accepted a position as an investigator for the District Attorney who covers the three counties in the northeastern corner of the state, including Red River. Within six months of taking the job, I was given a nice raise and a promotion to Chief Investigator. My position, along with my fellow investigators, is to serve as the detective for the many small police agencies in our jurisdiction that do not have detectives, as well as the traditional work that DA investigators normally do. It is a great job, but immediately threw me back into the world of death investigations, the forensic sciences, fingerprint examinations and chasing down the bad guys. With the history I had with Travis Ware, my friends and police associates in Lubbock find it pretty funny that I now actually work for a District Attorney!

My work as a major-crime investigator has expanded to include agencies outside of my primary jurisdiction that frequently ask me to assist with their cases for local, state and federal agencies. With my police instructor's certification from the New Mexico Department of Public Safety, I have also taught methodologies for homicide investigations across the state. All of this has been quite rewarding.

In addition, I have had the privilege of being able to go back and complete the one big "unfinished" in my life. On May 6, 2006, I received my master's degree in Theology from the Oral Roberts University School of Theology and Missions. Front and center at graduation were my mom and dad, who had waited nearly thirty years to see their badge-wearing, gun-toting baby boy complete the degree he started in 1976! Several people asked what I intend to *do* with that degree. My response: "Hang it on the wall!" No career changes are appearing on the horizon. A cop with a seminary degree—what a trip!

Debbie and I have been married for over twenty years now, and still enjoy the small-town mountain life. Her business has been blessed and continues to grow, all due to her hard work. I am now also married to a politician, as Debbie was elected in the spring of 2006 to the Red River Town Council. Yikes! Look out, White House!

Early one morning in May 1997, my home telephone started ringing. I had just finished a graveyard shift of patrol, so I was just settling in for that much-needed sleep. It is an hour *later* in West Texas, so ringing my phone at 7:00 A.M. was go-to-work time for my detective buddies at the Lubbock Police Department.

"Hub! You gotta see today's *A-J*!" I was told by at least a half-dozen callers. At their constant bidding, I went on and rolled out of bed to go to Debbie's office and get the fax they had sent. "Former DA Target of Assault in Park" was the headline. Travis Ware was in the news again.

The article said that Ware had agreed to meet a local cardiologist at a Lubbock park in order to "work out a personal problem." Before driving to the park, the doctor stopped at a sporting-goods store, where he bought an aluminum baseball bat. Upon arriving at the park, the doctor drove his SUV up onto the grass and over to Ware. He got out with his bat and commenced to "work out the personal problem" on the former DA. Some off-duty police officers were in the park, using the running track, and the doctor was arrested before he had inflicted much damage.

The next day's *Avalanche-Journal* headline was a real attention-getter: "Ware Helps Free Doctor from Jail after Attack." After the doctor had been booked into jail for the aggravated assault on Travis Ware, his lawyer—*Travis Ware*—came to arrange for his release. The standing joke around town was that the doctor had a used baseball bat for sale that only had a little "Ware" on it.

Who needs to write fiction when *fact* is this bizarre?

Travis Ware is still in private practice as an attorney in Lubbock.

Denette Vaughn is also still practicing law in West Texas. She is the Managing Attorney for several offices of the federally funded Advocacy, Incorporated; their purpose is to defend the rights of Americans with disabilities. She is also now Denette Sweeney, bringing to an end over twenty years of widowhood and single parenting, when she fell in love and married Ed Sweeney. I was privileged to be the photographer at their wedding in June 2002, and was heard to comment on how cool it was for me to be taking pictures of people who could *still move!* Homicide cops have the *worst* sense of humor.

Travis Ware's former First Assistant, Rebecca Atchley, and her husband divorced several years ago and she has since remarried. Rebecca is in private-practice law in Lubbock, but stays far away from any *criminal* law. Now, for the bizarre part: almost two years ago, Rebecca bought a mountain vacation home—*in Red River!*

Imagine my surprise in early 1998 when, out of the blue, I received a letter from Steve Losch. Steve had been one half of the powerful force joined with Millard Farmer in my first court appearance concerning the Erdmann matter in Canyon, Texas. Though Steve had been a huge help to our legal team, once the three of us had been indicted, we always stayed at arm's length on a personal level. He was an atheist Jew from Brooklyn and I am a charismatic Protestant from Albuquerque. Steve used to eye me suspiciously and ponder out loud, "Oral Roberts University, huh?"

The letter from Steve gave me reason for pause. In two short pages, he told of a complete turnaround in his life, which included meeting and marrying a lovely lady from Longview, Texas, whom he met while defending a death penalty case in Temple, Texas. Steve and Kaye became our very close friends. Steve's resolve to continue fighting the death penalty continued. We had stimulating conversations about legal matters, which lasted for *hours* on the phone . . . driving both of our wives crazy. I lost one of my closest friends in 2003, when Steve died unexpectedly. Criminal defendants lost a zealous advocate. When I scattered Steve's ashes atop Pikes Peak in Colorado in June of that year, I experienced yet another of the twists in life.

My fellow indictees, Millard Farmer and Pat Kelly, are both still plugging away in their respective professions. Millard is mostly retired now, still living in Atlanta, Georgia. He occasionally comes out of retirement in order to teach at conferences or to consult on difficult cases. Pat Kelly has continued to serve with distinction as a detective with the Lubbock Police Department. We were academy classmates in 1979, so Pat is nearing the twenty-seven-year mark . . . and looking forward to retirement.

My other two attorneys, Gerald Goldstein and Dan Hurley, are still in the trenches, doing battle for their clients. Dan, still in Lubbock, will always be in my heart for his words "Bill, you are the reason I went to law school." Gerald Goldstein, who lives in Aspen, Colorado, and *commutes* to San Antonio—as well as to anywhere else where constitutional rights are in jeopardy—calls our case the most important he ever had!

—Bill Hubbard
Red River, New Mexico
May 2006